2d95

CAPTURING CUSTOMERS

CAPTURING CUSTOMERS

HOW TO TARGET THE HOTTEST MARKETS OF THE '90s

BY

Peter Francese

AND

Rebecca Piirto

AMERICAN DEMOGRAPHICS BOOKS
ITHACA, NEW YORK

American Demographics Books
A Division of American Demographics, Inc.
127 West State Street, Ithaca, NY 14850

ISBN 0-936889-05-5

Library of Congress Catalog Number 90-232377
Library of Congress Call Number HF5415.2.F68 1990

LIBRARY OF CONGRESS CATALOGING IN PUBLICATION DATA

Francese, Peter, 1941–
Piirto, Rebecca, 1958–
Capturing customers

ISBN 0-936889-05-5

Printed in the United States of America

Designed and composited by Anne Kilgore

To all the hardworking people at American Demographics.

CONTENTS

Introduction

"The aim of marketing is to know your customers so well that when your prospects are confronted with your product, it fits them so exactly that it sells itself." —Peter Drucker

CAPTURING customers is what marketing is all about. Create a product, advertise it, and, if you can capture the customer's imagination, close the sale.

Marketing has always been that simple in concept but far more complex in execution. And it's getting more complex every year as growth slows and more consumer markets become saturated.

The purpose of this book is to show how information about consumers can be used to reduce the complexity of reaching consumers and increase the probability of making a sale. This is not a book about marketing. It's a book about using consumer information to improve marketing efficiency.

The premise of this book is that the more you know, in detail, about your potential customers and how they are changing, the more efficient you will be in targeting advertising or promotions to them and the more effective you will be when offering them products or services.

The key words above are "in detail." The general knowledge that your customer base was, say, women 18 to 49 years old, used to be sufficient information for a marketing plan. Not any more, because that once uniform demographic group has fragmented into employed women, nonemployed women, married women, single women, women with children, professional women, and nonprofessional women.

The media, of course, have fragmented to target those smaller segments. As a result, particular radio formats, TV shows, or specialty magazines attract demographically specific audiences. So choosing the media that most accurately target your market requires more detailed knowledge, not only of your customers' demographics but also their media preferences.

But the world's most precise target marketing program won't capture more customers unless the message cuts through the media clutter and speaks directly to the customers. Capturing the customers' imagination through words and images obviously requires a lot of creativity. But it also requires some understanding of the consumers' state of mind—their psychographics. Advertising messages are more likely to succeed if they are crafted to appeal to your target consumers' values, attitudes, or lifestyles.

Advertising and promotion are also going to be more successful if they are aimed at people whose past purchasing behavior indicates a willingness, or better yet, a recurring need, to buy your type of product or service.

So moving from the general knowledge of a consumer group to the specific details required to capture them as customers means obtaining information about their demographics, their psychographics, their media preferences, and their purchase behavior.

Gathering information is, of course, not enough. It must be processed, understood, and integrated into your marketing program.

Even before the 1990 census hits the computer tape there is a flood of consumer information and information providers out there. With more computer databases, people meters, scanner cash register data, and consumer surveys have come sophisticated software and computer systems to process all that data. But along with this growth of data, data providers, and information products comes the danger of getting swept into the torrent of data. The more detailed the information gets the more essential becomes the ability to simplify. One goal of this book is to help you look past the data files and focus on what's important—spending your marketing dollars on those people who are most likely to buy.

The format of this book follows the basic premise that the more you know about your target consumers the more successful you will be at capturing them as customers. Part I, Market and Consumer Trends, is about how business is adjusting to market changes, the characteristics of U.S. consumer markets, and how they will change over the next decade.

Part II, Consumer Information, details what each kind of data is for, where the numbers come from and how they can be processed and integrated with other information.

Part III, Consumer Marketing, provides specific examples of how to use the data and databases described in the previous chapters to improve your marketing performance.

PETER FRANCESE
Ithaca, New York, 1990

5

CHAPTER ONE

Splinters, Fragments and Finding Niches

SOMEWHERE in the American population is a group of people who would love to buy what you sell, if only you could reach them. The task of finding the right customers and getting the right message to them is the major challenge facing today's marketers.

Marketing is complicated by consumers themselves. It's hard to determine the needs and buying motivations of American consumers, because consumer markets are becoming increasingly diverse.

Not so long ago when the basic unit of society was the traditional nuclear family, there was something called the mass market. Today the norm is that there is no norm. The nuclear family has shattered into fragments. Consuming units can now be singles, gay couples, unrelated people, or childless dual-earner couples, as well as the traditional married couple with children.

It was easier to sell a product in the mass market. TV advertising was an effective net cast over the entire nation. In today's market, consumers in general and women in particular are much more sophisticated, and the embarrassment of dishpan hands just won't sell much soap. About three out of four women between the ages of 18 and 44 are in the labor force, and the state of their hands is the least of their worries. The old cliches not only don't work, they threaten to offend a significant portion of the people you hope to persuade. Shopping patterns are so altered that now it might be a teenage son who picks up groceries while both parents work. Rather than using a net, the soap company has to develop individual lines to each customer segment. It has to identify and locate actual and potential customers and fine tune the message to appeal to each.

Market Mayhem

These changes in the lives and attitudes of Americans have been accompanied by nearly simultaneous explosions in the media and consumer goods industries. Not only are there more types of consumers, there are many more vehicles and formats to convey an advertising message (television, cable, radio, print), and thousands of "new and improved" products are competing for the shortened attention span of the American consumer. So while increasing diversity in population makes it harder to identify the customer, fragmentation in the media challenges marketers to find the optimum vehicle.

Media fragmentation is partly a response to the diversification in the population and partly due to the rise of new technologies. A decade ago the networks held 92 percent of the prime time audience and 78 percent of the daytime audience. Today the networks' shares have fallen to 67 percent prime-time and 57 percent daytime according to Nielsen Media Research. The formerly homogeneous audience can now choose between a growing variety of viewing and reading options. Cable channels now reach half of all U.S. households, two-thirds of American homes have at least one videocassette recorder, and 2.2 million Americans have satellite dishes.

With the splintering of the mass audience, blanket advertising can no longer reach customers consistently enough to be cost effective. Mass marketing giants are pulling ad money from the networks and spending it on cable and syndication—often with more positive results. Cable TV's specialized health, finance and music channels have become more effective lines to certain markets. Ads on MTV, for example, helped H.J. Heinz Company's Ore-Ida Foods Inc. capture a younger market and reverse a long-term decline in the market share of its Steak-umm sandwich steaks. Further technological advances (such as the smaller, 18-inch satellite dish) are apt to splinter the viewing audience even further.

For advertisers, however, the old cliche that half of all ad spending is wasted is giving way to fears that the waste is even more pronounced. Advertisers now want proof that their ads are reaching their targets. Information services that measure ad and promotion effectiveness are enjoying growing revenues.

Many companies are looking for a better way to reach customers by changing their marketing approaches. Veteran mass marketers are finding order in the chaos of the post-modern marketplace by segmenting the total market into regions and devising different approaches for each region of the country.

In 1986, Campbell Soup Company reorganized its marketing force to emphasize regional and local marketing. It also altered some of its products such as its nacho cheese soup, which is spicier in the Southwest than in the Northeast. Campbell channeled more advertising and promotional funds to its 21 regional sales offices. The company also encouraged local salespeople to learn more about their customers and to look for local events as possible promotional opportunities. This regionalized effort has increased sales momentum in a flattening market.

The Jungle Out There

At the same time this fragmentation is happening, population growth is slowing to a crawl. There is no longer any leeway for marketing mistakes. In the past, robust population growth covered up some mistakes. Today many markets are actually declining. Often, companies find the only way to get bigger is to steal customers away from someone else.

Product proliferation, one of the consequences of market segmentation, is one way companies are trying to steal those customers. It has complicated the marketing equation further. Many companies try to appeal to smaller segments of the total market by introducing slightly different versions of their products. Veteran mass marketer Procter & Gamble has cooked up four different versions of the traditional Oreo cookie, one of which is called Double Stuf—for all the baby boomers out there who remember eating the creamy inside first.

In addition to saturating the airwaves, sellers now saturate the shelves and hope at least a few of the new products will hit their targets. *Gorman's New Product News* reports that in 1964, companies introduced 1,281 new products to supermarket shelves. Only 5 percent are still with us. Most of the 87,000 new products introduced since then have disappeared without a trace. This year alone, 8,000 to 10,000 new products, flavors and varieties will be launched on the American public at triple the marketing costs of 25 years ago. The majority of those new products will fail before the end of the first year.

Marketing has taken on an increasingly important role as the major competitors in most industries face similar production and distribution costs. If two companies can produce and distribute comparable products for roughly the same price, marketing becomes the crucial factor for success or failure.

Simply throwing more money into marketing, however, is no guarantee of success. Some companies today see their sales outpacing production costs but still don't show a profit because of soaring marketing costs. Regionalized marketing produces better results, but it also costs more. Production costs increase because product runs are shorter and there are more product variations. Data costs are higher because segmented marketing efforts require more sophisticated information. More efficient marketing is needed, and that is possible only through better use of consumer information. Consumer information is the marketer's magnifying glass.

Too Much Information

The sea of consumer information is at high tide. With computer databases, people meters, scanners, and panel surveys, there's more consumer information available today than ever before. It used to be that manufacturers waited weeks to get local sales results. Now with UPC product codes and laser scanners, manufacturers can get immediate feedback on the new product sales or the effectiveness of local ads or promotions. Combined with check-cashing cards, this information can reveal the exact purchase behavior of millions of consumers. The future potential is enormous.

Companies offering to help marketers find and analyze customers with demographic, psychographic (lifestyle), purchase behavior, and media preference data are growing in response to the booming demand. Many of these companies are database providers, that link data from various sources and package the information so it can be accessed via a desktop computer. With the 1990 census coming out on computer disks, even small companies will have direct access to the raw data.

Along with the growth of data, data providers, and information products, however, comes a danger. It's like trying to get a drink of water from a gushing fire hydrant. Without the right tools there is danger of drowning. To be useful, information has to be general enough to be understandable and specific enough to be usable.

The more complex things get, the more important it is to simplify. The goal is to focus marketing efforts on the people who are most likely to buy. Thus, from regionalized marketing we are going to local-, target-, niche-, or micro-marketing right down to the neighborhood level. To do this, we don't need more information. We need to understand how to use information to get results.

In this fragmented, media-saturated society, it is nearly impossible to get your message to your target audience unless you know not only who they are and where they live, but also what persuades them to buy. What are the words, ideas, or issues that will appeal to them? The right information will point out which media to use and what to say.

It's All in the Mind

Growing competition and change coupled with slower market growth mean that, more than ever, a miscalculation can be fatal. Why else would we be seeing so much verbal blood in current marketing literature, which urge their readers to swim with the sharks and to view marketing as combat?

As Al Ries and Jack Trout point out in their book *Marketing Warfare*, the battleground has become the consumer's mind. But, really, that's where it has always been. The difference is that slower market growth and other trends are making it vital that good customers stay happy and new customers be acquired. As the stakes increase, marketers must look for the tools that give them the competitive advantage. We believe that you can gain that edge by strategically combining information about your customers' demographics, psychographics, purchase behavior, and media preferences.

But marketers' attitudes must change first. Data-based marketing must be embraced as an opportunity rather than a necessity. Schools and companies must train marketers to be effective data users.

Target marketing is evolving with the emerging realities of the marketplace. The goal is to reach the most potential customers cost effectively, and to develop them as repeat customers. Once contact is established, the customer has to be convinced that one product or company is the better choice for reasons that appeal specifically to that customer. It is no longer enough to have a comparable product at a comparable price. You must know enough to establish a relationship with your customers.

Looking out for Number One

Some of the most successful American companies have never lost sight of the importance of customer satisfaction. L.L. Bean, Inc., for example, makes sure, through a slide show, that every employee knows precisely who the customers are. This desire to serve is L.L. Bean's competitive edge in the cutthroat mail-order business, and is what makes a customer order from L.L. Bean's catalog rather than from a competitor who was rude or botched the order. The easiest thing for a disgruntled customer to do is to throw away your catalog and buy from a competitor.

Handshake Marketing

In the new business environment, companies must return the customer to a position of honor. R. H. Macy started his first humble dry goods store on New York City's Sixth Avenue in 1858. His business grew because he knew each of his regular customers so well he could anticipate their needs and even make a sympathy call when one of them was sick. Size and the mass market have reduced the corporation's connection with its customers. The huge department store that bears Macy's name today can't turn back to the 1858 form of micro-marketing, but it can use modern technology to approximate it.

New charge cards called "smart cards" contain microchips that can store a customer's demographics and a record of every purchase he or she makes. Retailers get a readymade customer database and can use this information to target heavy buyers of a specific item with special discounts and promotions. Advanced Promotion Technologies Inc. (APT), a joint venture of Donnelley Marketing Information Services, Procter & Gamble, and Check Robot, is testing just such a smart-card program at a Des Moines supermarket chain.

In addition to its smart-card program, APT has paperless couponing systems at several chains in Ohio, which electronically process a customer's order and provide automatic discounts on certain products or issue coupons right at the checkout counter. Manufacturers and retailers are joining ranks to win customers, and you can bet that the manufacturers who master the information and get there first will be the ones with the biggest revenue gains.

Citicorp POS Information Services Inc. has set up customer card systems in more than 150 supermarkets in seven markets that allow each chain to offer their best customers automatic discounts. These scannable cards, special discounts, and a Valued Customer Program newsletter have helped Ukrop's Super Markets in Richmond, Virginia, increase business by 20 percent. Customers like being rewarded for buying and feel like they're members of a privileged group, says Ukrop's marketing director Carol Spivey. Ukrop's has gotten to know its market so well that it sends letters of apology to woo back lost customers.

Direct mailers can also benefit from database marketing by amassing computerized lists of customers and potential customers, segmenting the lists with data on demographics and buying patterns, and using the information to target new products, special coupons, or promotions at the people who will actually buy their products. Thus they can avoid mailing coupons for denture power to 25-year-olds or bubble gum to the elderly.

Database marketing deals with real people and real purchases with the ultimate goal of establishing a mutually satisfactory relationship. It can give companies the same detailed knowledge of customers that the wagon vendor once had. By deftly manipulating a database, marketers can cut through the clutter of nonprospects and focus on prospects—millions of them. More specific and focused promotions and products mean database marketing can also reduce waste. Considering there is no better salesperson than a satisfied customer, database marketing also could have spin-off promotional benefits.

As things get tougher, the leaders in nearly every industry are going to be the ones learning to use information technology to get back to basics—the customer.

Using Customer Intelligence

Focusing on the customer means doing three things: 1) understanding consumer trends; 2) mastering consumer information; and 3) learning to apply that knowledge to real-world consumer strategies.

This book gives you the guidelines for using information intelligently to make better marketing decisions. It is intended as a resource for navigating the high seas of consumer information. In the following chapters you will learn about consumer trends and opportunities in the 1990s. You will also be introduced to the various types of consumer information—demographics, psychographics, purchase behavior, and media preferences—and learn how to put this information together to solve marketing problems. The theme here is simply this: by managing consumer information more effectively you can make better marketing decisions.

Markets in the 1990s will be characterized by increasing variety. There is no reason to expect that the media will stop fragmenting, product proliferation will cease, or the flood of information will slow to a more manageable flow. As these processes continue, the organizations that learn to embrace and adjust to change will flourish. The tools for coping with change are within reach. What managers, planners, and marketers need is more precise knowledge about the who, what, where, when, and why of customers. What follows is a strategy for getting that knowledge and applying it to the real world.

CHAPTER TWO

Trends and Opportunities

A QUIET REVOLUTION is transforming the character of America. This revolution, as inevitable as the process of birth, aging, and death, will leave a profound impression on American life far into the next century. How well organizations prepare for the challenges presented by these demographic and lifestyle changes will to a large extent determine the future social and economic fabric of this nation.

The revolution is happening because of three major demographic trends: 1) the basic consuming units of our society—population and households—are growing more slowly every year, and our rate of growth will soon be at a record low; 2) our population is aging because of low birth rates and longer life spans; and 3) consumer markets are fragmenting. For example, suburban neighborhoods, once almost all traditional families, are now a mixture of singles, single parents, and people just living together, as well as married couples with children. Lifestyles, new products, and specialized media unheard of a generation ago are commonplace today.

The importance of these trends can't be overstated because they influence how consumers live, the media they are attracted to, and the products and services they buy. Each of today's consumer trends means new market opportunities and challenges for tomorrow.

Slowing Growth

The 1990 census counted 250 million people, representing a growth rate of only 1 percent per year since 1980. Population growth has been slipping for several decades and is expected to keep dropping. Our growth rate during the 1990s is projected by the Census Bureau to be a record low of only 7.1 percent, just below the old record low of 7.2 percent set during the Depression. Slower growth will be the theme of the 1990s for all regions of the country, even the former boom areas of the South and West. Annual population growth in the South, for example, is expected to slow from 16 percent in the 1980s to 11 percent in the 1990s. Likewise, growth in the West should slow from 21 percent to 14 percent. The Midwest, which grew a meager 1.5 percent during the 1980s, is projected to decline by 0.3 percent during the 1990s. Population growth in the Northeast will slip from 2.9 percent to 2.4 percent. Two of every three states are projected to grow less than 1 percent a year during the 1990s.

The reasons behind slowing population growth are: 1) women having fewer children; 2) an aging population; and 3) restrictive immigration laws. Birth rates are the lowest in American history. The current rate is estimated to be only about 70 births for every 1,000 women aged 18 to 44, compared with 118 births per 1,000 women in the 1960s. Women are having fewer children, and having them later, due to career and family income considerations.

Not only are the number of births per woman declining, but the number of women in the prime childbearing ages of 18 to 34 is expected to drop by 11 percent during the 1990s. So even if fertility rates do not slip further, the number of births is expected to fall throughout the 1990s, from about 4 million a year at the beginning of the decade to 3.4 million at the end.

The aging of the population means that the number of deaths will rise as the population of our oldest citizens, people aged 85 and older, increases rapidly. The Census Bureau projects the annual number of deaths to increase from 2.2 million in 1990 to 2.4 million in the year 2000 and 2.6 million in 2010. More deaths and fewer births mean that natural increase (births minus deaths) will contribute less to population growth while immigration will account for more.

People moving here from other countries, mostly from Latin America and Asia, currently add between 700,000 and 1,000,000 persons a year, depending on how illegal immigrants are counted. Assuming this level continues during the 1990s, immigration will probably contribute as many people to our population growth as natural increase. As immigration becomes a larger component of population growth, the racial and ethnic diversity of this country will increase. Today, people from Asian and Latin American countries make up nearly eight out of ten immigrants, up from about three of ten in the 1950s. Successful marketers must begin thinking in multicultural and even multilingual terms. Also, companies that have depended on population growth to find business growth will have to look for other ways to expand sales.

Almost no one is satisfied with sales growth of less than 1 percent a year. One strategy for continuing business expansion when population growth slows is to focus on market segments—both demographic and geographic— that are growing faster. This strategy has worked very well in the past couple of decades for companies that sold to households rather than to population. But now household growth is slowing as well.

Household Slowdown

For some businesses, slowing population growth is perhaps of secondary importance to slower household growth. Carpet cleaners, roof repairers, and thousands of other businesses market to America's 95 million households, not to individual customers. In the 1970s and 1980s, those businesses were lucky. The number of new households increased much faster than the population, fueling the demand for household products of every kind.

The gap between household and population growth, however, is slowing. Between 1990 and 2000, the number of U.S. households is projected to grow by 12 percent, while the population will rise by 7 percent. Compare that with the 1970s and the reason for the slowdown becomes apparent. In the 1970s the number of households grew by a remarkable 27 percent, while the population increased 11 percent. The economy was driven by this fast-paced household formation. Industries from housing and automobiles to packaged goods benefited from this expanding market for their products. Now that this artificial boost in demand is ending, businesses selling to households will need to adopt more consumer-oriented strategies to capture customers.

How is it mathematically possible for the number of households to increase faster than the population making up those households? Two factors are involved. There are now many more types of households, and they've gotten smaller.

The increasing number of household types was one of the most significant consumer trends of the 1970s and 1980s, transforming every aspect of consumer marketing. It was one of the reasons for the demise of the mass market. Today, being married with kids is no longer the only acceptable way to live. More people now live alone, with friends, or in other non-traditional arrangements. We've seen a pronounced decline in traditional family households—mom, dad and kids. Such family households have fallen from 40 percent of total households in 1970 to 26 percent in 1990, from nearly 26 million in 1970 to less than 25 million in 1990.

As household formation slows down, marketers have to watch the demographic trends and find new ways to increase sales. Fragmenting household types represent opportunity because each type of household has different wants, needs, and consumption patterns. In addition, some household types are growing faster than others.

There are five basic household types: 1) married couples with children under age 18 at home; 2) married couples with no children under 18 at home; 3) other family types like single parents and relatives sharing a house; 4) unrelated people living together; and 5) singles.

As household size decreases during the 1990s, it makes sense that the

15

Figure 2a: HOUSEHOLD TYPES
All households 1990 & 2000

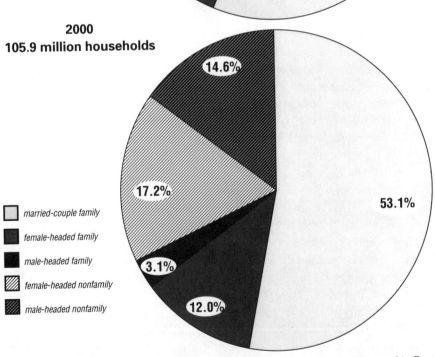

1990
94.2 million households

12.7%

16.5%

2.7%

11.8%

56.3%

2000
105.9 million households

14.6%

17.2%

3.1%

12.0%

53.1%

married-couple family

female-headed family

male-headed family

female-headed nonfamily

male-headed nonfamily

SOURCE: *1990-1991 Almanac of Consumer Markets*, © 1989, American Demographics Press.

smaller household types are growing the fastest. These are families headed by men (up 27 percent to 2.5 million in 2000) and unrelated people living together (up 33 percent to 4.5 million). Families headed by women are expected to increase 14 percent by 2000.

The largest household group is married couples without children at home, which are now about 30 percent of all households. Second is married couples with children, which are 27 percent of all households. Families headed by unmarried men and women make up 15 percent of total households, and unrelated people living together are 4 percent of the total. More Americans also are living alone. Singles have became the third largest household group, accounting for 24 percent of total households.

By 2000, nearly 28 million people will be living alone, and they will outnumber married-couple households with children by more than 6 million. This is not good news for durable goods manufacturers because, although every household probably needs a refrigerator, single-person households generally don't need two cars or two TVs. Over the long term the rise in the number of single-person households may mean new challenges for businesses because, on average, singles households have lower median incomes than married-couple households.

Perhaps the most significant trend into the 1990s will be the headlong growth of married couples without children. Between 1990 and 2000, married couples without children will increase by 21 percent, while married couples with children are expected to keep declining.

The 35 million childless married-couple households offer opportunities for marketers who figure out the specific wants and needs of this group. Most childless married-couple households have two earners and have correspondingly higher incomes. And many of these childless households will be in their peak earning years—ages 45 to 54.

More household types combined with low overall growth is driving the larger trend of consumer market segmentation. On the supply side, businesses are offering more products and services and adopting more targeted marketing campaigns to reach smaller consumer segments. On the demand side, the consumers' wants and needs are changing as household and population diversity increases.

Increasing Diversity

Americans not only embrace a greater variety of living arrangements, but the individuals themselves are becoming more diverse, a theme which runs throughout the population, affecting every facet of life—cultural, social, and economic.

Figure 2b: RACE AND ETHNICITY—U.S. Population

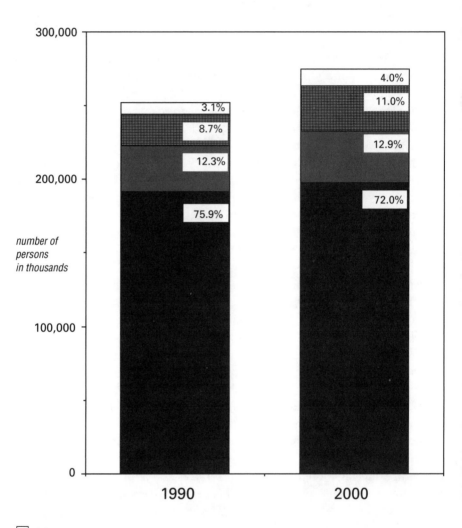

SOURCE: *1990-1991 Almanac of Consumer Markets,* © 1989, American Demographics Press.

As previously mentioned, ethnic and racial diversity is increasing along with immigration rates. This is compounded by another fact—a greater proportion of younger Americans will be minorities. This is reflected in their median ages: Hispanics' median age is 25.5 years, for blacks it's 27.5 years, and for Asians it's 28.4 years, compared with 33.2 years for whites.

The implications for the future composition of both the population and the labor force are dramatic. During the 1990s traditional entry-level workers, white males, will be outnumbered by women and minorities.

Minority communities will be pockets of robust growth within a nation that is growing more slowly, accounting for 87 percent of U.S. population growth between now and the year 2000. The minority population—Hispanics, blacks, Asians, Native Americans and others—made up 20 percent of the total population in 1980. By 1990 minorities were 24 percent. By 2000 they will comprise 28 percent, and by 2010 minorities will make up 32 percent of the total population.

Many U.S. cities are already feeling the effects. Miami, Los Angeles, Chicago, and New York (the metros with the largest minority populations) offer marketers a glimpse into the future. Miami is already struggling with the language and economic conflicts which have arisen from its population that is 42 percent Hispanic and 19 percent black.

However, the problems of new immigrants present opportunities for businesses that can provide training or language products to fill the gap between what government offers immigrants and what they need. By the same token, businesses that target and establish relationships with these communities now are likely to reap big rewards down the road, especially as the next generation becomes a bigger economic force. Surveys have shown higher than average brand loyalty among some minority populations.

The Education and Income Gaps

At the same time racial and ethnic diversity are increasing, there is a widening gap between the education and income levels of the poorest and richest Americans. In 1988, 21 percent of American households had incomes over $50,000. That's up from 16 percent in 1980, the most significant increase in any income group. However, the old image of the rich tycoon is no longer an accurate picture of most affluent Americans. Today, 59 percent of households with incomes of $50,000 or more are dual-earner couples

The dual-earner households are attractive targets for marketers. They represent a major market for luxury products, trade-up housing, private schools, and adult toys. And the incomes of these consumers are increasing faster than those of their traditional family counterparts. By 1988 the median income of working couples reached $43,800, while married couples with a non-working wife had a median household income of $34,200.

Middle-income households in the $25,000 to $50,000 range are now exactly one-third of all households. Since 1980 the share of households in this group has dropped from 35 to 33 percent.

At the same time, more people are very poor. Fifteen years ago, 11 percent of Americans had incomes below the poverty line. By 1988, the number had increased to over 13 percent. The share of households with incomes under $25,000, however, dropped from 49 percent in 1980 to 46 percent in 1988.

Some consumer attributes can determine income. Age and marital status play a role because income levels generally rise with age. But increasingly, income is tied to education. In the homogeneous 1940s, only 1 out of 20 Americans had a four-year college degree. Little academic training was required or even desirable for workers in a steel plant or on the automobile assembly lines in the era of American industrial supremacy. Today more than one out of five Americans has a college degree, and more than three out of four have a high school diploma.

As our economy continues to shift to a service base, education is becoming *the* determining factor in income. A college degree in today's job market, where skills are at a premium, is becoming what a high school degree was 20 years ago—a prerequisite for employment. Today as never before, people with the highest skill levels and the most specialized knowledge command the highest salaries.

The median household income of household heads with four or more years of college in 1987 was $43,100, an 11.4 percent increase since 1980. Those with some college had a median income of $30,400, a 6.5 percent increase over 1980. On the low end, however, householders with four years of high school showed a median income of $25,200, representing a 3 percent drop over eight years, while those who had not completed high school had a median household income of $13,000, a 6 percent decline since 1980.

The implication here is clear: without remedial training programs, less educated Americans stand to lose purchasing power to the more educated groups. For marketers with products geared toward higher income groups, this means they have to gear their messages toward a more information-oriented, sophisticated consumer—someone for whom patriotism in advertising, for example, may be seen as a cheap ploy.

Studies show that many people with lower educational and income levels are extremely brand conscious. They have less money to waste, so they will spend more to buy a brand they know, whose quality they believe they can trust. People with more disposable income may be willing to try a lesser-known brand because they can afford to be wrong.

Figure 2c: AGE CHANGE, 1990-2000

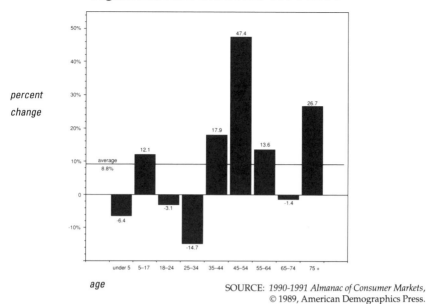

percent change

age

SOURCE: *1990-1991 Almanac of Consumer Markets,*
© 1989, American Demographics Press.

The Aging Population

Perhaps the most dominant theme in the demographic symphony is the gradual aging of our population. The population is getting older because the number of young adults is falling, while the number of middle-aged adults and very old people is rising rapidly. The consequences of these fluctuations are immense.

As people move through their lives, they develop different wants and needs and begin to vary the way they live their lives. Their consumption patterns shift along with their ages and budgets. Think about the aging of the population as the accelerating impact of millions of these tiny life changes, and you can begin to understand the magnitude of what's happening in economic terms.

The America of the future will be quite different. It will be an America of oversized door handles, large type, entrance ramps, nursing homes and hospices. The needs of older people will have a greater influence on everything, from which laws are passed and which programs receive funding, to which products and services are most in demand.

One of the best things about demographic projection is that it provides a simple yet effective way to measure the future. It's almost like having a crystal ball. We know everyone who will be 11 years old in the year 2000 is already alive today. We also know that the 30-year-old today will be 75 in 2034, and at each life stage he or she will make different demands on society.

Multiply those demands by the number of people in that age group and we can begin to determine what the future will hold. Compare the number of 75-year-olds today with the number in 2034 and we can identify the trend—decidedly upward.

The aging of a population hinges on the number of babies born who survive. A relatively young population has a high birth rate, many youngsters, and fewer old people, while older populations have low birth rates and a lot of adults who shift the average age upward. The aging of the U.S. population is now being driven by the progression of the baby-boom cohort (those born between 1946 and 1964) through the population's age structure.

The aging of America presents unprecedented challenges for both public policy makers and corporate planners. More of the income of younger workers will have to be transferred to the elderly, whose numbers are increasing due to the sheer size of their generation and their longer life spans.

When today's 62-year-old woman was born, America was entering the Depression and birth rates were falling. Following World War II, in 1946, the nation's birth rate began to rise sharply, and it stayed high until 1964, the last year of the baby boom. During that long period of high fertility, Americans had 76 million babies, a group that has had a profound impact on this country's economy, politics, and culture ever since.

In 1965 the number of births began dropping again. But the population shift (now known as the baby bust) ended in 1976, when today's 62-year-old woman was presented with her first grandchild. In the 1980s baby boomers began having children and fueled a baby boomlet that will peak in the early 1990s.

Because of these wide fluctuations in the number of births, the population has become increasingly segmented by age. Now we face a diverse and growing contingent over age 55, the ever-changing baby boomers, and a shrinking group of teens and young adults. As the years progress and each group enters new stages of life, they will strain some parts of the economy while presenting a boon to others.

In the 1990s the ranks of the very old will swell, the number of young adults will decline, and baby boomers will enter middle age. Overall, the median age of the U.S.—the age that divides the entire population in half—will rise from 33 in 1990 to 36 in 2000 and 39 in 2010, the first year of the baby boom's retirement. When the last baby boomer turns 65 in 2028, the U.S. median age will stand at 42, and one American in five will be aged 65 or older. Today that share is one in eight.

Since the number of people in any given age group is a major determinant of product demand, anyone selling a product or service should have a basic knowledge of these age group fluctuations, what they mean and how they are changing over time. Let's look first at the most positive of these trends for marketers.

Biggest Market: Middle-Aging Boomers

Aging baby boomers will spark the most dramatic rise in any age group during the 1990s. The ranks of 45-to-54-year-olds will swell by 46 percent. This alone is nothing new. Baby boomers caused a similar rise in the 35-to-44 age group during the 1980s. What's significant here has to do with the characteristics and behavior of 45-to-54-year-old consumers. This high-income age group also spends the most.

Rapid growth in this age group of big spenders is projected to boost consumer spending by at least $219 billion between 1990 and 2000. This immense buying spree will stem from the demographic phenomenon of the oldest baby boomers moving into middle age and a 50 percent increase in the number of households headed by people in this age group. Great opportunities await the entrepreneurs who supply them with the products and services they want.

One need only examine past evidence of the baby boom's influence to get an idea of what the future holds. America has been obsessed with youth since the 1950s. This is due to the attitudinal influence of the baby boomers, the generation that made the Beatles and the Rolling Stones multimillionaires. In the 1960s anyone older than 30 was suspect. In the 1980s being 30-something was the height of cool. In the 1990s, the new happening age will be 40 and counting.

By 2000 this free-spending group of 45-to-54-year-olds will be 14 percent of the entire U.S. population, and they'll possess more than one-fifth of all household wealth. The growth in their ranks will fuel demand for a host of new products and services. Before we discuss the probable consumption trends, let's get to know the growth group of the 1990s a little better.

Race As is true in the general population, the 45-to-54 age group will become more racially and ethnically diverse in the 1990s. The proportion of minorities will increase by 3 percent. Eleven percent of all people in this age group will be black, 8 percent will be Hispanic and 4 percent will be Asian. Meanwhile, the number of whites will decline to 77 percent of the total.

Geography Where will this group grow the fastest? In the Mountain states and the Northwest. The population of 45-to-54-year-olds in these regions will jump by 60 to 75 percent in the 1990s. The East North Central and the Middle Atlantic states will show the smallest increases (27 to 40 percent).

In every state, the number of residents in this age group will climb, but the biggest jumps will occur in Nevada (75.6 percent) and Arizona (up by 70.9

percent). New Mexico, Alaska, Colorado, and New Hampshire will show increases of 65 to 70 percent.

On the low end of the increase will be New York (up by 27.7 percent) and Iowa (up by 31.9 percent). Nebraska, Indiana, Illinois, Ohio, and Pennsylvania all will show increases of less than 36 percent in their 45-to-54-year-old populations.

Living Arrangements The me-first generation is now settling into relationships. Family households are 80 percent of households in this age group. And households are likely to include a married couple—66 percent. Only one-third of these married couples, however, have a child under age 18 at home.

Though this group's family urge is strong, they are increasingly likely to live in nontraditional households. The number of family households in this group will grow by 45 percent in the 1990s, slower than nonfamily households, which are expected to increase by 70 percent.

Marriage This is the most married age group—76 percent are married and living with their mates. Though marriage is popular, the marriages that occur in this stage of life are more likely to be their second or third. Fewer than 1 percent of first marriages occur among 45-to-54-year-olds. Their marriages are more stable than those of 35-to-45-year-olds, but less stable than marriages of the next oldest group, 55 to 64.

Education This group on the whole is well educated. Fully 55.3 percent have completed one or more years of college and 20 percent have four or more years of college.

Income By the time people reach this age group, their incomes are at or near the peak and the children may have left home, leaving more discretionary income to spend on luxuries. Median income for all households is $37,000, and for married couples it's $45,200. Sixty-three percent of these couples are dual earners at the top of the income ladder, with median incomes of $50,300.

For nonfamily households, those headed by white men have the highest incomes ($23,000), followed by those headed by white women ($17,375). Black nonfamily households in this age group have a median income of $12,300.

Assets People in this group are savers. Between 1983 and 1985 households headed by a member of this age group saw an increase of nearly $47,000 in net worth. Savings amounted to 16 percent of their median income.

As people enter the 45-to-54 age group, they are more likely to own their home—three-quarters of them do—although homeownership rates are higher among 55-to-74-year-olds.

Work Retirement is still a dream for this group. Fully 91 percent of men aged 45 to 54 work, while 69 percent of women are in the labor force. By 2000 three-fourths of women in this age group will work.

Spending Householders in this age group spend an average of $30,600 a year—35 percent more than the all-household average of $22,710. They spend more than average on food away from home, transportation, clothing, contributions, insurance and pensions. Their spending on housing, health care, and entertainment is below the national norm.

They also enjoy good food. Their weekly tab for food is 31 percent above the average; for beef, pork, fish, seafood, and eggs it's at least 40 percent higher.

Health The incidence of chronic health conditions, such as arthritis, digestive conditions, high blood pressure, and vision problems, begins to increase as people enter the 45-to-54 age group. They account for 16 percent of all cases of arthritis and high blood pressure. Arthritis is the most common chronic health complaint of women, and high blood pressure is the most frequently reported condition for men aged 45 to 54.

Vision and hearing impairments also start to increase among this age group, as do diabetes, ulcers, constipation, bladder disorders, and hemorrhoids. Prostate troubles and abdominal hernias become more common among men, and varicose veins and thyroid disorders increase among women. People in this stage of life are more likely to carry a few extra pounds—30 percent are overweight.

On a brighter note, fewer people of this age group suffer from bronchitis, sinusitis, or hay fever than people in the next younger age group (35 to 44). And the incidence of indigestion, colitis, spastic colon, and migraine headaches among women is lower for 45-to-54-year-olds than for 35-to-44-year-olds.

Death Heart disease accounts for one-third and cancer for 29 percent of deaths in the 45-to-54 age group. People in this age group are more likely to die of cerebrovascular disease, chronic liver disease, or from an accident, than are people in the next youngest group. But 45-to-54-year olds are less likely to be murdered or commit suicide than are 35-to-44-year-olds. There are some rewards that come with age.

Different Attitudes: The Younger Boomer Market

In 1990, most baby boomers were between the ages of 25 and 45. By 2000 they will be between 35 and 55. Older baby boomers will cause the biggest growth in any age group, but the youngest boomers should not be forgotten either. They will swell the ranks of the 35-to-44-year-old age group by 18 percent during the 1990s, making it 16 percent of the total population.

They will add fuel to the fire of consumption sparked by the older boomers. Their households will spend $121 billion more in 2000 than they did in 1990, and the number of households will grow by 19 percent. This 35-to-44-year-old group is the best educated and most highly employed group of Americans. Though they head only 21 percent of households, they account for 26 percent of all household income.

Geography The South and Southwest will show the greatest increases (20 to 35 percent) in the numbers of 35-to 44-year-old residents. Florida, Georgia, and Arizona will be the biggest gainers in this age group—all up by about 30 percent. California's 35-to-44-year-old population will grow by 20 percent. Losses will occur in only four states—Montana, Oregon, West Virginia, and Wyoming.

Living Arrangements Household formations among this group will increase by 19 percent during the 1990s. This is the life stage most solidly ensconced in childrearing and family building. The 10 million married couples in this age group with children under age 18 living at home account for 41 percent of all such families.

Fully 82 percent of householders in this age group are family heads, and two-thirds of the women have two or more children. They also have the largest average household size—3.33 persons per household.

Like the older boomers, however, many in this group opt for nontraditional living arrangements. The number of their nonfamily households will increase by about 50 percent in the 1990s, while family households will rise by only 12 percent. The fastest growing household segments in this group are those (both family and nonfamily) headed by men.

Marriage They are also very likely to be married, many for the second time; only 8 percent of first-time marriages occur during these years. Women account for 25 percent of all remarriages and men for 32 percent. Nine percent of of 35-to-44-year-olds have never married.

Education The most educated of all groups, nearly half of 35-to-44-year-olds have completed one to three years of college and 27 percent have finished four or more years.

Income In general, this group is on the way up the income ladder. Median income is $26,800, but half of all households headed by a 35-to-44-year-old bring in $35,000 or more, and 26 percent earn more than $50,000. Men in this age group are more likely than all income-producing men to have high incomes—32 percent bring home between $35,000 and $50,000.

The married couples have median incomes of $41,300. But income is even higher ($44,600) among the 68 percent of married couples who are dual earners.

Assets Saving goes along with family building, and this group is more likely than households in general to hold every type of asset except homes, CDs, and money market funds. About 64 percent own their own home and and 33 percent have IRAs or Keoghs. They are also much more likely than average to be in debt due to mortgages, college loans, or other debts.

Work Professionals and managers are the most common occupations among this age group—accounting for 32 percent of working men and 31 percent of working women aged 35 to 44. Women in this group are more likely than any others to be in the work force —75 percent of them are working and most of them are working full-time. During the 1990s the labor force participation rate of women in this age group will increase more than that of any other group. Men aged 35 to 44 have a 95 percent labor force participation rate, but this is expected to decline slightly in the 1990s.

Spending Households headed by people in this age group spend $29,195 a year. They are on the whole average spenders, but they spend more than average on food, housing, and clothing. They pay out about $900 more than average annually on insurance and pensions. They also like to be entertained, spending about $600 more than average on movie and concert tickets, electronic equipment, etc.

On a weekly basis, their tabs are 30 percent higher than average for all frequently purchased items. And they spend considerably more on food away from home, nonalcoholic beverages, poultry, beef, and housekeeping supplies than the average American household.

Health Weight is a problem for people in this age group—29 percent are overweight and 12 percent are severely overweight. The top acute ailments for men in this group are colds, open wounds, and cuts, while women say colds, sprains, and strains are their top ailments.

Chronic health problems are less common among this group than among the next oldest group. Sinusitis, high blood pressure, hay fever, hearing impairments, and back deformities top the list of frequent complaints for men. Women aged 35 to 44 add migraines and high blood pressure to these complaints. This group also suffers from disc disorders, psoriasis, dermatitis, indigestion, and hemorrhoids more than the next oldest group.

The Age of Opportunity

The demographic statistics above can be viewed in at least two ways: some may see them as mildly interesting but useless facts about a faceless group; others will be able to visualize glimpses of the products that will be most in demand in the 1990s.

What spurs people to buy? What clues lie in their personal characteristics that will help us capture them as customers? Fans of murder mysteries know that the perpetrator needs motive and opportunity. Likewise, the customers we want to capture need the desire to consume and the income to afford the product.

That's one reason why these two age groups will be so interesting in the future. Consider, for example, the most striking fact about 35-to-44 and 45-to-54-year-olds. Most of them are married (73 and 76 percent, respectively) and for the majority of those couples (68 and 63 percent), both work. That's an immense potential market which will grow as the ranks of these two age groups swell in the 1990s. Their dual-earner status gives them the highest household income so it's more likely that they can afford to buy whatever tickles their fancy. But what products will they want enough to buy?

No Time on Their Hands

We get a clue from their extremely high labor force participation rates, which are still rising, about these age groups' time use in the 1990s. Products that help reduce the time demands of housecleaning, washing clothes, and preparing food will be very appealing.

People in these age groups spend more than average on food, which means growth in demand for food products and services. They like to eat out to save time and avoid the hassle of food preparation. But when they have time, they like to cook elaborate meals. Any product that could combine these two desires better than microwaveable gourmet frozen meals could capture many customers. Take-out-style restaurant food sold through drive-in windows, gourmet deli shops, and prepared hot-food sections of grocery stores will do even better in the 1990s.

Convenience and service will be the keys to sales success as time management becomes more important. Retailers who find ways to reduce shopping time will gain a competitive edge. Local cable companies have been talking for years about installing interactive boxes to allow subscribers to order local products with the push of a button. The 1990s may well be the time for these channels. Grocery delivery services or professional shoppers will do well. This also will be a positive market for home-shopping television channels, mail-order businesses, and subscription food services.

Some companies are already jumping on the convenience bandwagon. In San Francisco, a company called Waiters on Wheels delivers hot meals from the city's restaurants to the homes of people who are too busy to cook. Similar concepts are being tested from Minneapolis to Phoenix.

Consumers are impatient. Nothing irritates baby boomers more than waiting in line or being put on hold. Businesses that show they recognize the value of their customers' time will win their loyalty. Banks, grocery stores, utility companies, and others that routinely take their customers' time for granted should learn from the lesson of Wells Fargo Bank in Los Angeles.

In the increasingly competitive banking environment of southern California, Wells Fargo started a simple test. It offered customers $5 if they had to wait in a teller line for more than five minutes. The bank recognized that better customer service was the way to increase accounts. Since implementing the reward, deposits at the bank have increased and other banks, sincere in their flattery, copied the idea.

Consumers also want service that continues after the purchase. The quickest way to lose repeat business is to make product returns and exchanges inconvenient. Rudeness also loses customers. Manufacturers who offer more and better warranties and retailers who stand behind their products will send more than a public relations message to these customers.

Family Affairs

Eating out and entertainment are big with the 35-to-44 age group. But many of them have families. The person who devises an entertaining family activity that doesn't require going to Disneyland or eating pizza with a giant mouse may well be hailed as a genius. Family vacation packages that make it easy to take the kids along and involve recreation or adventures will be popular. Products and services geared toward young families will continue to do well through the 1990s.

Although the preschool market will decline in the 1990s, the school-aged market is growing. By 2000, the number of 5-to-17-year-olds will be up by 12 percent. And these kids are becoming a more savvy bunch of consumers every year, thanks to the universal presence of television.

Since the majority of children now live in dual-earner households, they are taking on more household responsibilities and making more and bigger purchasing decisions. Many buy over the telephone or do the family grocery shopping with their parents' credit cards. This will mean growth for video games, preteen cosmetics, clothing, and, because they're impatient, microwaveable foods. This trend will accelerate as their working parents have less time but more money to spend.

Money and Education

The 35-to-54 age groups have a high percentage of dual-earner couples, and their spending power is growing. The reason it's growing, according to Census Bureau figures, is not because husbands are earning more, but because wives are. Women still earn less than men on the average, but the growing share of full-time working women, coupled with their increasing earnings, raised the wives' earnings relative to their husbands'. One in five wives in two-income couples now earns more than her husband.

In the 1990s the majority of the labor force will be either women or members of minority groups. Day care will become an essential ingredient of the best corporate benefit packages. Smart corporations are starting company day-care programs now and reaping the rewards of increased employee efficiency and fewer absences.

The growing number and economic clout of working women in the 1990s should also make marketers and planners pay closer attention to their needs. What do they want in a product? An advertisement? A company? One thing is sure. A product must offer real quality, and the appeal must be intelligent.

Both women and men in these age groups are big consumers of games that increase knowledge or involve creativity. *Trivial Pursuit* and *Pictionary* rode to success on boomers' spending patterns. Gadgets with unique designs, such as Braun coffee makers, also do well.

Items that improve the efficiency of doing business, at home and in the office, will continue to be in demand. Lap-top computers, facsimile machines, and cellular telephones help people stay in contact and conduct business whenever it is convenient.

Financial services are another very important growth area. Long-term investments interest people moving into their 40s who realize they only have about 20 more years until retirement. These educated consumers are concerned about their financial futures. They doubt Social Security will be there for them when they retire, and they want to build up their assets. The median age of investors in stocks and bonds in this country is 44.

Although this doesn't necessarily mean that baby boomers are suddenly going to become interested in stocks and bonds, they may buy more mutual funds and be more interested in making something above the regular savings account interest rate. This bodes well for financial planners, stock brokerages, insurance companies, and banks.

Financial products with a new twist, such as socially responsible investment funds, are popular with the generation that used to view making money as something the "establishment" did. These funds offer competitive interest rates and still appeal to this group's desire to further worthy causes such as inner city development, saving the rain forest, and wildlife protection.

Companies should also remember that because family households are increasing slower than nonfamily households in these age groups, financial products should be designed with nontraditional families—singles and unrelated people living together—in mind.

Older but Better

These consumers are highly sophisticated. In clothing and accessories, they want to make an individual statement. They demand quality, and they are willing to pay more for it.

As more Americans age, products that offer youthfulness without denigrating aging will do well. These consumers are not like their parents—they don't feel that older is ugly. For the most part they believe they've earned their wrinkles. They want to look their age, but better. Jane Fonda, Linda Evans, and Katherine Hepburn are champions of this attitude and magazines like *Lear's* do well by publicizing it. Products and services emphasizing the "older but better" theme can capture these customers in the 1990s.

The sheer increase in the number of aging and overweight Americans will mean an expanding market for diet foods and weight-loss services. However, educated consumers want to know a weight product has been tested and approved. They don't want to risk their health, but they want it to be simple to use. And like other consumers, they want the product to taste good and take weight off.

Chronic health conditions like arthritis, diabetes, and high blood pressure will become far more common in the 1990s, fueling the demand for over-the-counter drugs to handle the more minor complaints like bronchitis, hay fever, and headaches. Patents will be expiring on many brand-name drugs, so customers will increasingly turn to lower-cost generic alternatives, providing they are convinced the quality is the same.

It will be an era of the drive-in store-front doctor. Time-saving outpatient services and diagnostic centers will do a booming business with these consumers, as will products that allow people to check cholesterol levels or other health conditions in their homes.

Home Sweet Home

The biggest opportunity involves the home because people in their 30s and 40s show a greater interest in home and community and move less frequently.

As baby boomers put down roots, literally and figuratively, lawn, landscape, and home-improvement businesses will thrive. Rising community spirit could also spark interest in local companies and products. This suggests greater regional and local diversity and a rising demand for advertising with a local flavor and content.

More interest in the home also points to an increasing demand for delivery services and shopping by telephone. This desire to stay warm and cozy means people who would have gone to hear a band at a club five years ago now rent a video, order a pizza, and stay home. Quality time and togetherness will be a continued theme in the 1990s.

There are also opportunities for those who offer adventures. Traveling for pleasure is above average for people aged 35 to 54 and for people with incomes of $35,000 or above. These age groups also take more weekend trips, and they're the most likely to take a business trip. Travel agents and companies that can appeal to their desire to learn or experience something new can take the lead in this market.

Above all, marketers who want to capture these customers should remember that it's pointless to adopt a group approach because there is no mass mentality among baby boomers. While some are concerned about the environment—degradable plastics, fluorocarbons, and organic foods—others continue to use aerosol sprays and disposable diapers. If one trait of the boom generation is carved in stone, it's their individuality.

Coming Shortages: The Decline in Young Adults

There are two facets of our aging population that present challenges for both policy makers and business. In the 1990s the number of young adults will decline rapidly, while the number of very old Americans will increase sharply. Understanding the economic and labor force implications of these age fluctuations is of the utmost importance for businesses in the 1990s.

The number of young adults aged 18 to 24 peaked in the early 1980s and is projected to decline by nearly 4 percent during the 1990s. In 1980 they were 13 percent of the population; by 2000 they will be only 9 percent. This means there will be about 5 million fewer consumers of alcoholic beverages, motorcycles, cosmetics, and clothes in 2000 than there were in 1980. Put another way, the consumer spending generated by this group will drop by $3 billion between 1990 and 2000.

This group's expected decline in consumer spending may be partially offset by increasing wages. Desperate employers will have to pay more as entry-level workers become scarcer.

When the baby boomers started working in the 1960s and 1970s, the labor force grew by about 2.5 percent a year. In the 1990s the growth will be only 1 percent a year.

A population decline of this magnitude will have a negative impact on many areas of the economy, most obviously higher education, the housing industry, and employers depending on lower-priced young workers. Labor shortages are expected to occur in nearly every industry in the 1990s, but companies that have openings in service, sales, administrative support, operator, fabricator, or laborer jobs will be especially hard hit because these occupations rely heavily on 18-to-24-year-olds.

Some employers have already begun to look into incentive programs such as day-care programs and more extensive benefit packages to help attract coveted workers in a tightening labor market. Major employers and local governments in areas most affected by shortages can be expected to work together to stimulate construction of affordable housing for young workers, creating a big opportunity for builders.

Labor shortages will be especially acute for employers the Northeast and Midwest, which will experience the biggest declines in the under-25 population. These employers will have to find creative ways to woo younger workers from the West, where growth in this age group will be as high as 28 percent in some states.

Opportunity in Shortage

At the same time the number of young people is shrinking, their skill levels, and those of workers in general, are declining. Dropout and illiteracy rates are increasing. One study found most 17-year-olds could not summarize a news article, comprehend a bus schedule, or write a passable cover letter. A study by the Hudson Institute, *Workforce 2000*, found that fewer than half of 21-to-25-year olds can make the correct change for a two-item restaurant meal.

Fewer workers is a serious problem, but the declining pool of those with skills spells grave economic trouble. More American businesses are recognizing the threat and redirecting funds toward training employees. In 1989, the private sector spent $210 billion on training programs, and by 1995 that is expected to increase to $300 billion.

Entrepreneurial opportunity exists in education. With increased emphasis and investment in education, private companies that provide tutoring or specialized educational programs are thriving. Berlitz Schools of Languages Inc., of Princeton, New Jersey, has contracted with the Dade County (Florida) School District to fill Spanish teaching vacancies. And more teachers are becoming entrepreneurs, such as the Minneapolis naturalist who runs a business called "Whales in the Classroom."

As more school districts turn to tutoring to keep at-risk students in school, private tutoring companies will see their business climb. The three largest tutoring companies have seen strong growth since 1985. Sylvan Learningcenters, of Montgomery, Alabama, American Learning Corporation of Chicago, and Huntington Learning Centers, of Oradell, New Jersey, operate or franchise about 700 centers nationwide and the number is growing.

Educational systems not lucky enough to get corporate help will be looking for labor-saving devices to offset teacher shortages and rising labor costs.

Electronic systems using CD-ROM and other mass storage devices will be in greater demand, along with adult education classes, audio and video cassettes, booklets, and other things that help adults retrain or learn new skills.

The average American of the 1940s—a blue-collar worker with a ninth grade education—no longer has a secure place in our increasingly technological economy. By 2000 two of every five jobs will require more than basic literacy. Most will require some college. It is in the interest of businesses to take action to train the workers of the future now.

Old Folks at Home

Sharp contrasts among people aged 55 and older—from bedridden patients in nursing homes to big-spending tourists cruising the Caribbean—make this market one of the hardest to understand.

Twenty years ago, few marketers made the effort to target them because it was assumed they were poor and too old to buy anything more interesting than denture power. However, today's mature market controls a sizable portion of the nation's discretionary income, and surveys show that most of them see themselves as 10 to 15 years younger—and they spend accordingly.

The mature market is really three markets: pre-retirees (55 to 64), young retirees (65 to 74), and the fully retired (75 and older), who make up the fastest-growing segment of the three. The number of households headed by people aged 75 and older will rise 28 percent between 1990 and 2000, compared with a 1 percent drop among 65-to-74-year-olds.

Until now the 75-plus group has been largely written off because it was mistakenly believed to be poor or stingy. It's true that their incomes are below average, with a median household income below $20,000. Even couples in this group bring in only $17,000 a year, the lowest married-couple median income of any group.

However, the oldest Americans spend more than the all-household average on personal care, food, and housing, and fully 15 percent of their income goes to health care. With their inflating numbers, consumer spending in this age group is projected to grow by $28 billion between 1990 and 2000.

The youngest segment of the mature market, those aged 55 to 64, receives pension and investment checks along with, in some cases, Social Security. In addition, many have assets such as annuities and home equity. This is the most affluent segment of the mature market, and it will grow 14 percent by 2000. The median income of the group is $27,600, and their consumer spending is projected to grow by $38 billion between 1990 and 2000.

They also spend more freely than their older counterparts. Research has shown that people's attitudes are powerfully influenced by world events during their formative years. This is one reason why the different age groups among older Americans, even with roughly equivalent assets, manage their money in such different ways. For example, someone who is 55 in 1990 was 21 years old in 1956, a time of economic growth and social tranquility. That person may not place as much value on thrift as someone who became an adult during the Depression and turned 78 in 1990.

By the time people reach age 55, their mortgages are mostly paid off, debts are low, and the kids are gone, so more of their income is discretionary. This group spends more than average on food, transportation and utilities, insurance and retirement plans, health care, and contributions. They are the core market for cruises, American luxury automobiles, and recreational vehicles.

The diversity of attitudes, interests, and activities among this group will present new challenges for businesses offering everything from financial services to travel companies to health care.

Unlike baby boomers, mature consumers aren't pressed for time. Studies show they seldom use automatic teller machines, preferring to have contact with tellers and other customers. The common seating areas in some Florida banks serve as social centers where bank patrons can visit while waiting to conduct their business.

The ranks of Americans aged 85 and older are expected to climb 42 percent, from 3.2 million to 4.6 million, by 2000, making them one of the fastest growing age groups in the country. The number of Americans aged 100 or older will nearly double from 56,000 to 100,000.

How will we handle this rapid increase in the number of very old? How will we care for them and who will pay the bill? These are all valid questions that policy makers have only begun to address. Twenty percent of people aged 85 and older are in nursing homes or hospitals, and a full 80 percent of all nursing home residents are aged 75 or older.

Think of what an increase like this will mean for the health-care system. Assuming present levels of institutionalization, there will be a demand for more than one new 100-bed nursing home every single day for the foreseeable future just to accommodate the growth in this age group. Where will these beds come from when most long-term-care facilities are already filled to capacity? Where will these institutions find qualified workers to staff them?

There is an opportunity for builders and developers who can create self-contained communities that meet the seemingly conflicting needs of these oldest Americans. They need autonomy and independence and also require maintenance support and access to health care.

Seeing the possibilities, Marriott Corporation built Jefferson, a high-rise community outside the nation's capital. It offers meals, transportation, nursing care, and housekeeping for the upscale residents of the 350 apartments.

The hefty price tag for each two-bedroom unit is $240,000, but Marriott recognizes the growth in this market will also be at the low end of the scale. The company plans to build additional life-care complexes for couples aged 70 and older who have incomes in the $25,000 range.

Most elderly people prefer to stay in their homes for as long as they can. This will create an immense need for home maintenance and home-health-care services, and programs offering respite for family care providers. The aging of America presents policy makers with a test of insight. The growth in the number of very old people in the 1990s is only a preview of what will happen after 2030 when the oldest baby boomers turn 85. By taking note now of the needs of this growing group, both government and private business can anticipate our population's needs when the aging process intensifies in the next century.

Spotting Opportunity in Diversity

America is a nation of contrasts. Faster-growing minority populations, increasing fragmentation by age, income, and education, and wide ranging consumer attitudes all spell increasing diversity. Marketing in this age is becoming more of a shell game—find the group who wants what you sell. But there are companies that are mastering the game.

One of these is San Francisco-based Levi Strauss and Company. The history of the company goes back to the rugged work pants worn by the gold mining '49ers, but company fortunes really started to take off when the baby boom came of age. In the 1960s, patched, ragged, and hiphugging Levi's jeans perfectly fit the baby boom's desire for comfortable clothes that parents hated.

As the baby boom aged into business suits, Levi Strauss looked at the demographic trends and recognized the dilemma: how to keep baby-boom customers, while generating the interest of the teen and young adult market. They decided to do it all. They have ad campaigns directed at the 35-plus market as well as the 501 Blues ads showing young inner-city toughs moving to rap music.

"Our marketing efforts had to break through advertising clutter," says John Wyek, director of the office of strategic research. When the ads came out in 1984, the clutter was thick, but the 501 Blues campaign managed to cut through it by addressing the spirit of rebelliousness and independence inherent in jeans, while emphasizing the brand's unique fit and identity.

"Consumers say, 'Yeah, I know Levi's makes stuff my dad wears, but that's okay.' or, 'Yeah, I know Levi's are worn by wild and crazy kids, but it's still a quality product'" Wyek says. "The net result is 'Whoever I am, Levi's are for me.' That's an advantage we have over many other consumer product companies."

Part of the reason they have marketed successfully to diverse groups is that they have grown intimately acquainted with their market, especially the baby boomers. They make products that are relevant for their customers— 70,000 products in different colors, styles, silhouettes, sizes, and fabrics.

They have also noted the problem of expanding waistlines among their loyal older customers. Levi Strauss now makes jeans with larger waist sizes, fewer junior sizes, and more misses and women's larger sizes.

"Many apparel manufacturers and retailers have missed the obvious," Wyek says. "They kept producing styles to fit young bodies, to the point where women said, 'Enough—there's nothing in this store for me to buy.' We have to pay attention to the people who are buying our goods."

Paying attention to the changing needs of customers is something Levi Strauss knows will be even more important in the year 2000 when 100 million Americans are over age 45. "Think about the implications of that for selling jeans," Wyek says. "It means different messages, different media, different products, different sizes, different distribution."

The success of Levi Strauss is rooted in the company's clear understanding of the demographic trends. Recognizing the importance of the baby-boomer market, the company learned how to keep making relevant products. At the same time it also learned how to speak personally and directly to a diversifying market.

Capturing customers in the era of demographic diversity doesn't have to be a guessing game if you know who your customers are and how to reach them. This is where consumer information and customer databases come in. Consumer information tells you who your customers are and how they are changing, and your customer database tells you what they buy in the way of goods and services. More complicated consumer markets require more sophisticated consumer information and its integration into media buying and marketing decisions. Once you understand the trends, the next step is learning how to find consumer information and using it to make better business decisions.

CHAPTER THREE

Consumer Information

IF KNOWLEDGE is power, then knowing about your customers is market-place power. The better you know your customers, the more successful you will be at tailoring your products and promotions to them. In the 1990s, if you don't know who your customers are, your competitors probably will.

All knowledge starts with questions, and there are many questions about consumers that need answers. Who are they? How many are there? Where do they live? What do they want? What's on their minds? Where can you reach them? What are they buying now? Answering these and other specific questions is, of course, a never-ending process.

At the most fundamental level, people have attributes or characteristics and they engage in consumer behavior in the marketplace. The basic idea behind gathering and processing consumer information is to use the attributes about consumers to predict their behavior. If we know, for example, that families with preschool children (the attribute) buy at least one gallon of milk a week (the behavior), and if we can get a count of that type of family, and others, in a geographic marketing area, we should be able to predict milk sales. But the next question is what kind of milk? Regular? Skim? Low-fat? And how can you convince the families that your brand of milk is better? The questions seem endless, but fortunately there are a lot of data with which to answer them.

What Consumer Information Reveals

Four categories of consumer information address all those questions. The first two categories in the consumer information system describe consumer attributes—the basic facts of their daily lives, and their inner wants and needs. **Demographics** reveal who customers are, where they live, and how they differ from the general population. Demographics are their age, sex, ethnic background, labor force participation, education, income, the number of people in their household, and who the household head is.

The second category, psychographics, provides clues as to what the consumer thinks. Though much harder to quantify, **psychographics** show what attitudes and values motivate different consumers and why they buy.

Information about consumer attributes comes from the decennial census and numerous surveys taken by both public and private organizations. Demographics can also be obtained from driver's licenses, credit applications, or other business records where such things as address, age, sex, and family type are often recorded.

The other two categories describe consumer behavior. **Purchase behavior** information reveals what certain consumers buy. The amount they spend on certain items, how often they buy those items, how they buy them (store, mail, phone, etc.), and how they pay are all critical bits of information.

Media preference data tell where and how marketers can reach the customers they seek. They show whether people who buy certain things prefer newspapers, radio, or television and which magazines they read.

Media preferences and purchase behavior are often passively recorded as the consumer engages in a transaction or activity. People meters attached to a sample of television sets record what is being watched and in some cases who in the room is watching. Scanner cash registers in supermarkets can record the brand, size, color, and price of what the shopper takes out of the store after presumably paying for it with a check and identifying himself or herself with a scanner-coded check-cashing card.

The data collected in this manner are useful only because the consumer attributes of the card holder or the people-metered household are known, usually through a prior survey.

The point is that one kind of data is not very useful without the other. The reason for tabulating data on purchase behavior or media preferences is to be able to link the information to a particular demographic or psychographic group, so that in the future you will know better who to target and where you can reach them.

Figure 3a. illustrates the power of linking consumer information and also shows how the combination of information answers key questions about consumers and addresses specific marketing problems.

Think of consumers, the source of all this information, as the hub of a wheel and envision the four categories of consumer information radiating outward from the hub like the spokes of the wheel. Each type of consumer information answers different questions about consumer attributes and behavior. Information about attributes is best used to predict consumer behavior. Information about behavior helps the researcher understand what consumers actually do with their time and money, leading to more complete knowledge of the consumer.

Start at the first spoke, demographics and geography, and you get the foundation of your story. Who are your customers? Where do they live? For

Figure 3a.: THE 4 TYPES OF CONSUMER INFORMATION

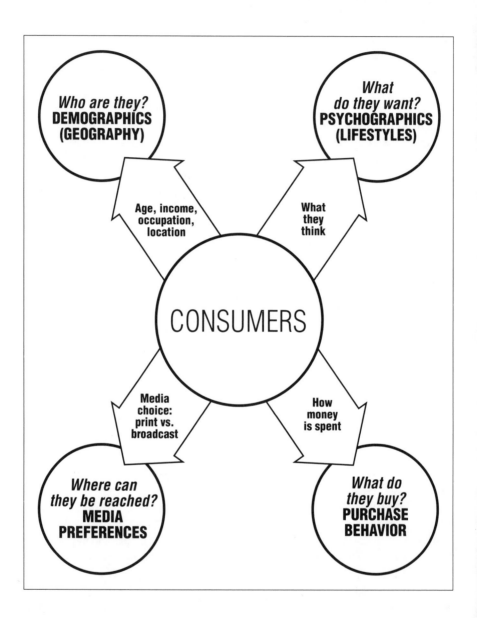

SOURCE: *The Insider's Guide to Demographic Know-How,* © 1990, American Demographics Books.

example, someone starting a cloth diaper service who wants to find out the potential market size would first look at the demographics. By identifying the number of women in their childbearing years, where women in this age group live, and projected birth rates, this entrepreneur can get some clues about market potential and location. But simply making inferences from demographics is not enough, because demographics are only one part of the story.

Demographics can tell you that two people each make $50,000 a year, live in $100,000 homes, are married, and have two children. But they can't tell you why one of them drives a three-quarter-ton Chevy pickup truck with a gun rack and custom roll bars, smokes Marlboros, and buys only Budweiser beer. And demographics can't tell you why the other one drives a top-of-the-line Mercedes, is a member of a wine-tasting club, and buys designer water.

People with similar demographics who live in the same neighborhood can have very different consumption patterns. Adding psychographic and life-style data can help any marketer understand what's on the customer's mind and answer the questions: What do they really want from my products, and what are the real reasons why they opt for one brand over another?

The purchase behavior of potential customers will answer the question about how customers spend their money. These kinds of data are often de-rived from a constantly updated customer database.

Then, when the most likely customers are identified, the question is: Where can I reach them most efficiently? For this, information about their media preferences would be most valuable.

Companies buy information to improve sales and marketing performance through geographic market analysis, product analysis, advertising, and stra-tegic planning. Each problem requires a different combination of informa-tion. Business people can better manage consumer information by research-ing alternative types of data and matching what is available with the specific tasks.

For example, combining sales records with easy-to-get federal data on buying patterns and demographics is a good, cheap way to estimate your market share, the total potential of the market, and which products and serv-ices will be in demand in the near future. Psychographics and purchase behavior information used together reveal how customers feel about specific products and how effective ads or promotions are. Using psychographics and media preference data can increase the effectiveness of advertising by helping you craft a message that is most likely to get through the media clut-ter to reach your customers.

What you see in figure 3a. is not a consumer information system but a blueprint for one. Just as you get a better house when you have a blueprint, you also get a better consumer information system when you have a blueprint. This blueprint includes some details, but it does not include all the technical specifications. The objective is to help you design the system for your specific needs.

By collecting consumer information, developing a consumer information system, and integrating it into your marketing system, you can gain a competitive edge by having data on everything from changing trading areas to the preferences of potential customers. The four types of consumer information are the basic building blocks of the consumer information system, but they are by no means the only components. The integrated system contains data on the general market, as well as in-house data on individual stores, target markets, and sales volume. An effective consumer information system also includes sales receipt data, new customer survey data, and other relevant internal and external information.

A consumer information system differs from the traditional idea of a marketing information or decision support system in that it contains specific details about the firm's customers. It is customer-oriented rather than product-oriented.

Whirlpool Corporation created an information "enclave" and improved the company's marketing information system in the 1970s. The same principle can be applied in the electronic age, only the enclave is now a series of integrated computer databases containing the corporate, marketing, and consumer information systems.

As the amount of data grows exponentially, it requires more time and money to maintain the database and keep it current. Some companies have attempted to tame the electronic tiger by creating a new position within the organization for an information integration specialist. Ultimately, these data integration wizards, perhaps a new breed of marketer, will become as essential to consumer service and marketing departments as controllers are to finance departments. Increasingly, these positions will require systems managers with marketing expertise who can crunch ideas along with numbers and create imaginative database tools designed especially to solve the firm's unique problems.

Better integration of consumer information can increase marketing efficiency and can create a competitive edge. Some of the nation's biggest companies recognized this early on and were the first to create massive in-house databases. These companies have databases containing internal data (generated by the firm), and external data (obtained from outside sources), as well as primary and secondary data. Primary data are gathered for a specific purpose and secondary data are all the data previously gathered for other purposes. These databases can become repositories for all relevant secondary data.

At the 1989 Information Industry Association conference, several of the firms at the cutting edge of information technology discussed their systems:

General Foods Corporation has a marketing information system designed especially to give its frozen-novelties sales force an edge. Forty people have direct on-line access to the system, which includes 20 marketing databases from several sources. Through their desktop computers, the staff can generate sales data, scanner data on product movement, couponing data, and competitive intelligence data.

Kraft Foods Inc. saved $5 million between 1986 and 1989 in data expenditures by developing its own in-house database with information designed to its own specifications. The database integrates proprietary, syndicated, commercial, and public databases, and effectively creates a one-stop information shopping system for the firm's marketers. Other advantages of the database have been faster response to market changes and greater attention to local differences among consumers. Kraft's Blair Peters said the firm was able to develop the database because the information suppliers the firm uses had better integrated their products and services.

These examples show the value of better consumer information management. But getting there can be a long, arduous road requiring a synthesis between the data information systems management and market research. Because the data and processing techniques are often incompatible, it may be necessary to start from scratch when building a system. But as many firms have discovered, automating marketing and sales information systems now will have a multiplier effect in the long term.

Data Providers

The consumer information system is the ultimate tool for marketing and sales people. Firms without the capability or intention of automating immediately, however, can also profit from effective use of consumer information.

Researchers with the time and expertise to compile and analyze raw data may prefer to buy CDs of the 1990 census and the software to manipulate them. Accessing demographic data directly will still mean the researcher must tap into other sources for psychographic, purchase behavior, and media preference data. Getting processed data and specialized reports from a full-service data firm costs more than doing the legwork yourself, but it can save time and may give you better information.

Apart from commercial data and research firms, other valuable sources are federal, state, and local governments, and trade associations and universities, which are discussed in more detail in chapters four and five.

Some firms are billing themselves as full-service data providers. By "full-service" these companies mean that they have access to every type of data and have separate business divisions to serve a wider variety of consumer research needs. Donnelley Marketing Information Services, for example, gets demographic information from the government, psychographic data from SRI International's VALS Program, and purchase behavior and media preference information from Simmons Market Research Bureau and Nielsen Media Research. It also compiles other databases and combines information into specially designed computer products.

The term "single-source," sometimes confused with full-service, entered the business lexicon in the early 1980s. Then it referred to the services that measure ad effectiveness by recording advertising exposure and tracing subsequent purchases of customers participating in panels. Using that meaning, there are only three electronically based single-source services: Arbitron's ScanAmerica, NPD/Nielsen's SCANTRACK and Information Resources' Infoscan. They all use checkout scanners to track purchases.

Getting and using information from a data firm can often be as easy as picking up the telephone and telling a representative what type of report or map is needed. The difficulty is not in getting the data, because all the necessary data can be obtained with relative ease. The problem lies in interpretation. Our ability to compile data has outstripped our ability to understand and use them. Often there's a gap between what a data or research firm can supply and what the client needs, so it's also important to understand the limitations of data sources.

The best way marketers can be sure to get the information they need is to know what it is they want. Getting what you need starts with a better understanding of the origins and capabilities of consumer information.

The following two chapters will help you master the basics—where to get the information, and what it can and can't tell you. Only by understanding the data beast can businesses tame it, manage information more efficiently, and become better equipped to capture more customers in the world of 2000 and beyond.

CHAPTER FOUR

Consumer Attributes: Demographics

DEMOGRAPHICS provide the basic picture of the customer and psychographic information adds color and depth to that picture. Used together, attribute information can predict what consumers are likely to want and buy in the future.

If you know, for example, that 18-to-24-year-olds are regular consumers of your hair mousse—they buy it at a certain rate—you can begin to project future unit sales. But rates of purchase may change because of fashion or attitude swings and the accuracy of your projection depends on what you know about the future demographics of 18-to-24-year-olds.

Understanding Demographics

The term "demographic" comes from two Greek roots: "graphein," which means "to write" and "demos," which means "people." The term reportedly was first coined by French political economist Achille Guillard in 1855.

For a quick definition of demographics, look at your driver's license. It lists your name, address, sex, and age—a description of an individual. That is basic demographics. As your needs become more complex, demographics can provide information on income level, type of dwelling, marital status, race, and many other factors that help distinguish one individual or group from the rest of the population.

Looking at the wider meaning, *Webster's Dictionary* defines something as "demographic" when it relates to the dynamic balance of a population. Demographers study the social and economic effects of a population's size, how many people are concentrated in various areas, how fast or slowly populations are growing, and how they move from place to place.

Analyzing shifts in national demographics reveals trends that transform the population. Because they identify opportunities, national demographics are essential for long-term strategic planning. By carefully considering the big picture, decision makers can learn what the needs and demands of future Americans will be.

Narrow the focus, however, and demographics prove invaluable for understanding individual consumers and smaller markets. Two important demographic attributes are age and income. If you know how old consumers are and how much money they have, you can get a pretty good idea of their propensity and ability to buy certain products and services. A married couple in their early 40s with a high income, for example, might spend a lot on furniture. If you know more about them, such as whether they have any young children in their household, then you can sharpen your prediction about the kinds of furniture they might buy.

Household type, education, and occupation are also valuable demographic factors for predicting consumer behavior. For example, the maker of home office products will look for market areas with high concentrations of the self-employed, while the maker of home furnishings will seek young married-couple households.

By segmenting the market this way, it becomes easier to quantify and understand. Demographics were the first segmentation device available for consumer goods manufacturers faced with the emergence of a market-oriented economy. They are still the most important and the most frequently used tool.

Demographic data were not widely used until businesses started to recognize the potential impact of the baby boom on product demand. Their median age, median income, and household formation rates became standard business terms. It has only been in the past decade that many of the nation's universities have started offering demographic courses as part of their business programs.

As the ability to identify and target products and messages to market segments becomes more crucial, demographics will grow in importance because they are the easiest type of data to get, the least expensive, and the most useful.

Demographics are a vital part of a consumer information system for these reasons:

1. They are universally available. No matter what tiny corner of the country your customers inhabit, you can get demographic statistics for it. Whether it's an irregular oblong-shaped trading area a mile long, a tiny ring around a convenience store, a whole state, or the entire country, you can get the demographic statistics that tell you who lives there.

2. The terms are standardized. The Census Bureau is the definitive source, and its terms are widely accepted. That means everyone who uses demographic statistics is talking about the same thing. The definition of a household is absolutely consistent from market research company to market research company. A household is an occupied dwelling unit. An empty dwelling is definitely not a household. All families are households but not all households are families. The standardization of terms means you can take a survey, code it in a certain way, and match it with demographic data from another source.

3. Many demographic characteristics are projectable. Today's 35-year-old American will be a 45-year-old in ten years. That statement will be absolutely true unless that person dies or leaves the country. This makes demographic projections quite accurate. When the demographic facts are projected into the future they can predict which populations will grow and which will decline.

4. They make market segmentation possible. With these standardized, readily available measurement units, it is possible to discern who is buying what. Because of the above reasons, demographics have become the starting point of business research activities from market and product analysis to advertising and strategic planning. But it is just the starting point. Demographics, when used for marketing purposes, must be combined with other types of data, such as purchase behavior, media preferences, and psychographics, to give a complete picture of the consumer. Demographics are not everything, but they are the skeleton of a consumer information system.

Where Demographics Come From

As the origin of the term suggests, demographic information comes from people. By responding to censuses or other surveys, Americans give us virtually all the demographic information that exists about them.

The U.S. Census Bureau is the primary source for demographic knowledge, because it is the only official service that enumerates all U.S. citizens. Every ten years the Census Bureau takes a headcount of Americans. By law, every household in America must answer the census questions. In addition to the decennial census, the bureau also conducts regular surveys, such as the annual Current Population Survey (CPS), which provides updated estimates of the most widely used data.

The CPS collects demographic and employment characteristics of 60,000 households each month, a much larger sample than any private corporation could afford to survey. For example, Mediamark Research, Inc., and Simmons Market Research Bureau, two of the most widely used syndicated research firms, base their data on annual surveys of about 20,000 adults.

Other demographic data come from surveys of representative population samples done by various organizations. We know, for example, that about 25 percent of adults in the U.S. are smokers because the National Center for Health Statistics took a survey. They sampled a group of adults large enough to represent the demographic characteristics of the U.S. population. Survey tabulations are really approximations of what the whole group is like, with statistically defined margins of error.

The U.S. Census

The type of information required from Americans has become more diverse since the first national census was taken in 1790. Changes in the questions reflect changes in American lifestyles.

In 1790 people were asked how they were related to the "family head." By 1940 the term was "household head" to enable researchers to distinguish subfamilies and nonfamilies, and for the first time people were asked how many times they had been married. The 1980 census was the first to include the more generic term "householder," in recognition of the growing number of female heads of households.

The 1990 census was the first census to include a category for "unmarried partner," so researchers can track the growing number of people living in nontraditional arrangements. The 1990 census was also the first to include categories for "natural born," "adopted," or "foster" children. This will help researchers estimate how many of the nation's families are products of divorce and remarriage. The 1990 census will also provide better data on alternative energy, the economic status of the elderly, people with disabilities, and second mortgages than any past census.

In April 1990, most households received the short questionnaire which consisted of seven population and seven housing questions. Every householder was asked to list the names and relations of all people in the household, along with their sex, age, race, marital status, the type of home or dwelling, and the cost of monthly rent or mortgage. A longer questionnaire, consisting of 26 additional population and 19 more housing questions was sent to a 17 percent sample of households.

The primary uses of census information are social and political. Census results are used to redistribute congressional seats among the states. The census results determine how federal funds are allocated to social and economic programs. State and local governments also use them for allocations, and universities base research on them.

But census data are the stuff that marketing dreams are made of. Once the Census Bureau has a handle on the sex, age, race, income, and educational attainment levels of the population, these data can be crunched and projected with a high degree of accuracy.

Key Demographics

Here is a list of key demographic variables used by the Census Bureau, along with their more widely used categories:

1. **Age:**

   under 5, 5–12, 13–17, 18–24, 25–34, 35–44, 45–54, 55–64, 65–74, 75–84, 85+

   Sex: • male   • female

2. **Race/Ethnicity:**
   - white
   - black
   - Asian
   - Hispanic (may be of any race)
   - other (includes Native Americans)

3. **Household Types:**

   Families:
   - married couple with children under age 18
   - married couple with no children under age 18
   - other family (includes single parents)

   Nonfamilies:
   - persons living alone
   - unrelated persons sharing living quarters

4. **Household Ownership:**
   - single-family, owner-occupied
   - two+-family owner-occupied
   - condominium or coop
   - rented unit
   - mobile home or trailer
   - other (includes houseboats, etc.)

5. **Educational Attainment:**
   - not high school graduate
   - high school graduate
   - some college (1 to 3 years)
   - college degree
   - advanced degree (master's degree, doctorate, etc.)

6. **Employment Status & Occupation:**
   - employed full-time
   - employed part-time
   - not employed
   - retired

   If Employed:
   - professional worker, executive/administrative/managerial
   - clerical/sales/technical
   - craft/repair/equipment operator
   - service worker (food service, etc.)
   - other

7. **Household Income:**
   - under $10,000
   - $10,000–$24,999
   - $25,000–$34,999
   - $35,000–$49,999
   - $50,000–$74,999
   - $75,000+

Income data can be difficult to collect because people often will not tell you their income. However, income is closely related to education and occupation, questions people are more likely to answer.

Purchase behavior will vary depending on what one or more of these variables show. Others may be important for specific products (number of bedrooms for bed and mattress sales, for example), but these demographics have the most general applications.

Geography

Geography is a vital factor determining the relevancy and availability of demographic data for marketers. For companies doing target marketing, the smaller the area the better, but often accurate small-area data are hard to find.

Think of an aerial view of the nation. The target marketer's job is to zero in on areas as small as a city block and figure out what consumers there are like and whether they fit the profile of the target group. The Census Bureau collects data on units of households as small as block groups or as large as states and the entire nation.

There are two major categories of geography for which census data are available:

1. Legal borders—town, village, city, county, state, region, and nation

2. Statistical areas—in ascending order: block groups (250 households), census tracts (1,200 households), and metropolitan statistical areas.

Statistical areas are more useful for targeting and understanding markets because they follow market area boundaries more closely. The most widely used statistical areas are metropolitan statistical areas (MSAs), which include data on the largest U.S. metropolitan areas defined by their component counties. The United States is made up not only of 50 states, but of 335 MSAs, about 68,000 census tracts, and about 254,000 block groups.

From a marketer's point of view, the most important advance in the 1990 census is TIGER. TIGER (Topologically Integrated Geographic Encoding and Referencing System) is a computerized map of the nation.

In the past, census takers used paper maps to find addresses and updated the maps by hand, which caused a lot of mistakes. After the 1980 count, bureau geographers began computerizing all of the U.S. Geological Survey's maps. They used an optical scanning machine that assigned geographic coordinates to waterways, political boundaries, rail lines, and streets.

The census's TIGER database contains only geographic data and address ranges for each city block. Once these data are linked with other types of data, however, its power increases. TIGER has the potential to show the street patterns around a potential site or identify physical barriers limiting customer access and decreasing sales.

Figure 4a: 1990 CENSUS GEOGRAPHY

The 1990 census will provide data for a variety of geographic areas, most of which are hierarchical—meaning the smaller areas are subunits of the next larger areas. These units range from the U.S. as a whole down to city blocks. Below is the geographic hierarchy in which most census data will be arranged, in descending order.

U.S.*	The 50 states and the District of Columbia.
Region	The four regions are the Northeast, South, Midwest, and West.
Division	The four regions are split into nine divisions. Individual states combine to form divisions.
State	The 50 states and the District of Columbia are subunits of the nine divisions.
County	Counties are subunits of states. The 3,141 counties are divided into two types of subunits: minor civil divisions (MCDs) or census county divisions (CCDs), and census tracts.
Minor civil division/ census county division	Minor civil divisions (MCDs) are county subunits. MCDs are defined by the municipal governments within each county. In the 21 states that are not subdivided into MCDs, the bureau creates census county divisions (CCDs). Every county is completely divided into MCDs or CCDs.
Place	Places include incorporated places and census designated places. Incorporated places are defined by the laws of states to include cities, boroughs, towns, and villages. Census designated places are created by the Census Bureau to include boundaries of closely settled population centers without corporate limits. Before 1980, census designated places were called unincorporated places. Places can cross MCD or county lines, but not state lines.
Census tract/block	Census tracts/block numbering areas are also county numbering area subunits. Census tracts are defined by local committees and follow guidelines prepared by the Census Bureau. Block numbering areas are defined by the bureau in areas that don't have census tracts. When first defined, these areas are to contain an average of 4,000 people, having generally similar socioeconomic characteristics.
Block group	Block groups are the subunits of census tracts or block numbering areas. Block groups have an average of 1,000 people living in them. They are new versions of the 1980 block groups or enumeration districts. Block groups combine to form census tracts and block numbering areas, which combine to form counties.
Block	Roughly equivalent to a city block, census blocks are the smallest level of census geography, but they are bounded by water, roads, railroads, and other physical features. Blocks combine to form block groups, which combine to form census tracts/block numbering areas. For 1990, the entire nation is divided into blocks.

*Puerto Rico, U.S. Virgin Islands, Guam, and outlying areas in the Pacific will not be included in U.S. totals, but similar reports will be available for these areas as for the states.

SOURCE: © 1989, American Demographics Magazine

Integrating TIGER and other consumer information databases results in a system that allows marketers to enter into a personal computer the geographic coordinate for any street intersection in the country. They can then call up a thematic data map of any size trade area around that intersection and print out demographic, purchase behavior, and media preference data related to it.

Compact Disk and TIGER

The 1990 census will be the first available on laser disks, also known as CD-ROMs. These CDs look just like the ones containing digitized music, but each CD contains data—the equivalent of 1,500 floppy disks. This means that if you have a reader (which costs less than $500), you can buy the disks and access the census data right from your desktop. It's slower than a mainframe, but it puts all that age, income, and household information within easy reach.

Cluster Segmentation Systems

Geodemographic segmenting, also called cluster analysis, is a process that analyzes the average demographic characteristics of the people living in a small geographic area and defines the area by the characteristics most common there. Businesses can use cluster analysis to quantify and categorize relatively small populations.

By linking demographic factors to lifestyle and buying data, cluster analysis systems can tell marketers that the majority of consumers in a certain ZIP Code, census tract, or block group buy more seafood than beef, or watch more TV than read magazines.

For direct mailers, however, a more refined level of postal geography is the carrier route. There are 180,000 carrier routes in the country, which are composed of about 480 households each. Carrier routes may also include many types of consumers, but the advantage is that they identify the location of these smaller groups with greater accuracy.   It is also possible to get the demographics of carrier routes by comparing them with census block groups that cover the same area.

To Cluster or Not to Cluster

Five companies now offer clustering systems, and each has a trade name. They are, in alphabetical order:
- ACORN, by CACI
- ClusterPLUS, by Donnelley Marketing Information Services
- OASYS, by National Demographics & Lifestyles
- PRIZM, by Claritas
- VISION, by Equifax Marketing Decision Systems

Despite some drawbacks inherent in using averages, cluster analysis has become a widely accepted marketing information tool. Some of the biggest consumer goods producers have used cluster analysis with great success to identify local and regional markets.

Cluster analysis is now available for almost any geographic level from the broadcast-oriented Areas of Dominant Influence (ADIs) to ZIPs, census tracts, census blocks, and postal carrier routes. The data firms link cluster data with syndicated surveys of psychographics, purchase behavior, and media use to produce more sophisticated profiles of the people who live in a neighborhood. One drawback, the once-in-a-decade nature of the small-area census data, is partially compensated for by regular projections and updates done by the data firms.

Other changes will be seen in the data industry with the greater availability of 1990 census data. Edward Spar, president of Market Statistics, a data firm based in New York City, calls what the Census Bureau is doing "data liberation." Because of this, he says, data firms are going to have to concentrate more on solving customers' problems and less on the data. That bodes well for all data users.

The Census Bureau makes the census data accessible, but it does not provide the software and systems needed to integrate their data with other consumer information. The Census Bureau is concerned primarily with the political and social uses of the data. Marketing information firms make the census useful to the business world.

Don't Know? Ask Them

The census is a wonderful instrument—a snapshot of the country that's versatile and full of potential for researchers with imagination. With the demographics of your current customers in hand, you can hunt through the census data for areas of similar people.

Gathering the names and addresses of current customers is like putting money in the bank. For a small fee, many of the data companies will take your customer list and assign each name and address to its unique census block code number. Geocoding is a fast and reasonable way to estimate the demographics of your current customers. It is only an estimate, however, because the confidentiality of the census prohibits release of data on individuals or households. Geocoding tells you where your customers are, and census data can tell you generally who they are, but you get their specific demographics through information provided on charge-card applications, sales receipts, product registration cards, or surveys. Then you need psychographics, purchase behavior, and media preference data to get the whole story on your actual customers.

The way to get the real first-hand story on your customers is to ask them. Take a survey and ask for their ages, incomes, and other demographics. Ask them how much of the product they buy, what makes them buy it, what they like to watch and read, and what would make them buy more or less of your product.

That sounds easy, but survey taking is a tricky business. There are procedures that must be followed to make the survey statistically accurate. One of the most common mistakes is surveying too few people, or surveying a group that is not representative of the whole. Because sample bias becomes worse as the sample gets smaller, asking a dozen customers (out of thousands) isn't enough. Decisions based on what a dozen customers tell you may be worse than not questioning them at all.

Even if the sample size is large enough, survey bias can render your results questionable. Survey bias means asking the wrong questions, asking them incorrectly, or recording them improperly. It could even be something as subtle as asking them in the wrong tone of voice. Survey taking is a precision science, and the possibilities for making mistakes are endless. There are many research firms that specialize in surveying customers face-to-face, by mail, or over the telephone.

Demographic Data Sources

Probably the easiest and fastest way to get a general demographic picture of an area is to order a report from a marketing information firm. To produce a printed report all that is usually required is an address or a geographic coordinate, such as a street intersection. A sample page from a general demographic report, which usually costs between $50 and $100 and takes a day or two to receive, appears in figure 4b.

These reports provide a demographic overview of any area from one to 20 miles around an intersection, including population size, household types, age, income, education, and other characteristics. The data firms can also provide similar data on one or two other areas to allow comparison. This is invaluable for market screening because potential target markets can be matched with an area where the product or service is already successful. By comparing target markets to the entire U.S. a researcher can gauge market potential by finding out what characteristics are present in higher or lower concentrations than the national average.

On a local level, a retailer who knows that fewer customers are coming from one region in his trading area could compare the demographics from the problem neighborhood with the demographics of the whole trade area. Perhaps the store has a stodgy, outdated image that can't attract the young, upscale residents who live in the problem area. By identifying who the cus-

Figure 4b: A DEMOGRAPHIC TREND REPORT

```
TREND REPORT
for Washington, D.C.
                                    Max Area Evaluation System
                                    1-800-234-5629     6-JUN-90

Study Area Summary

Trend Information (Including Household Income Distribution)

Population, Households, Families, and Year-round Housing Units
```

	1970 Census	1980 Census	% Chg 70-80	1990 (Est.)	% Chg 80-90	1995 (Proj.)	% Chg 90-95
Population	756510	638333	-15.6	612569	-4.0	597914	-2.4
Households	262539	253143	-3.6	247434	-2.3	240188	-2.9
Families		133643		125135	-6.4	118801	-5.1
Housing Units		276792		270277	-2.4	262291	-3.0
Household Size	2.72*	2.40	-11.9	2.36	-1.5	2.37	0.7
Group Quarters		31919		29015	-9.1	27728	-4.4

```
Income
```

	1969 (Census)	1979 (Census)	% Chg 69-79	1990 (Est.)	% Chg 79-90	1995 (Proj.)	% Chg 90-95
Agg. Income ($MM)	2906.5	5719.5	96.8	10489.0	83.4	13049.5	24.4
Per Capita ($)	3842	8960	133.2	17123	91.1	21825	27.5
Average HH ($)	10660	21982	106.2	41902	90.6	54014	28.9
Median HH ($)	8898	16219	82.3	32383	99.7	42018	29.8
Average HH Wealth ($)				111682		144684	
Median HH Wealth ($)				44225		64042	

```
Household Income Distribution
```

	1979 Count	1979 %	1990 Count	1990 %	1995 Count	1995 %
Less than $ 7,500	56936	22.5	27879	11.3	19038	7.9
$ 7,500-$ 9,999	20305	8.0	8942	3.6	8714	3.6
$ 10,000-$ 14,999	40284	15.9	19140	7.7	13892	5.8
$ 15,000-$ 19,999	34102	13.5	20595	8.3	14188	5.9
$ 20,000-$ 24,999	25291	10.0	19806	8.0	15826	6.6
$ 25,000-$ 29,999	19201	7.6	19202	7.8	15269	6.4
$ 30,000-$ 34,999	14425	5.7	17108	6.9	15020	6.3
$ 35,000-$ 39,999	9880	3.9	15699	6.3	12812	5.3
$ 40,000-$ 49,999	13124	5.2	24716	10.0	26439	11.0
$ 50,000-$ 74,999	12869	5.1	38742	15.7	40501	16.9
$ 75,000-$ 99,999	3576	1.4	16764	6.8	27254	11.3
$100,000-$149,999	2069	0.8	12969	5.2	18415	7.7
$150,000-$199,999	575	0.2	2884	1.2	8026	3.3
$200,000-$249,999	225	0.1	1322	0.5	1866	0.8
$250,000-$499,999	236	0.1	1389	0.6	2153	0.9
$500,000 and over	45	0.0	277	0.1	775	0.3

```
*1970 Household size is an estimate based on 1970 census data.
Data on income are expressed in "current" dollars for each respective year.

1990 estimates and 1995 projections produced by National Planning Data Corp.
```

tomers are and who they aren't, the retailer is on the way to solving the store's problem and capturing those customers.

A growing number of companies collect, process, and repackage data into products designed for diverse business uses. Most firms can provide all four types of consumer information and sell software products that link the data.

How to Get Demographic Data

Tracking down demographic data has five simple steps, according to Diane Crispell, associate national editor of *American Demographics* magazine.

1. Identify the species. To identify the best source of data, first you have to know what kind of data you need. For example, if you need health statistics, the National Center for Health Statistics or a state health department would be likely sources.

2. Mark off the territory. Identify the geography for which the data are required. Except for the Census Bureau, the Bureau of Labor Statistics, and the Bureau of Economic Analysis, most federal agencies only have national data. For up-to-date small-area data, look into state, local, commercial, or organizational sources. Or you could hire a survey firm or survey the market yourself.

3. Select the season. Data are available by census year, in current estimates, and by future projections. Not all data are available for all time periods. Projections are especially limited. Do you need data collected yesterday, or are census data current enough? Often, data on certain characteristics don't exist for periods in the past. And older data may not be compatible with current data due to definition changes. Generally, the data companies have the most up-to-date data, but the federal government also has extensive national- and state-level projections.

4. Check the format. Some government publications, like the Census Bureau's *Current Population Reports* and the Bureau of Labor Statistics' *Monthly Labor Review* are easy reads. The detailed census publications and tapes are not. Do you want complicated volumes of numerical tables or abbreviated reports and colorful maps? The data companies can provide the whole range, but the Census Bureau cannot.

5. Consider cost. As a rule, government data are older but cheaper than those sold by the data firms. If cost is a consideration and if you're able to, it's much cheaper to buy government data and manipulate them yourself. Most data firms, however, offer less expensive options—reports ranging from $50 to $100 that provide various types of data on one or two areas. As the clients' information needs become more complicated, the data price goes up. There are some problems that would take forever to solve using the raw data. If you need up-to-date local information for every area of the country, your only option is a private marketing information firm.

Demographic data can help measure the size and composition of current and potential markets. They can point out changes that may cause you trouble down the road or identify a terrific opportunity. But the next consumer attribute, psychographics, gives you the ability to predict how your customers will behave. Together, demographics and psychographics provide the most basic picture of your customers.

CHAPTER FIVE

Psychographics: Inside the Mind

IN THE HEYDAY of the mass market, demographics were enough to guide the marketing efforts of most companies. Today, the only thing two 34-year-old women may have in common is their age. One may be a single corporate executive with a heavy travel schedule. The other may be divorced and raising her two children with the help of an unmarried male or female partner. Both of them are single and 34; both may have similar incomes and educations. But they will demand totally different things from the goods and services they buy.

What's a marketer to do? One increasingly valuable option is to take a look into their minds. Does the corporate executive live in the fast lane but long for a slower-paced, more romantic existence? Does she pamper herself by buying jewelry and flowers? Or does she have little time or desire for anything but success and work?

Understanding Psychographics

Psychographics put flesh on the demographic skeleton to answer those questions. Demographics and psychographics share the Greek root, "graphein," which means "to write," and psyche is "mind" in Greek. In marketing analysis, psychographics focus on the mind of the consumer.

The origin of the term "psychographics" is decidedly hazy. Emmanuel H. Demby, president of Demby & Associates in New York City, has stated that he made up the word on the spur of the moment in 1965 when an executive in the firm he was working for asked him to define his research. Demby said he came up with the word by combining psychology and demographics. That may have been about the time the term entered the marketing lexicon with its current meaning. That same year the word "psychographics" appeared in *Grey Matter*, a Grey Advertising newsletter circulated to clients. It referred to the benefit segmentation work being done at Grey by Russell Haley and others. There is still some disagreement about who first coined the term.

Arnold Mitchell, the late founder of Stanford Research Institute's Values,

Attitudes and Lifestyles (VALS) Program, and a recognized pioneer in psychographic research, defines the term this way in his 1983 book *The Nine American Lifestyles*: "The entire constellation of a person's attitudes, beliefs, opinions, hopes, fears, prejudices, needs, desires, and aspirations that, taken together, govern how one behaves," and that in turn "finds holistic expression in a lifestyle."

The emergence of lifestyle as a concept parallels the rise of interest in psychographics as a market segmentation tool. Some consider psychographics to be lifestyle research. In the early 1960s, when social psychologists and market researchers first set out to segment American buyers by their values and attitudes, the concept of lifestyle was relatively new. Before then, people didn't have lifestyles, they just lived.

Lifestyles are a product of postwar U.S. affluence, the rebellions of the 1960s, and the machinations of social change. In his 1981 book *New Rules*, Daniel Yankelovich, cofounder of the Yankelovich Lifestyle Monitor, equates the social changes of the past 30 years to plate tectonics. On the surface, the unrests of the 1960s had very little effect on the lives of the majority of Americans. But by the 1970s, Yankelovich's surveys showed the idea of self-discovery and the search for fulfillment had permeated the consciousness of 80 percent of Americans. Like massive geological plates moving deep beneath the earth, the ideas of the 1960s eventually did transform the landscape of the American mind.

"It is as if tens of millions of people had decided simultaneously to conduct risky experiments in living, using the only materials that lay at hand— their own lives," Yankelovich wrote. This translated into more women entering the work force, more people going back to college, more divorces, and more lifestyle alternatives. Now lifestyles run the whole gamut—from the gay rights activist to the traditional wife and mother.

Psychographic research helps differentiate one customer from another in terms of personalities, opinions, interests, activities, attitudes, and values. It tells the researcher what the target group thinks—about themselves, about the product, the advertising, or the medium. It identifies the image that sticks in consumers' minds and allows businesses to create products and messages that hit their mark and bring in sales.

Used alone, psychographics are interesting. They tell you what a certain survey group thinks. But psychographics gain real power when they are tied to purchase behavior data. Then they can show that people who spend the most money on a specific product are more achievement-oriented than the rest of the population, or that they think of themselves as risk-takers. This gives the researcher definite clues about what types of appeals will work with those customers.

What's the Motive

To understand consumer behavior, you first have to look at product-related motivations. Except for those who shop as a hobby, most people are motivated to buy when an unmet need is stimulated. Some needs are biological, like food, shelter, and rest; and some needs are psychological, like the need for respect and the need to feel good about oneself.

A motivation to buy may be as simple as being hungry and buying a hot dog from a street vendor, or it can be the complex process of buying a big-ticket durable good such as an automobile. A woman decides she needs a new car, then she starts noticing cars around her and paying attention to ads. She reads articles on various models and brands, she tests different brands, and finally she buys.

The motivation changes depending on the product. Some products, like cars and clothing, induce high ego involvement from consumers, while other products, like laundry soap, require very little.

Whether the purchase is impulsive or planned, one constant remains: needs vary from person to person and over time. The automobile one customer buys for safety may be the same car someone else buys for prestige. Psychographics reveal both customers' needs so that products and advertisements can be tailored to meet those needs.

Psychographics can also help correct image problems. Once the decision to buy is made, the customer has to decide which brand or model to purchase. With durable goods and most consumer goods, a customer will buy the brand or model that seems the best. This is a purely subjective judgment based on the image in the customer's mind. Image is the critical factor that makes a motivated consumer choose one product or service over another.

Even when driven by hunger, some consumers will not buy a sidewalk vendor's hot dog because it contains preservatives and meat by-products. The image of the ballpark hot dog will never induce some consumers to buy. But alter the image by adding the words "gourmet," and "all natural," and even those reluctant consumers may give in to their hunger.

A company that encounters an image problem has two options: change the product or change the consumers' image of the product. Each solution begins with psychographics.

Changing the consumers' image is the more expensive and difficult alternative, but it has been done successfully. Honda did it upon first entering the U.S. motorcycle market. Consumers had the image of motorcycle riders as ruffians. Honda successfully instituted an ad campaign showing fresh-faced, all-American types riding motorcycles. MCI Telecommunications Corporation faced the image obstacle of convincing consumers that its technology and service were as good as leader AT&T's. MCI won market share from Goliath partly by successfully portraying itself as an aggressive, sophisticated company that was committed to offering better service. Absolut vodka used creative images of its crystal-clear bottle to buck the trends. Despite falling liquor consumption rates, Absolut's U.S. sales have risen from nothing in 1978 to 16 million bottles in 1988. Each company changed the way consumers thought about its products with strategic advertising and promotional campaigns.

Like the sidewalk vendor, most companies find that changing the product is the only way to fix a widespread image problem. But even product changes based on psychographic data can go awry if they aren't supported by demographics, purchase behavior, and media preference information.

This was the lesson learned by Anheuser-Busch after the release of a new beer called Natural Light. It seemed a sure thing because all the psychographic data revealed a real groundswell of consumer interest in natural products and healthy lifestyles. But the beer bombed. The product was positioned on the premise that beer drinkers cared about naturalness. As sales proved, they didn't. But the company hadn't bothered to ask the actual beer consumers. They made the mistake of extrapolating psychographic research about one segment of the market to another. They took solo psychographic research too far.

Trend or Segment?

Psychographic research comes in two very basic flavors: research that reveals trends and research designed to segment consumers by attitudes, values, or product attributes. Trend research will tell you that more American consumers feel they are pressed for time. Trend research can also tell you that your customers feel that same way. It can be about the general market or your customers, but it reveals only changing attitudes.

Psychographic segmentation research allows a business to segment its own customers or all the people who buy the product it sells by psychographic type. This provides a useful way to identify the differences between your customers and customers in general.

The cost of psychographic research is high because, unlike demographic research, the data are not available from the federal government. The only way to get valid psychographic data is to hire someone to take a survey. Sometimes low-cost psychographic trend data can be obtained from trade associations and other special interest groups. But in general, good psychographic data are expensive because the best come from researchers who have refined their methods through years of practice.

Companies with limited resources can, however, learn more about the thoughts and feelings of people in their markets. In some cases, a business can get valuable psychographic data through informal chats or semi-formal small group discussions called focus groups. In other cases, the only method that will work is a large-scale survey. For that, you need a specialist with a proven track record who understands the strengths and pitfalls of psychographic research.

Buyer Beware: Trick or Trend?

Psychographic research is trickier than demographic research because the researcher must find a quantitative way to get qualitative data about people. And there is no industry standard or set of Census Bureau definitions for psychographics. As a result, dozens of psychographic systems have emerged, each based upon a different definition and using different methodology.

Psychographics involve human nature, which is much less precise than age and income. Ask someone to describe their attitudes and beliefs at 8:00 a.m., when they're fresh and beginning a day at the office, and you're likely to find a charged-up business achiever. Ask them again at 9:00 p.m., when they're relaxing after work, dinner, and a couple of drinks, and you'll find someone more interested in security, warmth, and comfort. A person's age and income usually don't change with the time of day. But their psychographic makeup changes constantly, depending on shifting moods.

For these reasons, it is important to separate psychographic fact from fiction. Psychographic claims must be based on solid research, not hearsay. Take, for example, the media focus a few years ago on "cocooning," or the desire to spend more leisure time at home. In the late 1980s, a growing number of articles trumpeted the growth of the cocooning trend. Actually, Roper Organization polls at the time showed the number of respondents saying they preferred staying home to going out had remained stable at 42 percent. What the trend spotters may have noticed was a maturing of attitudes in one age group.

Marketers should be especially wary of exaggerated or unsupported claims when looking at information on attitudes and values. When you hear that "everybody" knows, likes, or dislikes something, ask exactly who "everybody" is. Is he a 19-year-old single man or a 65-year-old married woman? A Libertarian, a fundamentalist, someone who's happy, or depressed? Everybody's different, especially in the America of the 1990s.

When measuring values and lifestyles, look for systems that are clearly based on social science methods and operated by people with advanced social science training. Don't buy anything until you understand exactly how it works, and ask for comments from people who already use the data. There are a growing number of psychographic consultants who can guide you through this maze. If you spend a lot of money on product development and advertising, buying their services will be well worth it.

The Major Contenders

In the U.S., two companies are now on the market with psychographic descriptions of the entire U.S. market. Their products are called VALS 2 and Lifestyle Monitor. The heaviest users of these kinds of data are the major players in consumer packaged goods, banking, travel, health care, automobiles, and other businesses where the public image of products or services is important.

Both systems are based on surveys of a representative sample of 2,500 Americans. VALS is the most widely used and the only one directly linked to purchase behavior and media preferences through surveys conducted by Mediamark Research and Simmons Market Research Bureau. The VALS system is composed of eight psychographic types. Any consumer group, from the entire population to an individual store's customers, can be classified by these types and then compared with other groups.

The Yankelovich Lifestyle Monitor looks at the bigger picture. It is more fluid, and the types of attitudes and behaviors it identifies can change from year to year. The Monitor is designed to identify changes in consumer attitudes, which can be predictors of larger social changes. It attempts to show how these changes in consumer values affect businesses. The newly updated VALS program, however, is specially designed to provide corporate clients with a method of segmenting their customers according to their psychology.

The Monitor

The Monitor is the oldest continuing survey of consumer attitudes and behavior. It was started in 1970 by Harvard-educated psychologist Daniel Yankelovich and Florence Skelly, who were principals in the research firm Yankelovich, Skelly & White. Their firm was acquired by Saatchi & Saatchi and merged with Clancy and Shulman. Yankelovich Clancy Shulman (YCS) of Westport, Connecticut, now controls The Monitor, while Daniel Yankelovich and Florence Skelly left to form another firm, the Daniel Yankelovich Group, in New York.

Data for the Yankelovich Monitor are gathered through 90-minute home interviews with a representative national sample of 2,500 adults each year at 350 sites in the U.S. Some of the questions are designed to reveal social attitudes; these questions do not change from year to year, so they can be compared over time. Other questions address consumer behavior and are designed to fit the concerns of various industries.

The interviews track more than 50 social trends, such as "the search for community," "commitment to buy American," "anti-bigness," "the new romanticism," and "tolerance for chaos and disorder." Based on the trends, The Monitor outlines several major adaptive patterns that segment the American people: Traditionalists, Good Neighbors, Reachers, the New Establishment, and Anglers, who are subdivided into Entrepreneurs and Players. The groups are defined attitudinally but can also be examined in terms of their demographics and behavior.

The Monitor is a psychographic information tool designed to measure changing values and is based on empirical evidence. It is not a segmentation system like VALS. The Monitor, for example, looks at how a general social change, such as the entry of women into the labor force, alters specific consumer values, such as the social acceptability of bringing home take-out food. Through other questions a researcher can gain insight into whether male respondents who express positive feelings about women in the labor force also practice what they preach and split the house work 50/50 at home. "It explains the wider world, finds an appropriate target for the business and helps them decide how to approach the target," says YCS president Robert Shulman.

In the past several years, YCS has also introduced additional Monitor studies focusing on specific demographic groups. The Youth Monitor, which looks at attitudes, consumer behavior patterns, and aspirations of children between grades 1 and 12, started in 1987. The Senior Monitor started in 1988, and examines the attitudes and behavior of Americans over age 49. The Hispanic Monitor focuses on American Hispanics and started in 1988. Plans are in the works to develop an Asian Monitor, provided the obstacles of accessibility and language can be overcome, says YCS vice president Susan Hayward.

VALS 2

The Values and Lifestyles Program came out of research done by SRI International, a large private research firm in Menlo Park, California. VALS became a separate program in 1978 and its first survey was done in 1980.

The original VALS was devised by the late Arnold Mitchell, a social scientist who borrowed heavily from Abraham Maslow's theory of the hierarchy of human needs. Mitchell's original VALS "typology" divided the U.S. population into four major categories according to the way they related to the world, whether they looked outside themselves for fulfillment or relied on their inner resources. The four categories were: 1) **Outer-Directed**—those who seek external symbols of status; 2) **Inner-Directed**—those who seek self-fulfillment; 3) **Needs-Driven** or impoverished; and 4) a tiny, "superior" group at the top of the hierarchy—the **Integrated**—who combine the best elements of all other groups.

These four categories were further divided into nine lifestyle types such as Survivors, Belongers, Experientials, Achievers, and Societally Conscious. In the original VALS, a sample of adults were asked to state their feelings about 33 statements such as, "Communists should be prohibited from running for mayor of a city," and "I like to think I'm a bit of a swinger." The statements were designed to reveal the respondent's feelings about status, family, risk, and other personal issues, and to establish the lifestyle typology.

In the early 1980s, when VALS was combined with data from Simmons and Mediamark syndicated surveys, it gained an edge over The Monitor because its psychographic types could be linked to buying behavior and media use. This allowed researchers to begin to understand why certain people buy certain products. It has been found that Belongers, for example, drink a lot of beer. That's why the word "American" and flags are seen so often in beer commercials. Flag waving appeals to this group.

As VALS use spread, however, some companies began to find it was too general. It could classify consumers into typologies, but it couldn't really predict consumer behavior or solve specific marketing problems. In response, SRI changed the survey questions, administered them to two samples of 2,500 adults, and unveiled VALS 2 in early 1989.

VALS 2 looks at unchanging psychological stances rather than changeable attitudes and values. For example, the statements about the legalization of marijuana and attitudes about abortion were eliminated. Among the new statements respondents are asked to agree or disagree with are, "I am usually interested in abstract theories," and "I could stand to skin a dead animal."

VALS 2 categorizes people as to their self-identity (principle, status, or action orientation) and their resources (income, education, self-confidence, and energy level). The identity factor indicates three different ways of buying. Principle-oriented consumers, according to VALS, buy based on their world views; status-oriented consumers buy based on the opinions and actions of others; and action-oriented consumers buy based on a desire for social or physical activity, variety, and risk-taking.

SRI hopes the new typology will be more applicable to the real world because it links psychographic segmentation more closely to purchasing choices. Subscribers compare their customers with the larger group of buyers and media users in the Mediamark and Simmons surveys. Most of the cluster analysis products such as Claritas' PRIZM and Donnelley Marketing Information Services' ClusterPLUS are also available segmented by VALS types.

This increasing product linkage between information companies enhances researchers' ability to solve specific marketing problems. For example, suppose a company selling Fizz Water, a specific brand of bottled water, wanted to find out the psychological makeup of its customers. One way to proceed would be to subscribe to SRI International's VALS Program and categorize drinkers of Fizz Water by VALS types.

Suppose the VALS program shows that most people who buy Fizz Water fall into three segments: Fulfilled, Actualizers, and Experiencers. With that knowledge, Fizz Water researchers could then go to the Mediamark or Simmons databases, which are cross-tabulated by VALS types, and find out how Fizz Water drinkers compare with everyone else who drinks bottled water. If this step reveals that in addition to Fulfilled, Actualizers, and Experiencers, Achievers also buy a lot of bottled water, then Fizz Water researchers might want to find out why their brand isn't attracting Achievers. With this process, the company could learn a lot about who is and isn't buying Fizz Water.

The company has a number of choices once it separates customers from noncustomers. It could do more research into why the brand is failing with some and succeeding with others, and launch an advertising campaign designed to appeal to the missing segment. Or it could design a direct mail promotion using one of the cluster analysis products to locate neighborhoods with high concentrations of the VALs segments that are known customers of Fizz Water.

The Monitor and VALS are only two of the many psychographic surveys that exist. The main value of these two products is that they provide a way to better understand customers' psychological characteristics. Because they can be linked to purchase behavior and media preference data, they can be a valuable tool for measuring product performance and crafting effective advertising. The price of these systems (VALS costs between $25,000 and $50,000) may put them out of reach for smaller businesses. There are, however, less expensive options.

Other Psychographic Sources

One option is to look for existing surveys that fit your situation. For example, businesses that sell outdoor recreation clothing and equipment could purchase a 1986 study of *Americans Outdoors* from Market Opinion Research in Detroit. This survey divides the outdoor market into four groups: the Fitness Driven, who jog every morning at dawn; the Getaway Actives, who want to experience nature as often as possible; the Sociable Actives, who like to experience nature from the safety of a group; and finally, the Unstressed and Unmotivated, otherwise known as couch potatoes.

There are many other examples. One survey, released in 1989 by Strategic

Directions Planning in Minneapolis, segments adults over the age of 50 by their attitudes toward food, self image, and health. HealthFocus, a consulting group in Emmaus, Pennsylvania, has developed a technique for segmenting health-food consumers into five types. Other consultants specialize in tracking the cultural assimilation of Hispanics or the attitudes of working women. The list goes on and on.

If you need to know who wears out a pair of running shoes every six months, or about older shoppers, Hispanics, or working women, surveys like these are the best possible sources. They can give you a detailed picture of a targeted group's state of mind that can be useful in creating advertising or promotions.

There are literally thousands of polls and surveys released every month. So how can anyone keep up? A good source is the *American Public Opinion Index*, put out annually by Opinion Research Service of Boston. The book lists thousands of polls and surveys covering more than 1,600 topics.

Local Psychographics

Another option, if you operate in one of the top 75 broadcast markets in the country, is to find out whether any television or radio stations in your area have done psychographic studies of the market. Many stations in the biggest markets hire research firms such as Marshall Marketing & Communications of Pittsburgh, or Leigh Stowell & Company of Seattle to conduct telephone surveys of the market. These surveys typically include demographic, psychographic, media preference, and specific purchase behavior questions. Through the resulting database, a grocery store advertiser, for example, can discover the attitudes or the media use of people who shop in the company's stores. Usually the stations give the information to the advertisers free of charge, hoping it will induce them to buy air-time. Another company, Impact Resources of Columbus, Ohio, includes attitude questions in its non-proprietary surveys of the top broadcast markets. This database can be tapped by anyone for a fee.

Focus Groups

Smaller companies that can't afford VALS, Roper, or a custom-designed typology can get useful attitude and opinion information by conducting focus groups. A focus group is a meeting of up to ten people who discuss a topic with guidance from a trained moderator. The meeting is usually videotaped or watched secretly by the client. Focus groups are the most popular kind of psychographic research because they are usually less expensive and easier to arrange than large surveys. But they are often misused, and their results can be seriously misleading.

Focus group results should not be thought of as a representative sample of your customers or used to segment customers, but they can be invaluable tools to help identify the subtle and unexpected ways consumers react to your product or idea. They can never substitute for surveys, because the opinion of ten people might not mirror the reaction of the entire market.

One of the principles of statistical research is that as the size of a survey gets smaller, the possibility for error increases. And when you're talking about only 10, or even 50, people, the margin of error becomes so high as to render the results statistically meaningless. The basic value of focus groups is to stimulate managers or creative people to think about products or ideas in a different light.

Opinion Polls

Tracking public opinion is another way to explore the general mindset of your market. Established firms like The Gallup Organization, the Roper Organization, Louis Harris and Associates, R.H. Bruskin Associates, and others survey national samples of adults on virtually every issue. Pollsters say the difference between what they do and what SRI does is the difference between theory and reality. "We emphasize tracking actual behavior and drawing our conclusions from changes in behavioral patterns, rather than from presumed psychographic categories," says Roper executive Thomas Miller.

The oldest and largest of these firms, The Gallup Organization, gains its strength from asking the same questions year after year. Thanks to Gallup, we know that 76 percent of Americans think Jesus Christ is God or the son of God, up one percentage point from 1965. Gallup measures everything from Americans' trust in authority to what they order in restaurants. Special reports on religion, alcohol use, eating out, book buying, and leisure activities are available for $100 or less. Gallup also conducts custom surveys for clients.

The Roper Organization offers *Roper Reports*, which asks 2,000 adults once every five weeks for their opinions on advertising, fashion, packaging, vacations, and hundreds of other topics. Published since 1973, the reports are usually the best place to find details on opinion trends. For example, the results of a Roper survey early in 1990 reveal that a 53 percent majority of Americans give drug abuse top priority out of a list of 21 national concerns.

Clearly, opinion pollsters have the edge over psychographic segmentation systems when it comes to detail. But polls have one major drawback. They are based on opinions, which tend to change rapidly. Segmentation systems are based on beliefs that tend to change more slowly.

Polls can measure attitudes toward your product or service or whether your advertising is working. But creating more effective products, services, and advertising requires an in-depth knowledge of customers' motivations.

Consumer Attributes

As we've seen, demographics and psychographics describe consumer attributes. There are four major uses of consumer attribute information:

1. Measure the size of the current and potential market. By understanding the demographic attributes of customers, you can find out how many people in a trading area share those attributes.

2. Predict consumer behavior. Demographics alone can provide clues about what products and services will be hot in the 1990s. Psychographics will identify the state of mind of specific consumers that may predispose them to buy certain products over others.

3. Adapt products and advertisements as customers' tastes change. Through focus groups or surveys, managers can be alerted to mismatches between customers and products before they result in slumping profits.

4. Communicate more effectively. "Know thy customer" is the first commandment of successful business. Psychographics help marketers fine tune the message to the customers.

Consumer attributes are only half of the consumer information system. Once you find out who the customers are and what they think, you have to look at what they buy and what media they prefer.

CHAPTER SIX

Purchase Behavior: What Do They Buy?

THE NUMBER of choices consumers face every day is exploding. Never before have there been more things to buy, or a greater variety of media to watch, read, and listen to. And never before has the need for consumer information been so great.

While consumer attribute information tells you what consumers are likely to do, behavior data describe what consumers actually do. Demographics and psychographics reveal consumer profiles, and purchase behavior and media use data tell what people with those characteristics read, watch, or buy. To make sound decisions, managers need both types of information.

A crystal ball would be the most useful tool for marketers, who are in the business of making timely predictions. Their jobs depend on giving their firms the most accurate accounts of what consumers will be buying, reading, watching, and listening to in the coming years. Consumer behavior data are the closest thing we have to a crystal ball.

Knowing what customers buy and what media they prefer is essential for forming strategies and making advertising more efficient. These behavioral data help determine what actions a business can take to capture the most customers.

Understanding Purchase Behavior

Although customers' demographics and psychographics can give you an idea of what they buy, they are no guarantee. For example, educated people buy more mail-order products: they are willing to trust people they cannot see to deliver the product, and they have enough confidence to return something if it's not right. But not all educated consumers shop by mail. To predict what consumers will buy, you must look at the money value and the volume of their past purchases, and identify who the best customers are. The only way to do this is by looking at actual purchase behavior data.

Most data about purchases come from cash register receipts, laser scanners, or product registration cards—administrative data that are the result of buying a product. The other major source of purchase data is consumer surveys done by the government or syndicated survey firms.

The best source of purchase behavior data is often overlooked by many businesses—their own sales records. Although it's the easiest data to get and the most accurate, it's surprising how many research departments have no idea what kind of information the sales department collects on customers. This unfortunate lack of interdepartmental communication can mean losing out on purchase data that could be a marketing gold mine.

Purchase data and demographics are the foundation for the most effective database marketing systems. Internal sales records are the only accurate method of identifying your best customers. By knowing what separates them from other customers, you can craft effective appeals and turn mediocre customers into better ones and turn potential customers into actual ones.

A financial services firm, for example, has the names and addresses of its customers. The marketing department might already be sending them direct mail, but that's by no means the only value of those records. If the firm also has information about its customers' household income, age, marital status, and other demographic characteristics, it could then "geocode" the addresses so it could, for example, send information about college loans only to customers with children. Or it could blanket a high-income neighborhood with a mailing about its investment services.

Scan It

Most purchase data today come from laser scanners that record Universal Product Control (UPC) codes. Every time a customer buys something in a scanner-equipped store, the purchase is entered into the store's computer banks. Some stores also have check-cashing cards which assign a UPC code to each customer, making it possible to record everything that customer buys. Through scanners, the store knows how much beer a person buys and when he or she last bought dishwashing detergent. Conceivably, the store could send out reminders when it becomes time to buy another package.

This technology gives businesses all the information they need to alter their stores and advertising specifically to appeal to their customers. They have the actual data on what their customers buy, when and how much they spend. They also have the customers' names, addresses, and other demographic data the customers provided when they filled out the application for their check-cashing cards.

With this information, stores could measure the effectiveness of targeted advertising and promotions so precisely they could determine how many new customers were attracted from specific neighborhoods. They could also learn about their biggest customers, those who stopped shopping in the store, and what it would take to attract more customers. In short, the technology gives scanner-equipped retailers all the ingredients for more complete control over sales. So why were scanners in only 69 percent of all supermarkets by 1989?

Scanners are underused for the same reasons the massive amounts of data they generate are underused: lack of understanding and high costs. The volume of data generated by scanners is so staggering that most of it just accumulates untouched in computer storage systems. The future potential of these purchase behavior data is practically unlimited providing someone figures out a cost-effective way to process and use them.

The major players in the scanning data business are Nielsen Media Research, Information Resources Inc., and the Arbitron Company. The scanning services of Nielsen and Information Resources Inc. track purchases through supermarket checkouts for the packaged goods industry. All three companies have household panels equipped to collect purchase and TV viewing data which are used to measure advertising and promotion effectiveness.

Scanner data are some of the most accurate because they come from actual purchases. The scanner services can provide a wide array of detailed brand-specific data. Nielsen's SCANTRACK (a joint venture with the NDP Group), and Information Resource's BehaviorScan, and some other scanner-based products can provide detailed customer profiles of heavy, medium, and light users of a given product. They can also tell how well one brand is doing relative to the others by market and by each new variable, such as the entrance of a new product.

SCANTRACK collects purchase data through the checkout scanners of 3,000 supermarkets in 50 markets. Nielsen is integrating into this database information from its 15,000-household panel, whose members are equipped with hand-held scanners to record all of their purchases. Five-thousand of those households have TV meters to record viewing exposure as well as purchase behavior.

IRI's Infoscan tracks purchases through supermarket checkouts in 66 markets. This represents 27,000 supermarkets and about 60,000 households. The BehaviorScan program collects TV viewing data along with the purchase behavior of 3,000 households in six markets. To record their purchase, these consumers use coded cards which they present when checking out.

The single-source scanning-media behavior services will be discussed in more detail in the next chapter on media preferences. One of the reasons these services were developed was to help solve the perennial problem media companies and major advertisers have of measuring advertising and promotion effectiveness.

Getting Demographics

The main problem with most purchase data is that often they are merely a record of a purchase. Purchase data become most valuable when they are linked to demographics. The sales records must include more than an address. You must have information that tells you what type of person is doing the buying.

Where do you get the demographic information necessary to make the data useful? How do you get the demographics? One source is your own internal records. If the internal records have no demographics to help identify differences and similarities between your customers and the general population, you need to survey your customers. Some firms have had success with customer surveys by offering discounts or other incentives to those who voluntarily supply demographic information. Other options are check cashing cards, check surveys (sending a questionnaire by mail to the addresses on checks) or asking for more information at the time of purchase. Some companies are changing sales receipts so they at least include addresses. Once you have an address you can geocode the addresses and get general demographic data on the neighborhoods from one of the cluster analysis products. Still another option is to take a look at national purchase behavior data. One of the best and also one of the most underused sources of national purchase behavior data tied to demographics is the Consumer Expenditure Survey of the Bureau of Labor Statistics.

The Value of CEX

The Consumer Expenditure Survey (CEX) is an ongoing survey of the day-to-day spending of American households. In conducting the CEX, the Census Bureau surveys 10,000 households every year for the Bureau of Labor Statistics, which uses the data to calculate the Consumer Price Index. The government has been doing expenditure surveys every decade since the late 19th century, but it was not until 1980 that the CEX became a continuous survey with results published annually.

The CEX is actually two surveys—an interview survey and a diary. It is the only annual survey that asks consumers about what they buy. Not only that, it also shows what percentage of total expenditures and what percentage of total income went to purchase various products. Because the sample size of the CEX is large, it is a very accurate measure of purchase behavior. The CEX offers an easy way to determine the biggest consumers of your product.

Spending is categorized by age, income, household size, region of the country, and other demographic variables. This makes it possible to look at the CEX and determine, for example, that households headed by 35-to-44-

year-olds spend an average of $1,975 on entertainment, $360 more than the next biggest spenders—the 45-to-54-year-olds—and $646 more than the average. Or the CEX could reveal that married couples without children spent $1,014 in 1988 on cash contributions—more than any other group.

This gives businesses a good way to estimate the dollar values of various markets. A grocer who knows that the average household spends $2,136 a year on food at home is halfway to knowing how his store is doing. If there are 5,000 households in the store's trade area, the total potential market is over $10 million. If the store is doing less business than that after taking the competition into consideration, then it's apparent the store is doing something wrong.

The CEX can also shed light on hidden markets. It shows that households headed by 55-to-64-year-olds spend an average of $37 per year on clothing for children under the age of two. Multiply that by the expected 12.3 million households in that age group in 1990, and suddenly you've uncovered a $456 million national market for baby clothes hidden in households without young children.

The disadvantage of CEX data is that they aren't brand-specific. The survey looks at spending for product categories such as shoes, rather than Rockport shoes. Other sources of purchase behavior data, however, are brand specific. CREST, a survey conducted by NPD Group of Port Washington, New York, asks about restaurant usage by brand, such as McDonald's versus Burger King. The syndicated surveys of Simmons and Mediamark also ask about brand purchases, such as hair-care products by Clairol. But the CEX only asks about hair-care products in general.

Even though the CEX deals with categories rather than specific products, projections based on the data are extremely helpful for making sales forecasts.

Take the case of the clothing manufacturer who wants to determine who spends the most on apparel now. There are at least two ways to do this. First, the researcher could get all of the firm's internal sales records, hire data processors to do the arduous work of entering them into computers, hire programmers to write a program, and weeks later, find out what customers aged 25 to 34 spent on clothes in the company's stores.

Fortunately, there's an easier way. The researcher can flip through the CEX and find out easily what each age group spends. Not just customers, but what the entire apparel-buying public is doing. Then by comparing different years of the CEX, the researcher can track changes in the spending of each group on apparel. If one group is spending more and one less than the others consistently, that is the first clue about what the target market should and should not be. By projecting those purchase patterns into the future, re-

Figure 6a: SAMPLE PAGE OF THE CONSUMER EXPENDITURE SURVEY

Item	All consumer units	Under 25	25 - 34	35 - 44	45 - 54	55 - 64	65 and over	65 - 74	75 and over
Number of consumer units (in thousands)	94,862	7,216	21,985	19,911	13,601	12,546	19,603	11,319	8,284
Consumer unit characteristics:									
Average income before taxes 1/	$28,540	$14,827	$28,318	$36,428	$39,934	$29,979	$17,754	$20,704	$13,707
Average number of persons in consumer unit	2.6	1.8	2.8	3.3	2.9	2.2	1.8	2.0	1.5
Average age of reference person	47.0	21.7	29.7	39.3	49.2	59.6	73.9	69.2	80.3
Average number of earners	1.4	1.3	1.5	1.8	2.0	1.4	.5	.6	.2
Average number of vehicles	2.0	1.2	1.9	2.4	2.6	2.2	1.4	1.7	1.0
Percent homeowner	62	11	44	66	74	79	77	79	73
Average annual expenditures	$25,892	$16,373	$25,770	$33,078	$33,205	$25,765	$17,297	$20,120	$13,339
Food	3,748	2,455	3,664	4,636	4,815	3,952	2,581	3,013	1,939
Food at home	2,136	1,121	2,046	2,599	2,605	2,355	1,709	1,933	1,373
Cereals and bakery products	312	166	291	387	387	334	253	277	215
Meats, poultry, fish, and eggs	551	249	506	661	675	648	463	533	357
Dairy products	274	152	276	333	329	295	211	236	175
Fruits and vegetables	373	176	328	434	450	433	350	390	290
Other food at home	625	378	645	785	763	645	432	496	335
Food away from home	1,612	1,334	1,618	2,037	2,210	1,597	872	1,081	566
Alcoholic beverages	269	312	355	281	307	239	131	162	89
Housing	8,079	4,746	8,469	10,467	9,672	7,757	5,551	6,178	4,682
Shelter	4,493	3,004	4,942	6,147	5,232	3,929	2,705	3,018	2,276
Owned dwellings	2,569	440	2,384	3,946	3,345	2,630	1,582	1,889	1,163
Rented dwellings	1,468	2,396	2,253	1,519	1,179	770	841	772	937
Other lodging	456	168	305	682	708	529	281	358	176
Utilities, fuels, and public services	1,747	897	1,545	2,023	2,173	1,935	1,593	1,739	1,393
Household operations	394	141	483	528	349	327	324	306	349
Housekeeping supplies	361	166	347	411	450	383	329	382	249
Household furnishings and equipment	1,083	539	1,152	1,357	1,469	1,183	600	733	415
Apparel and services	1,489	1,042	1,504	2,015	2,112	1,355	763	977	451
Transportation	5,093	3,911	5,479	6,369	6,641	4,603	3,040	3,975	1,760
Vehicle purchases (net outlay)	2,361	2,039	2,794	2,931	3,016	1,749	1,350	1,849	667
Gasoline and motor oil	932	659	922	1,152	1,248	970	576	729	367
Other vehicle expenses	1,521	1,023	1,528	1,978	1,987	1,553	892	1,129	567
Public transportation	279	190	235	309	389	330	222	268	158
Health care	1,298	523	777	1,253	1,258	1,518	2,099	2,005	2,230
Entertainment	1,329	961	1,396	1,975	1,615	1,136	658	881	351
Personal care products and services	334	204	318	427	446	330	231	276	164
Reading	150	80	131	183	187	164	129	151	100
Education	342	646	247	454	678	234	60	81	31
Tobacco products and smoking supplies	242	183	246	277	334	268	142	185	84
Miscellaneous	578	217	515	783	775	600	424	512	301
Cash contributions	693	120	375	806	957	1,002	767	753	785
Personal insurance and pensions	2,249	972	2,293	3,150	3,409	2,609	720	972	375
Life and other personal insurance	314	47	241	394	418	418	275	290	255
Pensions and Social Security	1,935	926	2,052	2,756	2,991	2,191	444	682	119

SOURCE: Consumer Expenditures in 1988, USDL Press Release #90-96, Bureau of Labor Statistics

searchers can identify the biggest spenders ten years from now.

As this example suggests, both internal sales records and the CEX are useful, but for different purposes. The CEX offers a snapshot of the total market; the sales records show what specific customers are doing. The data are most powerful when used together for comparison. By comparing the differences between the behavior of these two groups, firms can measure the store's or a brand's performance.

Suppose, for example, that a women's clothing chain wants to find out why one store is failing. The CEX shows that 35-to-44-year-olds spend the most on clothes, although women's clothes take the biggest bite from the budgets of 45-to-54-year-olds. Meanwhile, the median age of the problem store's customers is 65. Further examination of the CEX shows that married-couple households with children over age 18 spend the most on women's clothing, followed closely by couples without children. Most of the store's customers, however, are single or widowed.

The manager then has to look at the areas around the store, determine where the younger married groups live, and figure out how to attract more of them to the store. At the same time, the manager should find out why older women like the store so much and make sure they continue to shop there.

We may miss the big picture if we restrict our information to large stacks of printouts from the sales department, but we'll need those printouts to decide the practical changes that need to be made in messages, products, and services to keep established customers and attract new ones. The CEX is a strategic weapon for doing this. It makes it possible to look at the whole market and ask, "How important is that consumer group to me today and how important will it be tomorrow?"

Another advantage of the CEX is that it is cheap and very accessible. The government puts out regular bulletins and news releases with CEX data. To order the bulletins, write the BLS Publications Sales Center, P. O. Box 2145, Chicago, IL 60690. To receive news releases, call (202) 272-5060. The price of the bulletins ranges from $3 to $10.

Syndicated Surveys

A growing number of private firms conduct national surveys of consumer buying behavior and sell that information. These syndicated surveys share one flaw with the CEX. Both are based on what consumers say they buy rather than on actual purchases. This tends to skew the data somewhat at the outset, because people underreport purchases of certain products like junk foods and overreport others. They also forget some purchases. Regardless of this drawback, surveys are valuable for getting the total picture of a market and making comparisons between a firm's customers and the national average.

Some companies specialize in processing purchase information for certain industries. NPD Group of Port Washington, New York, does ongoing purchase surveys of the following industries: toys, apparel, textiles, jewelry, sporting goods, health care, petroleum/automotive, and some electronic products. Their databases track the movements of these products through retail channels. The company's Custom Services business unit does client-specific research using a 250,000-household mail panel and telephone interviewing done through its central facility in College Park, Maryland. NPD Group is a partner with Nielsen Media Research in SCANTRACK.

Simmons and MRI

Simmons and Mediamark specialize in tracking buying behavior for the magazine industry, and their syndicated surveys are invaluable sources of buying data on thousands of product categories and specific brands.

These syndicated surveys go beyond purchase data alone, to include information on media usage, brand purchasing, leisure activities, VALS lifestyles, and geodemographic segmentation (cluster analysis). The data are presented in the form of usage indexes that compare the spending of various groups with the average and provide a quick way to gauge product preferences.

A usage index is a division of two percentages. For example, of all adults in the U.S., 24 percent are between the ages of 25 and 34. If 24 percent of the buyers of a brand of foreign car are between 25 and 34, the usage index for that product is 100, indicating average usage. The index is derived by dividing the two percentages. If, however, 50 percent of the buyers of that foreign car are between 25 and 34, the usage index is 208, indicating that people in that age group were more than twice as likely to buy that car than average. An index below 100 indicates below average usage, and the preference for the product rises as the index climbs above 100.

The biggest clients of the syndicated surveys are advertising agencies, major national advertisers, product and service marketers, magazines, newspapers, broadcast companies, and cable networks. Because the surveys link purchase behavior to media usage, demographics, and psychographics, they are powerful tools for tracking advertising and marketing effectiveness.

Simmons Market Research Bureau is a subsidiary of MRB Group of New York City. The firm's largest service is the Simmons Study of Media & Markets (SMM), which is now in its 26th year. The SMM is based on interviews

Figure 6b: SAMPLE PAGE FROM SIMMONS'

1989 Study of Media and Markets: Direct Mail & Other In-Home Shopping, Yellow Pages, Florists, Telegrams and Greeting Cards

Catalogs bought from in the last 12 months (adults)

	TOTAL U.S. '000	LILLIAN VERNON A '000	B % DOWN	C % ACROSS	D INDX	SEARS A '000	B % DOWN	C % ACROSS	D INDX	SPIEGEL A '000	B % DOWN	C % ACROSS	D INDX
TOTAL ADULTS	178193	5954	100.0	3.3	100	27045	100.0	15.2	100	5665	100.0	3.2	100
MALES	85056	1328	22.3	1.6	47	10375	38.4	12.2	80	1463	25.8	1.7	54
FEMALES	93136	4625	77.7	5.0	149	16671	61.6	17.9	118	4202	74.2	4.5	142
18 - 24	25713	**319	5.4	1.2	37	2620	9.7	10.2	67	*733	12.9	2.9	90
25 - 34	43283	1842	30.9	4.3	127	6248	23.1	14.4	95	1519	26.8	3.5	110
35 - 44	34804	1468	24.7	4.2	126	6784	25.1	19.5	128	1643	29.0	4.7	148
45 - 54	23902	897	15.1	3.8	112	4505	16.7	18.8	124	786	13.9	3.3	103
55 - 64	21733	765	12.8	3.5	105	3226	11.9	14.8	98	*508	9.0	2.3	74
65 OR OLDER	28756	663	11.1	2.3	69	3662	13.5	12.7	84	*476	8.4	1.7	52
18 - 34	68997	2161	36.3	3.1	94	8868	32.8	12.9	85	2252	39.8	3.3	103
18 - 49	115841	4038	67.8	3.5	104	17813	65.9	15.4	101	4306	76.0	3.7	117
25 - 54	101990	4207	70.7	4.1	123	17537	64.8	17.2	113	3948	69.7	3.9	122
35 - 49	46845	1877	31.5	4.0	120	8946	33.1	19.1	126	2055	36.3	4.4	138
50 OR OLDER	62351	1916	32.2	3.1	92	9232	34.1	14.8	98	1358	24.0	2.2	69
GRADUATED COLLEGE	32799	2051	34.4	6.3	187	5074	18.8	15.5	102	1638	28.9	5.0	157
ATTENDED COLLEGE	32672	1357	22.8	4.2	124	5539	20.5	17.0	112	1411	24.9	4.3	136
GRADUATED HIGH SCHOOL	70684	2018	33.9	2.9	85	11804	43.6	16.7	110	1895	33.5	2.7	84
DID NOT GRADUATE HIGH SCHOOL	42039	*528	8.9	1.3	38	4628	17.1	11.0	73	720	12.7	1.7	54
EMPLOYED MALES	60732	981	16.5	1.6	48	7850	29.0	12.9	85	1151	20.3	1.9	60
EMPLOYED FEMALES	49968	3177	53.4	6.4	190	10036	37.1	20.1	132	3172	56.0	6.3	200
EMPLOYED FULL-TIME	97991	3492	58.6	3.6	107	15384	56.9	15.7	103	3813	67.3	3.9	122
EMPLOYED PART-TIME	12710	*666	11.2	5.2	157	2501	9.2	19.7	130	*510	9.0	4.0	126
NOT EMPLOYED	67492	1796	30.2	2.7	80	9159	33.9	13.6	89	1342	23.7	2.0	63
PROFESSIONAL/MANAGER	29483	1855	31.2	6.3	188	5018	18.6	17.0	112	1600	28.2	5.4	171
TECH/CLERICAL/SALES	36012	1389	23.3	3.9	115	6241	23.1	17.3	114	1777	31.4	4.9	155
PRECISION/CRAFT	14266	*285	4.8	2.0	60	2223	8.2	15.6	103	*318	5.6	2.2	70
OTHER EMPLOYED	30939	629	10.6	2.0	61	4404	16.3	14.2	94	628	11.1	2.0	64
SINGLE	38354	529	8.9	1.4	41	3424	12.7	8.9	59	983	17.4	2.6	81
MARRIED	107815	4390	73.7	4.1	122	20105	74.3	18.6	123	3708	65.5	3.4	108
DIVORCED/SEPARATED/WIDOWED	32024	1034	17.4	3.2	97	3516	13.0	11.0	72	975	17.2	3.0	96
PARENTS	59509	2273	38.2	3.8	114	11442	42.7	19.4	128	2216	39.1	3.7	117
WHITE	153416	5580	93.7	3.6	109	24661	91.2	16.1	106	4966	87.7	3.2	102
BLACK	19771	*342	5.7	1.7	52	2099	7.8	10.6	70	567	10.0	2.9	90
OTHER	5005	**31	0.5	0.6	19	*285	1.1	5.7	38	**132	2.3	2.6	83
NORTHEAST-CENSUS	37709	1636	27.5	4.3	130	5251	19.4	13.9	92	1100	19.4	2.9	92
MIDWEST	43858	1448	24.3	3.3	99	8873	32.8	20.2	133	1741	30.7	4.0	125
SOUTH	61120	1692	28.4	2.8	83	9150	33.8	15.0	99	1816	32.1	3.0	93
WEST	35505	1177	19.8	3.3	99	3771	13.9	10.6	70	1008	17.8	2.8	89
NORTHEAST-MKTG.	39614	1748	29.4	4.4	132	5301	19.6	13.4	88	1193	21.1	3.0	95
EAST CENTRAL	25102	847	14.2	3.4	101	4402	16.3	17.5	116	720	12.7	2.9	90
WEST CENTRAL	29609	987	16.6	3.3	100	6291	23.3	21.2	140	1253	22.1	4.2	133
SOUTH	53267	1351	22.7	2.5	76	7820	28.9	14.7	97	1529	27.0	2.9	90
PACIFIC	30601	1021	17.1	3.3	100	3231	11.9	10.6	70	970	17.1	3.2	100
COUNTY SIZE A	74178	2980	50.1	4.0	120	8659	32.0	11.7	77	2641	46.6	3.6	112
COUNTY SIZE B	53234	1430	24.0	2.7	80	7090	26.2	13.3	88	1511	26.7	2.8	89
COUNTY SIZE C	26987	1068	17.9	4.0	118	5349	19.8	19.8	131	798	14.1	3.0	93
COUNTY SIZE D	23793	*475	8.0	2.0	60	5947	22.0	25.0	165	714	12.6	3.0	94
METRO CENTRAL CITY	54244	1329	22.3	2.5	73	5293	19.6	9.8	64	1744	30.8	3.2	101
METRO SUBURBAN	82717	3424	57.5	4.1	124	11947	44.2	14.4	95	2738	48.3	3.3	104
NON METRO	41232	1201	20.2	2.9	87	9806	36.3	23.8	157	1183	20.9	2.9	90
TOP 5 ADI'S	40038	1573	26.4	3.9	118	5027	18.6	12.6	83	1677	29.6	4.2	132
TOP 10 ADI'S	56175	2291	38.5	4.1	122	6906	25.5	12.3	81	2186	38.6	3.9	122
TOP 20 ADI'S	81501	3244	54.5	4.0	119	10667	39.4	13.1	86	2867	50.6	3.5	111
HSHLD INC. $60,000 OR MORE	19957	1286	21.6	6.4	193	3090	11.4	15.5	102	1031	18.2	5.2	163
$50,000 OR MORE	31697	1840	30.9	5.8	174	4956	18.3	15.6	103	1618	28.6	5.1	161
$40,000 OR MORE	53998	2867	48.2	5.3	159	9259	34.2	17.1	113	2780	49.1	5.1	162
$30,000 OR MORE	83793	3964	66.6	4.7	142	14767	54.6	17.6	116	3764	66.4	4.5	141
$30,000 - $39,999	29795	1097	18.4	3.7	110	5508	20.4	18.5	122	984	17.4	3.3	104
$20,000 - $29,999	34040	1031	17.3	3.0	91	5394	19.9	15.8	104	930	16.4	2.7	86
$10,000 - $19,999	38419	723	12.1	1.9	56	5000	18.5	13.0	86	641	11.3	1.7	52
UNDER $10,000	21942	*235	3.9	1.1	32	1884	7.0	8.6	57	*330	5.8	1.5	47
HOUSEHOLD OF 1 PERSON	22006	736	12.4	3.3	100	1770	6.5	8.0	53	511	9.0	2.3	73
2 PEOPLE	57453	2017	33.9	3.5	105	8842	32.7	15.4	101	1983	35.0	3.5	109
3 OR 4 PEOPLE	71838	2392	40.2	3.3	100	11601	42.9	16.1	106	2629	46.4	3.7	115
5 OR MORE PEOPLE	26896	809	13.6	3.0	90	4832	17.9	18.0	118	*542	9.6	2.0	63
NO CHILD IN HSHLD	106426	3460	58.1	3.3	97	13809	51.1	13.0	85	3070	54.2	2.9	91
CHILD(REN) UNDER 2 YRS	14122	*698	11.7	4.9	148	2232	8.3	15.8	104	*457	8.1	3.2	102
2 - 5 YEARS	26410	999	16.8	3.8	113	4677	17.3	17.7	117	889	15.7	3.4	106
6 - 11 YEARS	33185	1095	18.4	3.3	99	6464	23.9	19.5	128	960	16.9	2.9	91
12 - 17 YEARS	33008	895	15.0	2.7	81	6361	23.5	19.3	127	1118	19.7	3.4	107
RESIDENCE OWNED	122907	4984	83.7	4.1	121	22268	82.3	18.1	119	4518	79.8	3.7	116
VALUE: $70,000 OR MORE	60160	3203	53.8	5.3	159	10490	38.8	17.4	115	2579	45.5	4.3	135
VALUE: UNDER $70,000	62747	1781	29.9	2.8	85	11778	43.5	18.8	124	1939	34.2	3.1	97

SOURCE: © Simmons Market Research Bureau: *1989 Study of Media and Markets.*

with 19,000 adults and provides data on more than 800 product categories and 3,000 brands. Users are categorized by light, medium, or heavy usage, and quantity used. Results are also cross-tabulated by demographics, media usage, readership of 121 magazines, exposure to outdoor advertising, cable and radio formats, and viewership of more than 100 different TV programs, including news and sporting events. It also breaks down information on the number of sole, primary, and secondary users of many brands and whether they're men or women.

Simmons also looks at purchasing behavior of households with incomes above $70,000 in its Affluent Study. Clients can receive Simmons data in printed reports, via commercial on-line computer services, or through CHOICES. The company also does custom studies for clients.

Mediamark Research Inc. of New York City was founded in 1979. It bases its syndicated survey of media exposure and product consumption on personal interviews with 20,000 adults and a leave-behind questionnaire. Mediamark gathers buying data on about 450 product categories, 1,900 product types, and 5,700 individual brands.

Respondents record the brands, types, and varieties of products used during the last six months and the quantities used in the last seven days. The results categorize users as light, medium, or heavy buyers, their exposure to television and radio by day part, formats, by 18 cable channels, and readership of 140 magazines. Some of the product data are also categorized by female or male homemaker (whoever makes the buying decision). The data can be accessed through the company's annual 20-volume set of printed reports, or through Mediamark's proprietary PC-based MEMRI software system. On-line access is also possible through several computer service companies

Although syndicated survey data are more expensive than the CEX, these surveys offer several advantages. One of the most obvious advantages is that they provide detailed brand-specific data. They also give information about other products that customers use. Knowing what other things your customers buy can provide clues on where to find similar customers and how to appeal to them in ads and promotions.

For example, suppose the owner of a chain of fast-food restaurants looked at data from either syndicated survey and noticed that the demographics of the heaviest consumers of fast food matched the heaviest buyers of Chevrolets. That restaurateur could use the information in at least two ways: he could go to a list supplier such as R. L. Polk and get the names and addresses of all Chevy owners in the area and send ads or coupons to them. Or the restaurant's ads could show happy customers leaving in a Chevy.

Another advantage of syndicated buying data is that they are frequently

Figure 6c: SAMPLE PAGE FROM MEDIAMARK'S PET & BABY PRODUCTS REPORT

CAT LITTER

POUNDS/LAST 30 DAYS

BASE: FEMALE HOMEMAKERS	TOTAL U.S. '000	ALL A '000	B % DOWN	C % ACROSS	D INDEX	HEAVY MORE THAN 20 A '000	B % DOWN	C % ACROSS	D INDEX	MEDIUM 6-20 A '000	B % DOWN	C % ACROSS	D INDEX	LIGHT LESS THAN 6 A '000	B % DOWN	C % ACROSS	D INDEX
ALL FEMALE HOMEMAKERS	79236	12580	100.0	15.9	100	2924	100.0	3.7	100	5084	100.0	6.4	100	4553	100.0	5.7	100
WOMEN	79236	12580	100.0	15.9	100	2924	100.0	3.7	100	5084	100.0	6.4	100	4553	100.0	5.7	100
HOUSEHOLD HEADS	27114	3709	29.5	13.7	86	817	27.9	3.0	82	1570	30.9	5.8	90	1321	29.0	4.9	85
HOMEMAKERS	79236	12580	100.0	15.9	100	2924	100.0	3.7	100	5084	100.0	6.4	100	4553	100.0	5.7	100
GRADUATED COLLEGE	12005	2626	20.9	21.9	138	599	20.5	5.0	135	1195	23.5	10.0	155	832	18.3	6.9	121
ATTENDED COLLEGE	13697	2379	18.9	17.4	110	536	18.3	3.9	106	1031	20.3	7.5	117	812	17.8	5.9	103
GRADUATED HIGH SCHOOL	33217	5072	40.4	15.3	96	1248	42.7	3.8	102	2024	39.8	6.1	95	1801	39.6	5.4	94
DID NOT GRADUATE HIGH SCHOOL	20318	2482	19.8	12.2	77	*541	18.5	2.7	72	834	16.4	4.1	64	1108	24.3	5.5	95
18-24	7140	1379	11.0	19.3	122	*349	11.9	4.9	132	688	13.5	9.6	150	*342	7.5	4.8	83
25-34	19497	3710	29.5	19.0	120	807	27.6	4.1	112	1432	28.2	7.3	114	1471	32.3	7.5	131
35-44	15715	3029	24.1	19.3	122	714	24.4	4.5	123	1222	24.0	7.8	121	1093	24.0	7.0	121
45-54	11324	1925	15.3	17.0	107	481	16.5	4.2	115	927	18.2	8.2	128	517	11.4	4.6	79
55-64	11154	1360	10.9	12.3	77	353	12.1	3.2	86	451	8.9	4.0	63	565	12.4	5.1	88
65 OR OVER	14406	1150	9.2	8.0	50	*220	7.5	1.5	41	363	7.1	2.5	39	566	12.4	3.9	68
18-34	26637	5089	40.5	19.1	121	1156	39.5	4.3	118	2120	41.7	8.0	124	1813	39.8	6.8	118
18-49	48167	9240	73.6	19.2	121	2117	72.4	4.4	119	3897	76.7	8.1	126	3226	70.9	6.7	117
25-54	46536	8663	69.0	18.6	117	2002	68.5	4.3	117	3582	70.5	7.7	120	3080	67.6	6.6	115
EMPLOYED FULL TIME	34842	6594	52.5	18.9	119	1527	52.2	4.4	119	2828	55.6	8.1	126	2239	49.2	6.4	112
PART-TIME	7143	1416	11.3	19.8	125	*325	11.1	4.5	123	580	11.4	8.1	127	*510	11.2	7.1	124
NOT EMPLOYED	37251	4551	36.2	12.2	77	1071	36.6	2.9	78	1676	33.0	4.5	70	1804	39.6	4.8	84
PROFESSIONAL	6473	1515	12.1	23.4	148	*315	10.8	4.9	132	867	13.1	10.3	161	533	11.7	8.2	143
EXECUTIVE/ADMIN./MANAGERIAL	4555	843	6.7	18.5	117	*190	6.8	4.4	118	401	7.9	8.8	137	*244	5.4	5.4	93
CLERICAL/SALES/TECHNICAL	18435	3353	26.7	18.2	115	880	30.1	4.8	129	1459	28.7	7.9	123	1014	22.3	5.5	96
PRECISION/CRAFTS/REPAIR	1000	*192	1.5	19.2	121	*41	1.4	4.1	111	*90	1.8	9.0	140	*62	1.4	6.2	108
OTHER EMPLOYED	11522	2107	16.8	18.3	115	*417	14.3	3.6	98	792	15.6	6.9	107	898	19.7	7.8	136
H/D INCOME $50,000 OR MORE	14304	2651	21.1	18.5	117	569	19.5	4.0	108	1142	22.5	8.0	124	940	20.6	6.6	114
$40,000 - 49,999	9821	1969	15.7	20.0	126	*489	16.7	5.0	135	785	15.4	8.0	125	694	15.2	7.1	123
$35,000 - 39,999	6500	1296	10.3	19.9	126	*479	16.4	7.4	200	*363	7.1	5.6	87	*454	10.0	7.0	122
$25,000 - 24,999	13806	2188	17.4	15.8	100	483	16.5	3.5	95	1052	20.7	7.6	119	653	14.3	4.7	82
$15,000 - 24,999	15616	2287	18.0	14.5	92	495	16.9	3.2	86	985	19.0	6.2	96	807	17.7	5.2	90
LESS THAN $15,000	19190	2190	17.4	11.4	72	410	14.0	2.1	58	776	15.3	4.0	63	1005	22.1	5.2	91
CENSUS REGION: NORTH EAST	16966	3351	26.7	19.8	125	823	28.1	4.9	131	1387	27.3	8.2	127	1142	25.1	6.7	117
NORTH CENTRAL	19582	3392	27.0	17.3	109	880	30.1	4.5	122	1521	29.9	7.8	121	990	21.7	5.1	88
SOUTH	27346	3371	26.8	12.3	78	579	19.8	2.1	57	1220	24.0	4.5	70	1572	34.5	5.7	100
WEST	15342	2446	19.5	15.9	101	641	21.9	4.2	113	955	18.8	6.2	97	849	18.6	5.5	96
MARKETING REG.: NEW ENGLAND	4656	936	7.5	20.1	127	*147	5.0	3.2	86	476	9.4	10.2	159	*314	6.9	6.7	117
MIDDLE ATLANTIC	13652	2615	20.8	19.2	121	717	24.5	5.3	142	1027	20.2	7.5	117	871	19.1	6.4	111
EAST CENTRAL	11204	1851	14.7	16.5	104	458	15.7	4.1	111	632	12.4	5.6	88	761	16.7	6.8	118
WEST CENTRAL	12679	2330	18.6	18.4	116	605	20.7	4.8	129	1132	22.3	8.9	139	593	13.0	4.7	81
SOUTH EAST	14499	1827	14.5	12.6	79	*313	10.7	2.2	59	700	13.8	4.8	75	814	17.9	5.6	98
SOUTH WEST	9288	920	7.3	9.9	62	*178	6.1	1.9	52	*290	5.7	3.1	49	*452	9.9	4.9	85
PACIFIC	13258	2081	16.6	15.7	99					826	16.2	6.2	97	748	16.4	5.6	98
COUNTY SIZE A	32384	5267	41.9	16.3	103	1410	48.2	4.4	118	1987	39.1	6.1	96	1870	41.1	5.8	100
COUNTY SIZE B	23508	3986	31.6	16.9	106	932	31.9	4.0	107	1624	31.9	6.9	108	1411	31.0	6.0	104
COUNTY SIZE C	12456	1967	15.7	15.8	100	*396	13.5	3.2	86	891	17.5	7.2	111	680	14.9	5.5	95
COUNTY SIZE D	10888	1360	10.8	12.5	79	*186	6.4	1.7	46	582	11.4	5.3	83	*592	13.0	5.4	95
MSA CENTRAL CITY	28381	4277	34.1	15.1	95	1008	34.4	3.5	96	1674	32.9	5.9	92	1596	35.1	5.6	98
MSA SUBURBAN	32254	5003	44.0	17.4	110	1525	52.2	4.7	128	2047	40.3	6.3	99	2032	44.6	6.3	110
NON-MSA	18601	2680	21.3	14.4	91	*393	13.4	2.1	57	1362	26.8	7.3	114	925	20.3	5.0	87
SINGLE	8850	1461	11.6	16.5	104	*249	8.5	2.8	76	610	12.0	6.9	107	602	13.2	6.8	118
MARRIED	50063	8428	67.1	16.8	106	1917	65.6	3.8	104	3520	69.2	7.0	110	2991	65.7	6.0	104
OTHER	20323	2871	21.3	13.1	83	757	25.9	3.7	101	954	18.8	4.7	73	960	21.1	4.7	82
PARENTS	31882	5304	42.2	16.6	105	1087	37.5	3.4	93	2231	43.9	7.0	109	1976	43.4	6.2	108
WORKING PARENTS	19985	3515	28.0	17.6	111	679	23.2	3.4	92	1554	30.6	7.8	121	1281	28.1	6.4	112
HOUSEHOLD SIZE: 1 PERSON	13148	1458	11.6	11.1	70	348	11.9	2.6	72	575	11.3	4.4	68	535	11.8	4.1	71
2 PERSONS	23406	3980	31.7	17.0	107	1100	37.9	4.7	128	1501	29.5	6.4	100	1371	30.1	5.9	102
3 OR MORE	42682	7122	56.7	16.7	105	1467	50.2	3.4	93	3008	59.2	7.0	110	2646	58.1	6.2	108
ANY CHILD IN HOUSEHOLD	34747	5649	45.0	16.3	103	1165	39.8	3.4	91	2306	45.4	6.6	103	2178	47.8	6.3	109
UNDER 2 YEARS	5971	752	6.0	12.6	79	*256	8.8	4.3	116	*256	5.0	4.3	67	*240	5.3	4.0	70
2-5 YEARS	13551	2282	18.2	16.8	106	509	17.4	3.8	102	841	16.5	6.2	97	932	20.5	6.9	120
6-11 YEARS	16228	2641	21.0	16.3	103	630	21.5	3.9	105	1005	19.8	6.2	97	1006	22.1	6.2	108
12-17 YEARS	15479	2696	21.5	17.4	110	583	19.9	3.8	102	1110	21.8	7.2	112	1003	22.0	6.5	113
WHITE	68615	11776	93.8	17.2	108	2744	93.8	4.0	108	4845	95.3	7.1	110	4187	92.0	6.1	106
BLACK	8816	664	5.3	7.5	48	*166	5.7	1.9	52	*187	3.7	2.1	33	*310	6.8	3.5	61
HOME OWNED	54889	8703	69.3	15.9	100	1918	65.6	3.5	95	3878	76.3	7.1	110	2907	63.8	5.3	92
DAILY NEWSPAPERS: READ ANY	46387	7717	61.4	16.6	105	1946	66.6	4.2	114	3065	60.3	6.6	103	2706	59.4	5.8	102
READ ONE DAILY	37130	5977	47.6	16.1	102	1548	52.9	4.2	113	2340	46.0	6.3	98	2089	45.9	5.6	98
READ TWO OR MORE DAILIES	9258	1740	13.9	18.8	119	398	13.6	4.3	116	725	14.3	7.8	122	617	13.6	6.7	116
SUNDAY NEWSPAPERS: READ ANY	49444	8219	65.4	16.6	105	2130	73.2	4.3	117	3312	65.1	6.7	104	2769	60.8	5.6	97
READ ONE SUNDAY	43413	7289	58.0	16.8	106	1876	64.2	4.3	117	2953	58.1	6.8	106	2459	54.0	5.7	99
READ TWO OR MORE SUNDAYS	6031	930	7.4	15.4	97	*282	9.0	4.3	118	358	7.0	5.9	93	*310	6.8	5.1	89
HEAVY MAGAZINES - HEAVY TV	20671	3037	24.2	14.7	93	788	26.9	3.8	103	1323	26.0	6.4	100	926	20.3	4.5	78
HEAVY MAGAZINES - LIGHT TV	18757	3589	28.6	19.1	121	849	29.0	4.5	123	1535	30.2	8.2	128	1208	26.5	6.4	112
LIGHT MAGAZINES - HEAVY TV	20250	2586	20.7	12.8	81	680	22.6	3.3	88	831	16.3	4.1	64	1105	24.3	5.5	95
LIGHT MAGAZINES - LIGHT TV	19558	3337	26.6	17.1	108	626	21.4	3.2	87	1394	27.4	7.1	111	1317	28.9	6.7	117

80

linked with a cluster system. This lets researchers identify the dominant buying behavior in areas as small as census block groups or neighborhoods.

The following is an example of purchase behavior from Simmons arranged within the demographic cluster groups of Donnelley Marketing Information Service's ClusterPLUS. It is important to note here that the other companies with cluster analysis products also link their systems to Mediamark and Simmons.

In this case, we see that the people in the top cluster are two and a half times more likely than average to buy imported beer. They are also big consumers of 35-mm color film, videocassettes, and English muffins, while the average consumer in cluster four buys domestic beer and motor oil and would never buy imported beer or English muffins. Compare these tastes with those of the people in cluster seven. For them, the beverages of choice are malt liquor and flavored milk, and they are not very likely to care about dishwasher detergent or color film.

The value of these combined data is that they not only start to identify customers through their demographics and purchase patterns, but they can pinpoint where those customers live. With the added geographic component you can identify the types of products and services likely to be hits or bombs in certain geographic areas.

Proprietary Customer Databases

Another method of acquiring demographic data linked to purchase data is to build a proprietary customer database. One company, National Demographics & Lifestyles (NDL), based in Denver, Colorado, offers a database marketing service that uses product registration cards as a vehicle to capture demographic, psychographic, purchase, and behavioral data from buyers of consumer goods and services.

After purchasing a product at the retail level, a consumer will voluntarily fill out a questionnaire, supplying purchase and behavioral information related to that purchase, as well as individual and household demographic and lifestyle data. The information is entered into a database which companies use to improve the effectiveness of their sales and product planning, advertising, direct mail, dealer support, sales promotion, and customer service.

List Enhancement Services

Several companies offer list enhancement services which are designed to "tag" demographic, lifestyle, and socioeconomic data to an existing customer list, helping consumer marketers understand their customers better and access them more effectively.

One company, Infobase Services, based in Little Rock, Arkansas, builds

Figure 6d: PURCHASE BEHAVIOR BY CLUSTER

Demographic Cluster Group	Above Average Use		Below Average Use	
	Index	*Product*	*Index*	*Product*
1. *Highest social and economic indicators, 8 percent of U.S. households.* Demographic/Lifestyle description: highest income, very well educated, professionally employed, in high value single family owned homes. Travel frequently, prefer tennis or golf, heavily use financial	250	Imported Beer	54	Denture cleaners
	206	35 mm color film & cameras	62	Home permanents
	196	Imported & domestic wine	67	Disposable diapers
	186	Dishwasher detergent	69	Flavored milk & buttermilk
	179	Videocassettes	69	Snack candy & candy bars
	171	Expensive cosmetics	70	Toilet bowl fresheners
	171	Gourmet food	70	Canned spaghetti or soups
	154	English muffins & rye bread	71	Laxatives & indigestion aids
	150	Bottled spring water	72	Regular colas
	141	Low fat/skim milk	73	Dishwashing liquid
	136	Paperback books	74	Malt liquor
	131	Converted rice	78	Canned vegetables
	131	Decaffeinated ground coffee	78	Flavored breakfast drinks
	130	Yogurt & natural cheeses	78	Air fresheners
	128	Cat food & cat litter	78	Cold remedies
4. *Average social and economic indicators, 18 percent of U.S. households.* Demographic/Lifestyle description: blue collar or service workers with average income and education, families with children in owned or rented homes. Watch VCR or cable, prefer domestic cars or trucks, own pets, occasionally go hunting.	125	Cartridge film & camera	46	Light beer
	116	Domestic beer	72	English muffins & rye bread
	115	Cologne/perfume	73	Imported wine
	114	Dishwashing liquid	74	Imported beer
	114	Motor oil & car wax	76	Video cassettes
	114	Hair rinse/conditioner	77	Specialty mustard
	113	Buttermilk	79	Gourmet food
	113	Regular ground coffee	80	Mayonnaise
	112	Disposable diapers	80	Flavored/seasoned rice
	111	Dry catfood	83	Bottled spring water
	110	Laxatives	83	Ginger ale
	108	Denture cleaners	83	Scented hand soaps
7. *Lowest social and economic indicators, 6 percent of U.S. households.* Demographic/Lifestyle description: urban poor, unskilled, often unemployed, in older apartments, heavily consume hard liquor & cigarettes, and use insecticides.	240	Malt liquor	38	Dishwasher detergent
	211	Flavored milk	38	Color film
	164	Disposable diapers	41	Lipstick/lip gloss
	160	Butter	48	Motor oil or car wax
	160	Orange juice- bottles/cartons	48	Cat food or cat litter
	148	Snack candy & hard candy	51	Support pantyhose
	147	Toilet bowl fresheners	53	Dog food
	142	Flavored/seasoned rice	53	Instant pudding
	139	Indigestion aids	53	Low fat/skim milk
	132	Laxatives	57	Hair rinse/conditioner
	131	Cologne/perfume	57	Domestic/imported wine
	131	Air freshener spray	58	Ground coffee
	128	Hot breakfast cereal		
	126	Home permanents		

SOURCE: © 1988, American Demographics, Inc.

Consumer Infobase, which has information on more than 170 million individual American consumers, and almost all U. S. households. The information contained in Consumer Infobase is provided by firms such as R. L. Polk, National Demographics & Lifestyles, Database America, SmartNames, and many other companies. This multi-source database is used to enhance any existing customer list or database, whether it contains only name and address or purchase behavior information in addition to name and address.

Other companies, such as May and Speh in Chicago, and North American Communications in Armonk, New York, offer list enhancement services. If a company already has detailed purchase data, list enhancement can provide the link to demographic and lifestyle data. Many consumer marketers are taking advantage of these services to learn more about their existing customers, to communicate with them more effectively, and to reach new prospects.

Purchase behavior data are an invaluable tool for finding out who the best customers are and determining current and potential market shares. But there are also other uses that only become apparent when trying to solve specific problems. We'll be examining some of these variations in the final chapters. One thing should be growing apparent. The possibilities for creative use of data for better business decision making are limited only by the creativity of the user.

Three sections of the complicated consumer information puzzle are now in place. Demographics and psychographics painted a picture of your customers, and the purchase data revealed their spending patterns. The missing piece will tell you how to capture them with your messages.

CHAPTER SEVEN

Media: Do They Watch, Read, or Listen?

BY NOW, demographics have revealed who the customers are. Psychographics have shown what they want in products and messages, and purchase behavior data have identified what and how much they buy. But a very important piece of information is missing. We don't yet know how to reach them. Media preferences are the last piece of the consumer information puzzle and in some ways the most important. Without an effective means of communicating with customers, products remain in inventory and services stay unused.

Communicating with customers is no easy task in these days of media fragmentation, message clutter, and technological revolution. In one generation, the media environment has gone from drought to deluge. National television used to consist of three major networks; now there are dozens of cable channels. In most urban markets the venerable daily newspaper now faces competition from suburban newspapers, weeklies, regional and city magazines, and special interest publications targeted at women, seniors, or business people. Add in billboards, festivals, sports sponsorship, brand exposure in major motion pictures, multiple sets of Yellow Pages, and point-of-purchase ads, and the cacophony of competing messages becomes deafening. In our message-saturated society, even toilets and fruit can be media options, as ads grace the doors of public restrooms and bananas come with stickers advertising cereal.

Consumers, however, focus their attention on a selected mix of media. Your optimal consumer may only watch certain programs or no TV at all. She might depend on National Public Radio for all her news coverage.

That's where media preference information comes in. It helps determine the communication vehicle that will get your message most directly and cost effectively to the people who will buy what you sell. Media data point out the most direct way to put the buying bug in your customer's ear.

Media preference data have two major purposes and therein lies their greatest flaw. While on the one hand media preference data allow advertisers to find the most efficient media for their message, the data were developed by those very media companies as a way to woo advertisers.

Understanding Media Preferences

Much of the media data in existence are really a measurement of the size of audiences of various media in various markets at various times of day. Today, in each of 220 television markets, you can get a precise breakdown of what proportion of the "The Cosby Show" audience is white men older than age 55. Or you can find out the show's ratings points—what portion of the total audience it captures. A slip of one ratings point in prime-time can represent the loss of millions in advertising revenues. But these measurements that are so essential for media survival today didn't even exist 40 years ago. They weren't needed then because the mass market hadn't yet disintegrated, and the number of media choices had yet to explode.

Preference data were developed to give the media a way of measuring consumption of their products. Measuring readers of print media is relatively easy because a newspaper or magazine is a tangible product that must be purchased. To measure readership, you count sales and compile subscriber lists. To get demographics on readers and find out how you're doing, you take a survey or mail a questionnaire.

Measuring exposure to broadcast media, however, is much more complicated. The message is carried on invisible airwaves that anyone can access. In the infancy of the broadcast media, advertisers and audiences were cornered. Advertisers took it on faith that they were getting what they were paying for. Audiences could only watch or listen to the few stations available.

Today advertisers can no longer afford to take it on faith. They are raising legitimate questions about ad effectiveness. Consumers are faced with more media options and there is growing evidence that they are reaching a saturation point. A company needs some proof, then, that its messages are getting through before buying advertising time or space.

Audience measurement is one way to address the demand for proof. Fortunately, technology is providing ever-more accurate ways to measure consumer use of and attention to broadcast media, so the media companies, the advertising agencies, and the major advertisers are getting better information about ad exposure.

Major Suppliers

Audience measurement is a big business that's getting even bigger. A. C. Nielsen, the leading U.S. research company, reported revenues of $880 million in 1988—up 20.5 percent from the previous year. Nielsen is also the leader in the field of television audience measurement. The Arbitron Company, with $320 million in 1988 revenues, is the largest supplier of television and radio ratings. Birch/Scarborough Research ($13.2 million in 1988) is a major player in radio audience measurement and newspaper readership.

Mediamark and Simmons are the leaders in magazine readership measurement.

The major national audience measurement firms use different techniques to collect their data.

Television Measurement

Even when there were only a few thousand television sets in U.S. households, NBC sent set owners program schedules that had a mail-back postcard to indicate which programs they watched. Rudimentary as it was, it was the first TV measurement system. Most of the focus was on radio then and even the leading radio measurement firm, C. E. Hooper, was doubtful about the possibilities of the new medium. In 1950, however, Hooper sold its national radio and TV measurement services to Nielsen. Nielsen has been the leader in TV measurement ever since and now supplies viewing reports for each of 210 TV markets in the country at least four times a year.

A subsidiary of Dun & Bradstreet, Nielsen Media Research measures TV viewing through diary and/or meter-equipped household panels. Nielsen records the viewing habits (including cable TV, syndicated programming and videocassette usage) of 4,200 households in 22 national TV markets. Before 1987 there were 1,800 "Nielsen families." Meters attached to their TV sets recorded when the set was on and what channel it was tuned to, and the family filled out a diary of programs watched. Now the process has changed. The panel families are hooked up to a "people meter" which allows each viewer to clock in and out on a keypad when entering or leaving the room.

The problem with this method is that often the viewers fail to use their people meters and diaries. In mid-1989, the children's cable channel, Nickelodeon, sponsored a telephone survey to check on people-meter estimates. The survey respondents rated Nickelodeon 24 percent higher among children aged 2 to 11 than the electronic ratings had done. Other follow-up surveys have found serious underreporting of adolescents and men. These groups may be watching, but they won't tell you about it unless you catch them in the act.

The solution to this chronic problem is a people-proof people meter. A working model of this device, called the "passive people meter" was unveiled by Nielsen in 1989. When mounted on top of a television, the device can identify various household members and record, second by second, when they watch the television, when they leave the room, and when they look away to talk or read. Nielsen officials say that the new meters may be producing data by the mid-1990s.

Arbitron also measures cable and television audiences in 214 markets through mail diaries and people- and household-meter equipped households. The audience data are available to radio and TV stations, advertisers, and ad agencies in printed reports or a computer-based electronic book system.

Except for the handful of companies using people meters, most audience measurement is done with viewer-kept diaries and other kinds of surveys. The passive people meter will take care of the problem for large-scale network television, but radio, local TV, cable, print, and promotional media are likely to continue to do things the old way—surveying the audience through various means.

Radio Measurement

Most radio audience measurements come from diaries and telephone surveys. In measuring radio audiences, Arbitron selects random samples of households in each of 259 radio markets. The top markets are surveyed continuously. After the households have agreed to participate, Arbitron mails them one-week individual diaries so household members can record all of their listening choices during the survey week. An interviewer also calls the household to make sure they understand the procedure.

Birch Radio measures audiences in 150 markets around the U.S., 109 of which are measured on a continuous basis. Using a single telephone recall interview, Birch provides estimates of yesterday listening and average weekly cumulative audiences of people aged 12 and older. For each reported listen Birch reports the start and stop, where they listened (car, home, etc.) and listening by daypart. Audiences are measured by age, sex, race, ZIP Code and county of residence.

In the continuously measured markets Birch gets more demographic detail such as household income, education, occupation, other media usage and some purchase intention data. Birch Radio offers Target Market Reports that analyze black listenership in 41 markets, Hispanic Listenership in 16 markets and the Airline Target Market Report that measures 101 markets. Like the other ratings data, Birch data is available to subscribers only.

Print Measurement

The Scarborough half of Birch/Scarborough surveys newspaper readership in 31 markets every year. Scarborough researchers survey random samples of people by telephone to determine newspaper preference, and respondents are sent a product information book to record purchases and a weekly TV diary to record viewing patterns. The survey results are available to subscribers. Birch/Scarborough has plans to expand to 50 newspaper markets in the future.

Mediamark and Simmons Market Research Bureau connect purchase behavior data to magazine readership and to other media usage. They may

Figure 7a: SAMPLE PAGE FROM ARBITRON'S RADIO RATINGS FOR DENVER-BOULDER

Specific Audience
MONDAY - FRIDAY   6AM - 10AM

	Persons 12+	Persons 18+	Men 18+	Men 18-24	Men 25-34	Men 35-44	Men 45-54	Men 55-64	Women 18+	Women 18-24	Women 25-34	Women 35-44	Women 45-54	Women 55-64	Teens 12-17
KAZY															
MET AQH PERSONS	147	141	111	36	40	35			30	16	3	10	1		6
MET AQH RATING	.9	1.0	1.6	3.3	1.8	2.2			.4	1.5	.1	.6	.1		.4
MET AQH SHARE	3.8	3.8	6.2	17.0	6.9	7.0			1.6	6.4	.6	2.6	.4		3.4
MET CUME PERSONS	975	874	585	219	281	85			289	144	72	63	10		101
MET CUME RATING	6.1	6.1	8.3	19.8	13.0	5.3			3.9	13.7	3.5	4.0	1.1		6.7
TSA AQH PERSONS	162	156	123	38	50	35			33	18	4	10	1		6
TSA CUME PERSONS	1155	1035	678	250	343	85			357	194	90	63	10		120
KBCO															
MET AQH PERSONS	14	14	11		4	7			3			3			
MET AQH RATING	.1	.1	.2		.2	.4						.1			
MET AQH SHARE	.4	.4	.6		.7	1.4			.2			.6			
MET CUME PERSONS	164	164	129		59	70			35			35			
MET CUME RATING	1.0	1.1	1.8		2.7	4.4			.5			1.7			
TSA AQH PERSONS	19	19	16		4	12			3			3			
TSA CUME PERSONS	198	198	159		74	79		6	39			35			4
KBCO-FM															
MET AQH PERSONS	268	267	167	26	94	43	4		100	12	62	23	2	1	1
MET AQH RATING	1.7	1.9	2.4	2.4	4.3	2.7	.4		1.4	1.1	3.0	1.5	.2	.1	.1
MET AQH SHARE	6.9	7.2	9.3	12.3	16.3	8.6	1.7		5.3	4.8	11.5	6.0	.7	.5	.6
MET CUME PERSONS	1365	1343	768	97	399	240	32		575	91	325	130	22	7	22
MET CUME RATING	8.6	9.3	10.9	8.8	18.4	15.0	3.5		7.8	8.7	15.6	8.2	2.4	1.0	1.5
TSA AQH PERSONS	285	284	176	32	95	45	4		108	19	62	24	2	1	1
TSA CUME PERSONS	1491	1469	818	128	413	245	32		651	162	325	135	22	7	22
A/F TOT															
MET AQH PERSONS	282	281	178	26	98	50	4		103	12	65	23	2	1	1
MET AQH RATING	1.8	1.9	2.5	2.4	4.5	3.1	.4		1.4	1.1	3.1	1.5	.2	.1	.1
MET AQH SHARE	7.3	7.6	9.9	12.3	17.0	10.0	1.7		5.4	4.8	12.1	6.0	.7	.5	.6
MET CUME PERSONS	1470	1448	850	97	438	283	32		598	91	348	130	22	7	22
MET CUME RATING	9.2	10.0	12.0	8.8	20.2	17.7	3.5		8.1	8.7	16.7	8.2	2.4	1.0	1.5
TSA AQH PERSONS	304	303	192	32	99	57	4		111	19	65	24	2	1	1
TSA CUME PERSONS	1629	1607	929	128	466	297	32	6	678	162	348	135	22	11	22
KBPI															
MET AQH PERSONS	123	118	83	31	42	10			35	11	20	2	2		5
MET AQH RATING	.8	.8	1.2	2.8	1.9	.6			.5	1.0	1.0	.1	.2		.3
MET AQH SHARE	3.2	3.2	4.6	14.6	7.3	2.0			1.8	4.4	3.7	.5	.7		2.8
MET CUME PERSONS	1081	997	549	178	303	68			448	205	181	56	6		84
MET CUME RATING	6.8	6.9	7.8	16.1	14.0	4.2			6.1	19.5	8.7	3.5	.6		5.5
TSA AQH PERSONS	125	119	84	32	42	10			35	11	20	2	2		6
TSA CUME PERSONS	1147	1054	599	228	303	68			455	205	181	63	6		93
KBXG															
MET AQH PERSONS	96	96	50		5	13	7		46	7	2	12	4		13
MET AQH RATING	.6	.7	.7	.1	.2	.8	.8	2.1	.6	.7	.1	.8	.4		1.8
MET AQH SHARE	2.5	2.6	2.8	.5	.9	2.6	2.9	8.0	2.4	2.8	.4	3.1	1.4		6.2
MET CUME PERSONS	394	394	203	21	53	51	22	19	191	15	14	49	17		40
MET CUME RATING	2.5	2.7	2.9	1.9	2.4	3.2	2.4	2.9	2.6	1.4		7	3.1	1.8	5.7
TSA AQH PERSONS	116	116	53	1	5	15	8	14	63	7	2	21	4		15
TSA CUME PERSONS	484	484	224	21	53	59	35	19	260	15	14	79	34		45
KDEN															
MET AQH PERSONS	26	26	9			3	1		17		5				1
MET AQH RATING	.2	.2	.1			.2	.1		.2		.3				.1
MET AQH SHARE	.7	.7	.5			.6	.4		.9		1.3				.5
MET CUME PERSONS	218	218	87			28	8	7	131		30				13
MET CUME RATING	1.4	1.5	1.2			1.7	.9	1.1	1.8		1.9				1.8
TSA AQH PERSONS	29	29	9			3	1		20		5				1
TSA CUME PERSONS	225	225	87			28	8	7	138		30				13
KDHT															
MET AQH PERSONS	29	29	12		7	3	2		17		17				
MET AQH RATING	.2	.2	.2		.3	.2	.2		.2		.8				
MET AQH SHARE	.7	.7	.7		1.2	.6	.8		.9		3.2				
MET CUME PERSONS	178	169	81		24	50	7		88		74	7		7	9
MET CUME RATING	1.1	1.2	1.1		1.1	3.1	.8		1.2		3.6	.4		1.0	.6
TSA AQH PERSONS	36	36	15	1	7	5	2		21	4	17			7	9
TSA CUME PERSONS	241	232	119	31	24	57	7		113	16	83	7			9
KDKO															
MET AQH PERSONS	18	17	2			2			15	5	8	2			1
MET AQH RATING	.1	.1				.1			.2	.4	.4	.1			.1
MET AQH SHARE	.5	.5	.1			.3			.8	2.0	1.5	.5			.6
MET CUME PERSONS	201	181	33			24			148	37	85	10	16		20
MET CUME RATING	1.3	1.3	.5			1.1		9	2.0	3.5	4.1	.6	1.7		1.3
TSA AQH PERSONS	18	17	2			2			15	5	8	2			1
TSA CUME PERSONS	201	181	33			24			148	37	85	10	16		20
KEZW															
MET AQH PERSONS	84	83	41		2	5	5	21	42			12	6	16	
MET AQH RATING	.5	.6	.6		.1	.3	.5	3.2	.6			.8	.6	2.3	.1
MET AQH SHARE	2.2	2.2	2.3		.3	1.0	2.1	12.0	2.2			3.1	2.1	7.7	.6
MET CUME PERSONS	435	411	216		14	18	27	90	195			31	23	78	24
MET CUME RATING	2.7	2.9	3.1		.6	1.1	2.9	13.8	2.7			2.0	2.5	11.0	1.6
TSA AQH PERSONS	87	86	43		2	6	5	22	43			13	6	16	
TSA CUME PERSONS	480	456	241		14	32	27	101	215			45	23	78	24

Footnote Symbols: * Audience estimates adjusted for actual broadcast schedule + Station(s) changed call letters since the prior survey - see Page 5B
Both of the previous footnotes apply.

ask, for example, "Do you drink imported wine?" The respondents who say they do are then asked about what magazines, newspapers, networks, cable channels, and radio formats they listen to. The surveys ask which magazines people have read or seen in the last six months, and the results are cross tabulated with demographics. To measure newspaper readership, the consumers are interviewed twice and asked which papers they read yesterday or which Sunday sections they read.

The surveys measure TV audiences by two-week diaries of personal viewing, which produce data on viewers of specific programs, total audiences, and viewing frequency. They measure radio audiences through two interviews, either in person or by telephone. Radio measures include total daily cumulative radio audience and yesterday listening by dayparts, formats, and networks.

The Mediamark and Simmons audience data on magazine, newspaper, outdoor, radio, and TV are divided into quintiles (the total audience divided into five equal parts by total exposure to the medium). Consumers in the top television quintile may account for 45 percent of the TV audience, while the bottom quintile accounts for just one percent. Arranging the data this way and cross-referencing them with purchase information makes it simple to see which medium is preferred most by buyers of a product.

How to Get Preferences

The above firms supply data to most of the biggest media companies, advertising agencies, and consumer goods and service companies. But what if you want to find out what's the best media option in one local market? There are several ways to do this. For larger markets, one way is to subscribe to the Nielsen, Arbitron, or Birch/Scarborough services. This will result in accurate ratings data, but it may not be cost effective for smaller advertisers, and it may not tell you enough about who the audiences are in smaller markets. To find out who is watching, reading, or listening, you need more detailed data.

Ratings data can also be obtained from the local television and radio stations that subscribe to ratings services. These stations buy the reports hoping the results will show they deliver more viewers per advertising dollar than the competition. Local newspapers are also a source of information on readership, and local cable companies are very willing to tell advertisers about their subscribers.

There are several points to consider when collecting media preference data. Often the audience measurements are inaccurate or misleading because the company selling advertising is the only one with ratings data. Local stations or print media may not be entirely unbiased purveyors of ratings news, especially if they aren't coming in first in the ratings race.

Second, surveys cost money, and a small local media company may have used an audience sample that is too small to be statistically reliable. Third, if too few issues or episodes of a publication or program are measured, the results may be skewed. Networks try to skew their audience measurements by scheduling blockbuster programs during the ratings period. Publishers do the same by scheduling special issues, and radio stations fund contests and promotions to boost their audiences during "the book."

Local media will have access to ratings and subscriber information, and if they want to sell you some ad space or time, they're going to put the data together in glowing charts showing why their medium is best for you. If you are dealing with a persistent number two or three, it may be frustrating trying to differentiate between the truth and the hype.

For that you have to get a look at the unadorned information from one of the media preference firms or the original local surveys. Check the sample size and make sure the survey was taken by a reputable firm. Ask about promotion or special programs that may have run during the survey period and understand the inherent limitations of the measurement techniques.

Local market data are available from TV or radio stations in many of the top 75 media markets around the country. Many stations hire outside research firms such as Marshall Marketing & Communications of Pittsburgh, and Leigh Stowell & Co. of Seattle, to conduct a market survey. Demographics, psychographics, purchase behavior, and media preference questions are all included in those surveys. In many cases the stations include specific questions about advertisers' products. A grocery company, for example, could link people who said they used its stores with their attitudes and media preferences to find out what kind of appeal would win them and in what medium to place their ads. Impact Resources of Columbus, Ohio, makes similar market data available through its MA*RT database which consists of information from annual market surveys in the top 50 media markets.

The Problem with Ratings

Local stations and advertisers are turning to original local surveys because of the inherent limitations of ratings data. The ratings tell you how many people are watching or listening at given times and how frequently they watch. But apart from some vague age and sex data, they do very little to tell you exactly *who* is watching what station.

Advertisers now demand more than the basic numbers, and local television and radio stations are hiring their own research firms to find out who is watching and listening. This move toward local market research is only going to intensify as regional competition for advertisers heats up. Radio and television stations and newspapers are selling essentially one product to their advertisers—their audiences. The more they know about the demographics, psychographics, and purchase behavior of their respective audiences, the better they will know their own products, and the easier it will be to convince a retailer trying to target a specific customer group that a specific show on a specific station can deliver those customers.

The best advice for the advertiser is "know thy customer." An advertiser who has formed the most highly detailed profile of his customers and who demands to know how many of those customers each medium can reach is the one who is likely to get the most bang for his advertising buck.

The Power of Demographics

The goal of all audience measurement firms is to produce an accurate demographic profile of media audiences by medium and area. But add purchase behavior to the combination, and media preference data take on real power.

The traditional way to choose media has been to calculate the cost of exposing one person to your message and to go with the lowest-cost option. This no longer makes sense in the era of micromarketing. Ad and promotional spending is all but wasted if the person it reaches will never buy your product. By looking at media preference data and purchase behavior, you can determine the cost per thousand *customers*, rather than merely the cost per thousand readers or viewers.

Suppose you sell dry cat food and you know that your prime customers are professional women aged 35 to 54. How do you take the first step to determine how to reach them? Look at the Mediamark or Simmons reports and you will see that the heaviest buyers of your product read or listen to the radio rather than watch TV, and they are most likely to listen in the morning. Turn the page and you will see that the heavy users of the product (those who use more than 8 pounds of dry cat food in 30 days) are over three times more likely than average to subscribe to *Mother Earth News* or *Natural History* magazines. If you want to market nationally, those magazines might prove to be good vehicles for your messages.

This information can even work on the local level. Let's say the owner of a pet store wanted to promote a new array of cat-care products. A look at Mediamark or Simmons would provide valuable insights. It shows that cat owners are more likely than average to be professionals, and they are working parents between the ages of 35 and 54 who earn more than $35,000 a year. They are heavy magazine readers and they listen to the radio, but they are

Figure 7b: SAMPLE PAGE FROM MEDIAMARK'S PET & BABY PRODUCTS REPORT

PET OWNERSHIP

BASE: FEMALE HOMEMAKERS	TOTAL U.S. '000	OWN CAT(S) A '000	B % DOWN	C % ACROSS	D INDEX	OWN DOG(S) A '000	B % DOWN	C % ACROSS	D INDEX	OWN OTHER PETS A '000	B % DOWN	C % ACROSS	D INDEX
ALL FEMALE HOMEMAKERS	79236	17834	100.0	22.5	100	25343	100.0	32.0	100	7387	100.0	9.3	100
QUINTILE I - NEWSPAPERS	15995	3846	21.6	24.0	107	5669	22.4	35.4	111	1463	19.8	9.1	98
QUINTILE II	16180	3410	19.1	21.1	94	5170	20.4	32.0	100	1611	21.8	10.0	107
QUINTILE III	15913	3549	19.9	22.3	99	5460	21.5	34.3	107	1037	14.0	6.5	70
QUINTILE IV	15578	3629	20.3	23.3	104	4722	18.6	30.3	95	1793	24.3	11.5	123
QUINTILE V	15571	3400	19.1	21.8	97	4322	17.1	27.8	87	1483	20.1	9.5	102
QUINTILE I - RADIO	14915	3596	20.2	24.1	107	5124	20.2	34.4	107	1571	21.3	10.5	113
QUINTILE II	15953	3638	20.4	22.8	101	5116	20.2	32.1	100	1643	22.2	10.3	110
QUINTILE III	15994	3474	19.5	21.7	97	5050	19.9	31.6	99	1445	19.6	9.0	97
QUINTILE IV	16206	3901	21.9	24.1	107	5355	21.1	33.0	103	1521	20.6	9.4	101
QUINTILE V	16169	3224	18.1	19.9	89	4698	18.5	29.1	91	1207	16.3	7.5	80
QUINTILE I - TV (TOTAL)	16081	2906	16.7	18.6	82	5047	19.9	31.4	98	1373	18.6	8.5	92
QUINTILE II	16635	3266	18.3	19.6	87	5300	20.9	31.9	100	1232	16.7	7.4	79
QUINTILE III	15833	3908	21.9	24.7	110	5057	20.0	31.9	100	1623	22.0	10.3	110
QUINTILE IV	15262	3784	21.2	24.8	110	4778	18.9	31.3	98	1491	20.2	9.8	105
QUINTILE V	15425	3889	21.8	25.2	112	5161	20.4	33.5	105	1669	22.6	10.8	116
RADIO WKDAY: 6-10:00 AM CUME	45107	10649	59.7	23.6	105	14989	59.1	33.2	104	4153	56.2	9.2	99
10:00 AM - 3:00 PM	28138	6665	37.4	23.7	105	9799	38.7	34.8	109	3055	41.4	10.9	116
3:00 PM - 7:00 PM	28380	7114	39.9	25.1	111	9759	38.5	34.4	108	3227	43.7	11.4	122
7:00 PM - MIDNIGHT	11776	3011	16.9	25.6	114	4008	15.8	34.0	106	1430	19.4	12.1	130
RADIO AVERAGE WEEKDAY CUME	61019	14148	79.3	23.2	103	20181	79.6	33.1	103	6021	81.5	9.9	106
RADIO AVG. WEEKEND DAY CUME	51317	11529	64.6	22.5	100	16233	64.1	31.6	99	4676	63.3	9.1	98
RADIO FORMATS: ADULT CONTEMP	20565	4838	27.1	23.5	105	7362	29.0	35.8	112	2419	32.7	11.8	126
ALBUM ORIENTED ROCK (AOR)	7130	1977	11.1	27.7	123	2374	9.4	33.3	104	848	11.5	11.9	128
ALL NEWS	2636	475	2.7	18.0	80	637	2.5	24.2	76	*177	2.4	6.7	72
BLACK	2071	*231	1.3	11.2	50	*414	1.6	20.0	63	*139	1.9	6.7	72
CLASSICAL	1948	454	2.5	23.3	104	529	2.1	27.2	85	*225	3.0	11.6	124
CHR/ROCK	13663	3590	20.1	26.3	117	4682	18.5	34.3	107	1487	20.1	10.9	117
COUNTRY	14237	4037	22.6	28.4	126	5879	23.2	41.3	129	1689	22.9	11.9	127
EASY LISTENING	7216	1693	9.5	23.5	104	2280	9.0	31.6	99	467	6.3	6.5	69
GOLDEN OLDIES	2876	659	3.7	22.9	102	1075	4.2	37.4	117	323	4.4	11.2	120
MOR/NOSTALGIA	4109	844	4.7	20.5	91	1254	4.9	30.5	95	*246	3.3	6.0	64
NEWS/TALK	5386	995	5.6	18.5	82	1296	5.1	24.1	75	488	6.6	9.1	97
URBAN CONTEMPORARY	3270	539	3.0	16.5	73	586	2.3	17.9	56	*256	3.5	7.8	84
RADIO NETWORKS: ABC CONTEMP	4434	1078	6.0	24.3	108	1581	6.2	35.7	111	564	7.6	12.7	136
ABC DIRECTION	3493	806	4.5	23.1	103	1381	5.4	39.5	124	*329	4.5	9.4	101
ABC ENTERTAINMENT	5261	1172	6.6	22.3	99	1911	7.5	36.3	114	476	6.4	9.0	97
ABC FM	2808	577	3.2	20.5	91	1042	4.1	37.1	116	*277	3.7	9.9	106
ABC INFORMATION	7527	1699	9.5	22.6	100	2510	9.9	33.3	104	695	9.4	9.2	99
ABC ROCK	3370	814	4.6	24.2	107	1184	4.7	35.1	110	476	6.4	14.1	152
CBS	5188	1108	6.2	21.4	95	1666	6.6	32.1	100	385	5.2	7.4	80
CONCERT MUSIC NETWORK	900	*199	1.1	22.1	98	*231	.9	25.7	80	*103	1.4	11.4	123
INTERNET	23077	5288	29.7	22.9	102	7438	29.3	32.2	101	2409	32.6	10.4	112
KATZ RADIO GROUP	25173	5793	32.5	23.0	102	8114	32.0	32.2	101	2407	32.6	9.6	103
MUTUAL	6769	1188	6.7	17.6	78	2209	8.7	32.6	102	654	8.9	9.7	104
NBC	4808	1073	6.0	22.3	99	1546	6.1	32.2	101	372	5.0	7.7	83
NBN	1407	*181	1.0	12.9	57	*177	.7	12.6	39	*68	.9	4.8	52
RADIORADIO	3198	753	4.2	23.5	105	915	3.6	28.6	89	*359	4.9	11.2	120
SATELLITE MUSIC NETWORK	3680	894	5.0	24.3	108	1137	4.5	30.9	97	365	4.9	9.9	106
SHERIDAN	1787	*144	.8	8.1	36	*192	.8	10.7	34	*83	1.1	4.6	50
THE SOURCE	3294	933	5.2	28.3	126	988	3.9	30.0	94	392	5.3	11.9	128
SUPERNET	16028	3988	22.3	24.8	110	5338	21.1	33.3	104	1831	24.8	11.4	123
TRANSTAR	4324	1015	5.7	23.5	104	1362	5.4	31.5	98	375	5.1	8.7	93
US1	4060	1005	5.6	24.8	110	1155	4.6	28.4	89	419	5.7	10.3	111
US2	4128	783	4.4	19.0	84	1278	5.0	31.0	97	366	5.0	8.9	95
WALL STREET JOURNAL NETWORK	3222	546	3.1	16.9	75	842	3.3	26.1	82	*260	3.5	8.1	87
TV WKDAY AV 1/2 HR:7-10:00AM	7432	1562	8.8	21.0	93	2396	9.5	32.2	101	776	10.5	10.4	112
10:00 AM - 4:30 PM	12732	2528	14.2	19.9	88	4484	17.7	35.3	110	856	11.6	6.7	72
4:30 PM - 7:30 PM	20201	3901	21.9	19.3	86	5999	23.7	29.7	93	1785	24.2	8.8	95
7:30 PM - 8:00 PM	31577	6522	36.6	20.7	92	9819	38.7	31.1	97	2579	34.9	8.2	88
8:00 PM - 11:00 PM	37214	7914	44.4	21.3	94	11656	46.0	31.3	98	3249	44.0	8.7	94
11:00 PM - 11:30 PM	23262	5086	28.5	21.9	97	7223	28.5	31.1	97	1966	26.6	8.5	91
11:30 PM - 1:00 AM	6802	1573	8.8	23.1	103	1949	7.7	28.7	90	608	8.2	8.9	96
TV PRIME TIME CUME	63663	14338	80.4	22.5	100	20112	79.4	31.6	99	5754	77.9	9.0	97
PROGRAM-TYPES:DAYTIME DRAMAS	7150	1409	7.9	19.7	88	2243	8.9	31.4	98	765	10.4	10.7	115
DAYTIME GAME SHOWS	3743	765	4.3	20.4	91	1377	5.4	36.8	115	*375	5.1	10.0	107
EARLY MORNING TALK/INFO/NEWS	5875	1260	7.1	21.4	95	2013	7.9	34.3	107	557	7.5	9.5	102
EARLY EVE. NETWK NEWS - M-F	11664	2320	13.0	19.9	88	4037	15.9	34.6	108	943	12.8	8.1	87
FEATURE FILMS - PRIME	11260	2700	15.1	24.0	107	4072	16.1	36.2	113	1249	16.9	11.1	119
GENERAL DRAMA - PRIME	11800	2636	14.8	22.3	99	3689	14.6	31.3	98	1106	15.0	9.4	101
PVT DET/SUSP/MYST/POL.-PRIME	11952	2897	16.2	24.2	108	3708	14.6	31.0	97	944	12.8	7.9	85
SITUATION COMEDIES - PRIME	9559	2438	13.7	25.5	113	3365	13.3	35.2	110	902	12.2	9.4	101
CABLE TV	36901	8719	48.9	23.6	105	13120	51.8	35.6	111	3519	47.6	9.5	102
PAY TV	20291	5495	30.8	27.1	120	8051	31.8	39.7	124	2286	30.9	11.3	121
HEAVY CABLE VIEWING (15+ HR)	12402	3055	17.1	24.6	109	4976	19.6	40.1	125	1482	20.1	11.9	128
CABLE NETWORKS: A&E	4381	1274	7.1	29.1	129	1610	6.4	36.7	115	398	5.4	9.1	97
BET (BLACK ENTERTAINMENT TV)	973	*104	.6	10.7	47	*175	.7	18.0	56	*33	.4	3.4	36
CNN (CABLE NEWS NETWORK)	14023	3269	18.3	23.3	104	4800	19.0	34.3	107	1442	19.5	10.3	110
CNN HEADLINE NEWS	9263	1890	10.5	20.3	90	3223	12.7	34.8	109	762	10.3	8.2	88
CBN CABLE NETWORK	6935	1499	8.4	21.6	96	2673	10.5	38.5	121	671	9.1	9.7	104
THE DISCOVERY CHANNEL	4376	1167	6.5	26.7	118	1763	7.0	40.3	126	659	8.9	15.1	162
ESPN	11260	2875	16.1	25.5	113	4010	15.8	35.6	111	1216	16.5	10.8	116
FNN (FINANCIAL NEWS NETW'K)	642	*96	.5	15.0	66	*184	.7	28.7	90	*80	.8	9.3	100
THE LEARNING CHANNEL	993	*275	1.5	27.7	123	*368	1.5	37.1	116	*142	1.9	14.3	153
LIFETIME	6205	1632	9.2	26.3	117	2304	9.1	37.1	116	649	8.8	10.5	112
MTV	7162	2058	11.5	28.7	128	2624	10.4	36.6	115	926	12.5	12.9	139
THE NASHVILLE NETWORK	7147	1765	9.9	24.7	110	2813	11.1	39.4	123	756	10.2	10.6	113
NICK AT NITE	3628	1046	5.9	28.8	128	1568	6.2	43.2	135	464	6.3	12.8	137
NICKELODEON	5936	1423	8.0	24.0	107	2255	8.9	38.0	119	681	9.2	11.5	123
USA NETWORK	8059	2075	11.6	25.7	114	3056	12.1	37.9	119	878	11.9	10.9	117
VH-1 (VIDEO HITS ONE)	2138	572	3.2	26.8	119	866	3.4	40.5	127	*279	3.8	13.0	140
THE WEATHER CHANNEL	9846	2419	13.6	24.6	109	3686	14.5	37.4	117	992	13.4	10.1	108
WTBS	13102	3011	16.9	23.0	102	4848	19.1	37.0	116	1075	14.6	8.2	88

SOURCE: © Mediamark Research Inc. *Pet & Baby Products Report, Spring 1988.* All rights reserved.

light television watchers. And they like classical music and news programs.

This provides the general scenario. Next the advertiser goes comparison shopping. By matching the reader and listener profiles of the local media to the profile of cat owners, the store owner can determine where to place the ads. Suppose the classical radio station reports that 65 percent of its audience match the profile, while the regional magazine shows a 55 percent match. The monthly magazine ads cost $1,000 for a full page, while the radio station will give you five spots a day for $500 a week. Compare your costs with the number of potential customers in each audience, and the choice is made.

Media + Purchase = Ad Tracking

As competition among media increases, so will the quality of their information, especially if it is the advertisers who begin demanding more specific data. One solution is ad tracking.

An ad tracking system works like this: At home in the participating households, a device registers all programs and advertisements seen and who sees them. Their purchases are tracked either with portable scanners that the Nielsen participants use to record the UPC codes of all the products they buy, or with special codes or I.D. cards recorded at the checkouts of participating grocery stores (IRI uses these).

Such services are offering something new—a way to quantify people's subjective responses to images and messages. Ad tracking services have developed numerous ways for manufacturers and retailers to put scanner data to work.

Participating grocery chains, for example, can get valuable information on how each store is performing by comparing product movement, costs, sales, and profits in different markets. Consumer goods manufacturers have an immediate way to measure the effect of promotions or advertisements on sales. They can compare the number of people who bought due to coupons with those who responded to in-store displays or other appeals. When a brand is losing buyers, scanning services can analyze whether the problem is due to distribution changes, advertising, promotions, or pricing. In short, the potential of these services is just starting to be realized.

But scanners also have some limitations. At least for now, their use is restricted to sales of certain goods. Businesses that sell financial planning, education, or some other kind of consumer service don't have scanners at their cash registers, because no machine can attach scanner codes to stocks, investments, or consulting services, and measure sales volumes and ad effectiveness. But who knows? The technological equivalent to scanners that can offer similar measurement accuracy to services could appear sometime in this decade.

Future Shock

Advances in response measurement techniques already raise the analysis of the electronic media to new levels. Some companies are finding out how to fine tune audience reaction to ads and programs by measuring, in a controlled experiment, their moment-by-moment individual responses. Some techniques use hand-held dials with ten gradations. As a taped program or presentation progresses, selected viewers rate how positive or negative they feel by turning the dial one way or the other. Other measurement systems use portable buttons, positive in the right hand and negative in the left hand.

With these methods, ad people learn from a sample of viewers exactly when they lose the viewer and exactly what words or images cause the problem. If the majority don't like the look of the actor, or if a word has too many syllables, they find a more effective alternative. For marketing uses, this is just a refinement of the idea that the customer is always right.

As the science of response measurement gains sophistication, TV advertising can become ever more effective. More effective ads bode well for the large buyer of advertising, providing these improvements are accompanied by better methods of measuring that effectiveness. But television ads don't work for all products. For some advertisers, the major problem will be finding the right vehicle to reach the most customers. That involves weighing the value of one vehicle over the others in terms of costs, and will always require media preference data.

Trends in the Media

Some media are better positioned than others to take advantage of the shift from national to regional and local advertising. As producers of goods and services learn more about precisely defined regional and local markets, the media will be called upon to deliver these markets effectively. Four media stand to gain the most from the push toward micromarketing:

Radio Wins in Local Markets

Ad revenues and employment in the radio industry climbed in the 1980s and should continue to remain strong in the 1990s. Why? Radio delivers an attractive local market consistently. Radio audiences are more upscale, and a higher proportion of them are young people, working women, professionals, and executives than are found in TV audiences. And radio formats make the segment that buys American beer and listens to country music easy to distinguish from the white-wine segment listening to classical music. Different types of consumers tune in to specific formats and programs, which makes them easy to locate. In addition, people tend to listen to the radio regularly at certain times of the day, such as in the early morning on the way to work.

An audience in transit is a captive audience. And radio reportedly is the reigning medium during lunch hour.

Newspapers in Decline

Although newspaper readership has declined, demographic trends hold better news for the future. Readership dropped from about 98 percent of American households in 1970 to less than 70 percent in the mid-1980s. Demographics were to blame. The people who have a higher propensity to read newspapers are in the 45-to-64-year-old age groups. These were not growth groups in the last 20 years. The age group that was growing the fastest, 18-to-34-year-olds, reads fewer newspapers. But the 45-to-54-year-old group will be *the* growth group of the 1990s. The future of newspapers could be good, considering they are uniquely positioned to reach large proportions of entire market areas every day. In addition, newspapers can specifically target ad sections to smaller regional areas. However, the challenges are substantial. Newspapers have to develop better plans for fostering the newspaper reading habit in young children, especially minority children, to combat the influence of television and to keep readership levels high as the population diversifies.

Cable TV Targets Audiences

Cable ad revenues have grown as local firms recognized them as a lower cost alternative to the network affiliate stations. Like radio, ads on cable can be placed by format to reach more targeted audiences. For example, an ad for a chiropractic client can run on the Lifetime network during a show about back pain and can get a direct line to the customers who already have an interest in the topic. Or a diaper service could run its ad on the Family Channel during a show about parenting.

Cable reaches audiences that are very attractive from a marketing standpoint. Cable subscribers tend to be more upscale than audiences for free television, simply because they have to pay for the service. And in general, the subscribers with the most pay channels are the ones who have the highest incomes. What's more, cable companies know where their customers live, and often can provide advertisers with breakdowns of penetration by neighborhoods. Advertisers could use these penetration figures to follow up ads with direct-mail promotions or coupons to increase the number of customers coming from underrepresented local areas.

Direct Marketing Still Growing

Direct mail was an exploding field in the 1980s and will continue to be a cost-effective way to sell goods and services. Barring prohibitive postal rate increases, more firms will be marketing through the mails. The beauty of this medium is that ads, promotions, and other appeals are sent directly to people, and most people open their mail. The key to better use of direct mail lies in making sure the people it reaches are those who buy the products or services pitched. Junk mail is only junk if the person who opens it has no use for the product or service—coupons for baby diapers going to a 75-year-old, for example. With direct mail, the most crucial point is choosing to whom to send the message. Another advantage of this medium is that measuring effectiveness, or response rates, is easy. With coupons, a simple code can identify where the new customers are coming from. As companies develop customer databases, direct mail ads and promotions will be more widely used.

Now that you have a basic understanding of the four types of consumer information, you need to see how they work together to solve marketing problems. The best use by far for the four types of consumer information—demographics, psychographics, purchase behavior, and media preferences—is to maximize the effectiveness of your marketing. Better marketing uses consumer information to focus on potential customers, communicate with them, and persuade them to buy. The following chapters take a problem-oriented approach to using consumer information.

CHAPTER EIGHT

Marketing Smarter: Putting It All Together

ALL BUSINESSES today are essentially in the information business. Now, more than ever before, knowledge is power and customers are the key to that power. Smart use of consumer information narrows the gap between producers of goods and services and their customers.

The shoemaker in preindustrial society made shoes to the exact specifications of individual customers. He knew the needs of his customers because they were his neighbors. Their families were similar, they lived close together, and they had similar needs and wants. Marketing and planning were very efficient back then because business owners could make effective first-hand decisions about what customers would buy. The business owner could adjust when the time was right because he and his customers experienced disasters and prosperity simultaneously.

These days a shoe company has to make hundreds of styles of shoes in the fashion of the moment. But the importance of the customer has never changed. Providing what buyers want is just as crucial today as it was in preindustrial society. Only today it's much harder for corporate decision makers to hear what their customers are saying.

As competition both at home and from abroad intensifies, successful firms are rethinking their corporate information channels. Customers' needs have to be positioned at the top of the corporate hierarchy, and the lines of communication have to be clearly defined to give decision makers on-going knowledge of their customers. To keep ahead of the market and make effective decisions, managers have to learn to take their orders more directly from customers. And to understand what the customers are saying, managers need interpreters.

Closing the Information Gap

Marketing developed to fill that interpreter role, to bridge the modern information gap between managers and customers. Marketers provide intelligence about the attributes and behavior of customers that comes right from the source. They get the customer and the decision maker back together and give the modern business the next best thing to the shoemaker's knowledge of his customers' needs.

As noted in previous chapters, business success is not a function of the quantity of information gathered or the size of the marketing budget. Success is determined by the efficiency of the business's decision-making system. Does the decision-making network provide the right information to solve the problems, and does that information get to the right people? This decision-making network starts at the information gathering or research level and continues up to the top decision makers in the corporate hierarchy.

Market misjudgments happen when some key part of the information-gathering network is missing or fails to function. This network can break down at any point from the research level to the executive level. If the researcher fails to get the right information, the decision-making process is compromised. But even executives who are presented with the correct view of the market may make the wrong decisions.

Because there are so many potential points at which the network can break down and essential information can get lost or overlooked, it is imperative that the corporate purpose is clear to every link in the decision-making chain. Better business decisions are possible only if every link in the decision-making chain understands what consumer information is and what problems it can solve.

What's the Problem?

To function properly, the decision-making network requires a solid corporate commitment to information-based decision making. This means that company leaders must make it clear to each member of the decision-making network what the company wants to accomplish. The next step in this information-based approach involves identifying the problems that prevent the company from reaching its goals.

Successful business management at its simplest is the ability to solve problems before they become problems, and to identify opportunities. At each stage of business development, new problems develop and new opportunities will emerge.

In future chapters we will discuss four major problem areas of executive decision making: market analysis, product or service analysis, advertising and promotion, and strategic planning. In most cases, businesses do each of these analyses on a need basis. But as we will see, each area should not be viewed in isolation. The information that can solve one kind of problem is often applicable to other areas.

For the purposes of this discussion, it will be best to view each problem area as a series of questions. Problems of all types are easier to face if they are reduced to basic components—questions that must be answered to reach goals.

This view of problems makes finding solutions easier. It is a short step from knowing the questions to choosing the consumer information tool that will provide the answers to each question. The long and the short of it is that: problems are simply questions without answers. Demographics, psychographics, purchase behavior, and media preference information provide the answers.

The crucial factor to grasp here is the way that your consumer information system will become an ongoing resource whose value is enhanced as information is added. To get an idea about how this information-based decision-making system can work, let's look at the goals of one hypothetical company. This company has a successful string of gourmet pizza delivery franchises in one market and is considering entering another market. The goal is to expand into the best possible market. To do this, the company would do a market analysis that answers questions about the size and potential of each location being considered.

After selecting and entering a new market, this company might set the goal of maximizing the product's appeal to the most potential customers. For this they will do a product analysis to identify these potential customers and what they like or don't like about the product.

With a media analysis, the company can determine if a change of advertising image or media would attract additional customers. Then, once the market penetration goal is reached, the company needs to commit to an ongoing strategic planning program to meet long-term goals. Let's say the company has set long-term goals of expanding into a new market every few years. Avoiding overextension requires careful strategic planning to identify how the product's sales and customer base are changing over time.

Each problem area is a new challenge for the decision-making system. But the most effective decision is only a few steps away. Set up the problem as an organized series of questions and then choose the consumer information tools that will best answer the questions. Once the information is in place, you can explore your options. If, for example, maximum penetration of one market depends on overcoming consumer resistance to gourmet pizza, figure in the cost of offering a less expensive regular pizza in that market versus changing the image of your pizza.

Market analysis is the assessment of market potential in each geographic area, the allocation of sales territories by market potential, and the choosing of sites for sales outlets or distribution points. The questions you need to ask are:

- *What groups are present in the market?*
- *What is the size of the potential market?*
- *How much of that potential can I capture?*
- *Who are my customers?*
- *Where do my customers come from?*
- *Who are the competition's customers?*
- *What is keeping me from attracting more customers?*
- *How can I choose one location or unit of geography over another?*

Product or **service analysis** calculates a product's potential as well as the manufacturer's market share, and determines the characteristics of the people who buy the product or service (the prime market segments) and the dollar amount of the product or service purchased by each market segment. You need to find out:

- *Who are the primary and secondary customers?*
- *How much and how often do they buy?*
- *What are their needs for the product/service?*
- *What are the characteristics of the product/service?*
- *How does the product/service meet the needs of each group?*
- *How are my customers changing?*
- *How are their needs for the product or service changing?*
- *Can I alter the product/service to better meet their needs?*

Advertising and promotional analysis helps in selecting the most cost-effective media (TV, radio, print, direct mail) and developing a message that will get the consumer's attention and sell the goods. The questions that must be addressed here include:

- *What media can best reach my customers?*
- *Will a combination of media optimize sales?*
- *What formats and programs reach my customers?*
- *What messages will induce them to buy?*
- *What ads or promotions get results?*

Strategic planning is done to track the growth or decline of existing markets and to discover what new or existing products or services will be successful in those markets. It identifies emerging markets and the products and services they will demand. Here you need to know:

- *How are my customers changing?*
- *How are all segments of the market changing?*
- *What are the fastest growing markets/customer groups?*
- *Are there products/services they will want that I can deliver?*
- *What sales growth can I expect from my existing markets?*
- *Judging from trends, in which departments or new lines of business should I increase my investments?*

Figure 8a: PUTTING CONSUMER INFORMATION TO WORK

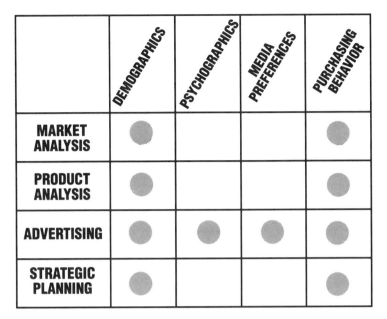

	DEMOGRAPHICS	PSYCHOGRAPHICS	MEDIA PREFERENCES	PURCHASING BEHAVIOR
MARKET ANALYSIS	●			●
PRODUCT ANALYSIS	●			●
ADVERTISING	●	●	●	●
STRATEGIC PLANNING	●			●

SOURCE: *The Insider's Guide to Demographic Know-How,* © 1990, American Demographics Press.

Consumer information is the key to solving each business puzzle, and combinations of the different types of information are used to solve various problems.

In doing a market analysis, for example, psychographics or media preference information won't be of much use. You will need demographics and purchase behavior data, because you will be concerned primarily with determining size and potential. You'll need to know about customers in the market and what they buy.

Product or service analysis requires the same information but uses it in a different way. In this analysis, you will be concerned with identifying the best consumer groups for a specific product. Demographics and purchase behavior remain the most useful tools, but your focus will narrow to a certain product market. In sophisticated product analysis, psychographics may be useful to help identify the features of the product that appeal to customers in certain psychographic groups.

All four types of information are useful when it comes to maximizing advertising and promotion effectiveness. This is perhaps the most difficult problem to solve correctly, because there are so many subjective variables that go into determining why one message works, and another bombs.

With strategic planning, understanding demographic trends is most important. The combination of demographic trend information and current purchasing patterns allows a planner to forecast demand for existing products or services and to discover emerging markets.

Nothing Out of Place

Using consumer information to make better business decisions is like building a radio. All of the transmitters and wires have to be in the right places, hooked up correctly, or it won't work. If a piece is missing, nothing happens when you turn it on. If you're missing a key piece of demographic knowledge and you're trying to find out what market potential is, the answer will be incomplete. Pieces are interdependent: the information that provides the answer to one problem will give you a more complete understanding of the next problem that arises. You can't really do good strategic planning without some basic market analysis. But a carefully built system is like a communication device that helps businesses reach their customers.

What happens when this system breaks down? Some companies have lost money because they neglected core markets in favor of smaller fringe markets or ignored shifts in consumer demands. Others have failed to recognize a peaking market in time to get out, or have lost competitive ground because they misdirected new products.

Most market misjudgments originate with poorly informed decision making. At their worst, these mistakes can lead to bankruptcy or force a company to play permanent catch-up with the competition. At the very least, market misjudgments compromise otherwise promising careers.

Opportunity Lost

Opportunity is a fleeting possibility, a window that is opened and quickly closed. Making the most of an opportunity takes two abilities: first recognizing the opportunity and then acting on it. This is the real value of consumer information—it gives decision makers the ability to recognize opportunity and act on it to capture more customers before it's too late.

A company that fails to reach its potential in any market is suffering from opportunity loss. If the right actions are taken, the company could increase its sales. If no action is taken, the status quo remains. The company is really not much worse off if it misses one opportunity, or is it?

How long can a company that rests on past successes and doesn't respond to market shifts remain competitive? Only as long as it takes for customers to become dissatisfied.

Armed with the right consumer intelligence, corporate decision makers can seize opportunity. What's even more important, the consumer information system provides a method of measuring the size and quality of the window of opportunity.

By calling on the simple tools of demographics and purchase behavior, a company presented with the chance of entering the rap music business, for example, could determine the size of the potential market for rap music and see how much of that potential it is positioned to capture.

The power lies in the potential. Let's say that you sell compact disk players and stereos. Most of your customers will be college-educated people who earn more than $25,000 a year. The census or a private vendor can provide an estimate of the number of households that fit that profile in each of your sales territories. A report from an information supplier can tell you the average amount that households in that category spend on compact disk products each year. Multiply the number of households in your territories by the average amount spent, and you have a rough estimate of the sales potential for that market.

Let's suppose doing this in a three-mile-wide trade area shows you that there is a possibility of $2 million in sales, and you already know there is only one other similar store. You decide there is enough potential to build a store.

There is more you can do by examining the potential. Suppose you build the store, and after the first year you feel that your sales could be better. You look at the competition and they seem to be doing much more business than you are. Your sales are less than $500,000, but you know a potential of at least $1 million exists. The next question you ask is, "What is wrong with my marketing plan?"

Measuring Performance

The beauty of a data-based marketing system is that it can work to maximize marketing efficiency at the local level just as effectively as it can at the national level. For retailers, performance measurement starts with a comparison of the market potential of a store with its actual sales. The size of the gap between those two figures is an accurate measurement of marketing performance.

If performance is consistently below expectations, it may be time to do a more detailed geographic market analysis to determine where customers are and aren't coming from. Sales performance can be improved by identifying which localities produce the most actual customers and targeting ads and promotions to underrepresented areas. New customers from those areas can be identified and if their entrance brings increased sales, the targeting efforts will have paid off.

In the beginning chapters, you learned about the elements in a consumer information system and about the major demographic trends affecting the nation. In chapters three through seven, the focus was on managing consumer information and the four basic types of consumer information needed to capture customers.

The next four chapters outline a systematic method of gathering information and applying it creatively to solve market analysis, product and service analysis, advertising and promotion analysis, and strategic planning problems. These chapters can be used alone, but they become more powerful when used together, as part of an information-based decision-making system. We believe that creative, information-based decisions are at the root of each business success.

CHAPTER NINE

Market Analysis

ONE TRAIT that most competitive U.S. business managers share is a thorough awareness of what is going on in their markets. With the most successful companies, this desire to know borders on obsession. But it's a reasonable obsession: the fastest way to fall behind is to fall out of step with the marketplace.

In the relatively stable business environment of the past, it was probably enough if a company did a market analysis once when entering a market and left it at that. Today, with consumer diversity increasing and demand shifting, a vigilant store manager does frequent market analysis in quickly growing markets and a similar analysis once every two years in more stable markets. The reason for erring on the side of over-analysis is simple. When markets are changing quickly, every day a company misses its market, it loses sales. Only with up-to-date information that provides a thorough understanding of the marketplace can a business operate optimally over time.

Market analysis means using consumer information to estimate the size and character of a market. This is done to determine how much business is coming from a market now and to estimate the behavior of that market in the future.

A market can be anything from a small trading area around one store to an entire country. It can also represent a geographically unrestricted group of customers who buy a particular product. For the purposes of this discussion we will define "market" in geographical terms. A market is a piece of geography determined by present or future business activity.

Market analysis consists of analyzing a single new or existing site, while market potential or territory analysis involves multiple sites. Each type of analysis reveals:

- **Who are my potential customers?**
- **What groups are present in the market?**
- **What is the size/growth of the potential market?**
- **How much of that potential can I capture?**
- **Where do my customers come from?**
- **Who are the competition's customers?**
- **Am I operating up to my potential?**

A market analysis should be done when entering a new market or when sales problems develop at an existing location. When the market to be analyzed is a series of distribution points or a number of different markets, the analysis determines how well each market or territory is performing in terms of its potential. The nature of your problem will dictate the kind of analysis you need.

Data for the analysis are manipulated according to the technique you employ. Basically, though, the power of the data in market analysis comes through making comparisons. One market area may be compared with another, a core trading area compared with a larger market area, or actual sales compared with market potential.

Trading Area Analysis

A trading area is defined as the area from which a store draws the majority (60 to 80 percent, depending on the industry) of its business. It can be a one- or 20-mile radius depending on the store. A potential trading area is an area from which you can reasonably expect to draw customers.

There are three basic types of trading area analyses: 1) new-site analysis, done when starting a new business or upon entering a new market, 2) site selection, done when a business must choose one new location over all the other potential sites, and 3) existing site analysis, done when an established business has declining sales or when one store consistently performs below the company's other stores.

Purpose: Determine if the proposed area will be favorable for your business.

Tools: Demographic and purchase behavior data.

Concept: Potential sales in a given trading area can be estimated by looking at the size of relevant demographic segments, applying purchase rates to each segment, and summing the results.

Formula: Number of households **x** household expenditures = potential sales.

By looking at the Consumer Expenditure Survey of the Bureau of Labor

106

Statistics, we can find out that the average U.S. household spends $50 a week on food eaten at home. If we know there are 6,000 households in the trading area it is a simple task to multiply the two numbers together to get the basic potential of the area. In this case there would be a potential $300,000 per week in food-store sales.

This estimate would be accurate only if the trading area is exactly like the national average, which is unlikely. More probably, your trading area differs in some key respects from the national average and your sales potential will be either higher or lower than the norm. Demographics will start the process of distinguishing your trading area from the national averages.

The accuracy of your estimate will improve with each additional demographic variable. On a most obvious level, the presence of large numbers of two-earner families with many children will increase food-store sales more than the presence of many single, retired people living on a fixed income. Even by adding one variable—age—we can refine our estimate of sales potential.

Age of Head	Number of Households	Weekly Spending	Total Spending/ Food at Home
under 25	2,280	$25	$57,000
25 - 34	1,400	47	65,800
35 - 44	1,150	60	69,000
45 - 54	380	65	24,700
55 - 64	250	52	13,000
65 and older	540	38	20,500
TOTALS	6,000	$50	$250,000

By including an age variable in our calculation, we learn that the sales potential of this area is $50,000 below the national average because of the inordinately large proportion of people under age 25. Households headed by under-25-year-olds spend less than the national average on food at home.

By adding more demographic variables to our estimate, we can improve its accuracy. For example, suppose husband-wife families with children aged 6 to 17 spend $72 a week, and households with annual incomes over $50,000 spend $74 a week. The census or a private data vendor can estimate the number of households with those two demographic characteristics in each of your markets. By multiplying the number of those households in the trading area by the amount they spend and figuring it into the total market calculation, the estimate can be tailored to the realities of the area.

Method: Demographic variables will be more or less relevant for different types of businesses. Age, income, education, sex, marital status, and household types play diverse roles in consumption of goods and services.

The first task in any market analysis is to determine what demographic variables are most important to your business. To do this you must answer the question:

Who are my customers?

1. Develop a customer profile. To identify the important demographic characteristics of your market, you have to develop a profile of your current customers. A number of methods can be used. Start by tapping all existing in-house customer records. Do these records give clues as to age, income, sex, etc.?

If internal records are lacking, consider surveying customers as they make purchases or leave the store. Try to identify what demographic characteristics your customers share. Are they mostly women aged 35 to 44 with children at home? Identifying the crucial demographic traits of your customers is a prerequisite to all the analysis techniques that follow.

Another, less specific method of getting a basic customer profile is to go to the Consumer Expenditure Report or one of the syndicated purchase behavior surveys. These sources will give you the age group, sex, income, and household type of the people who buy the most of your product.

Once you know your customers' demographics, the next task is to find out what the demographic characteristics are of the trade area. To do this you answer the question:

What groups are present in the market?

2. Identify the major segments present. The goal here is to get a demographic profile of the residents and to identify outstanding characteristics of your trading area. What makes it different than other areas such as the county or state where your company does business? Look for factors that set this area apart from the average American neighborhood or the surrounding area. Are there a higher proportion of college students or new immigrants living there? Are there a higher-than-usual number of people living in mobile homes? Is there a prison or large institution in the market? These and other factors may limit this market's potential by reducing the consumption of certain items.

Look at household growth, average household size, marital status, and educational levels of the population. These factors will tell you a lot about what consumers in this market buy. If households are growing faster than the population, you can expect higher demand for certain items like appliances. If household size is decreasing, consumers may demand smaller portions and more convenience products. Consumption patterns differ greatly depending on marital status and education as well.

One easy way to gather the necessary demographic data about a trading area is to order reports or maps over the phone from one of the data firms. These products range in price from $50 to $200.

To get the right information from the data firm, the researcher must have two factors clearly in mind: the size and shape of the area, and the most important demographic variables to examine for each area. A complete demographic trend report should include the following demographic data:

- Population and household count for 1980, current year and five years from now.
- Income figures for 1980, current year and five years from now.
- Current distribution of households by size.
- Average household size.
- Population count by race and Hispanic origin.
- Age and sex of the population.
- Housing characteristics—occupancy rate and owners vs. renters.
- Group quarters population (the percent of the population living in prison or institutional arrangements)

These are the data necessary to get an overview of the trading area. The answer to this question will be contained in the demographic report:

What is the size/growth of the potential market?

3. Look at the trends. Demographics tell us not only what groups are present in the market and their size but how they are changing. Market size is defined here as the number of consumers in a given market or market segment.

To determine growth, look at what has happened to the overall market and various population segments over time. Is the group you are most interested in growing or declining in number? An examination of population figures ten years ago compared with today and five years from now will tell you the answer. What is happening to their income? Are these groups getting richer or poorer; i.e., are they more or less able to buy what you sell? Look at the income figures over time and you can get a good idea. Is there a larger proportion of Hispanics, women, younger, or older people?

4. Choose a benchmark. Another important factor to consider in using a demographic report is what benchmark to use for comparison. You need to compare the area under examination with a larger area such as the United States to find out how the market differs from the national average. This helps to identify the characteristics that make the market area special and might offer business opportunities. State, county, city, and metropolitan area numbers are also good benchmarks.

Next it is necessary to look at the demographic realities of the market to answer the next question:

How much of that potential can I capture?

5. Compare the demographic trend report with your customer profile. How many customers in this market fit your customer profile? Examine the numbers for ten years ago, today, and five years from now. Will the segment that represents the majority of your customers grow, decline, or stay the same?

For example, suppose that the biggest customers for your product, jewelry, are concentrated in the 35 to 44 age group, and the report shows that the number of residents aged 35 to 44 in the market will increase by 25 percent in the next five years. In addition, the report shows that income levels are rising among this group.

Growth rates tell you how fast a particular segment is growing, but you also need to consider the actual numeric increase of the group and how this age segment will change relative to other age groups. If the 35 to 44 age group represents a relatively small share of local residents, then its rapid growth may not have much impact on your jewelry business. Perhaps 60 percent of the consumers in this market are elderly, and they are growing by just 5 percent. Even though the growth of the elderly is slower, they will represent a bigger share of the total market than 35-to-44-year-olds.

6. Examine consumption trends. This market may be a positive one for you, but next you need to look at the consumption trends. Examine the rate at which the people in this market consume your product. A retail potential report can provide this information.

Purchase behavior information is necessary to determine the monetary value of the market and its present and future potential. As outlined in chapter six, there are many sources of this information, but for simplicity's sake we will use a sales potential report ordered from a demographic data firm. The information in this one comes from the Consumer Expenditure Survey.

This particular report includes eight different categories, but data from different firms can differ greatly in form and content. The data companies have the most detailed consumption data on the grocery industry, convenience stores, drug stores, and restaurants because extensive databases on these industries already exist. The firms have simply purchased the right to repackage the data from those databases for their own use. For an industry like retail jewelry, the best small-area data will probably include only total spending on jewelry in the area, a per capita figure, and an index comparing the local spending with the national average.

ANNUAL SALES POTENTIAL, 1989

	Aggregate (000)	Per Capita	Market Index
Variety Stores	$7,491	$52.85	138
Grocery Stores	191,099	1,348.31	631
Apparel Stores	51,343	362.25	139
Shoe Stores	8,248	58.19	125
Jewerly Stores	10,790	76.13	163
Restaurants	109,807	774.75	159
Drug Stores	38,032	268.33	133
Liquor Stores	26,288	185.48	138

SOURCE: Urban Decision Systems

For small areas, the only data that exist on consumption levels deal with the total population. In most of the smaller geographical areas such as block groups the data on consumption by age group do not exist. Better data are available on entire metros, counties, and states. But general figures like the ones above will give you an idea about how consumption levels for major retail categories in this area compare with the national average. For example, residents of the above trade area buy 63 percent more jewelry than average, and they spend about $76 a year each, adding up to total spending on jewelry of nearly $11 million.

Both population and consumption trends on the surface look positive for our trade area. Here's where a more in-depth analysis is needed to answer the question:

Who are the competition's customers?

7. Size up the competition. It is essential in any trade analysis to consider the existing competition. Even if both demographic and consumption trends in the market are positive indicators for your business, the market may be a poor risk if there are already too many competitors. A complete trade area analysis will require competitive data, which can often be acquired from the state labor department, the local chamber of commerce, or the municipal or county governments.

To identify how much of the potential can be captured by the proposed store, divide the size of the total market by the number of competitors. In addition, major competitors should be given more weight than smaller, less significant firms.

Data firms can supply some competitive data. For example, Donnelley Marketing Information Services has a BusinessLINE database that lists 7.6 million U.S. businesses including name, city, state, ZIP-associated census geographies, employees, and sales volumes. The Census of Retail Trade from the Census Bureau is also useful.

Most other data firms can provide sales information on various industries. Again the data are often more detailed for businesses such as restaurants and grocery stores, because they already exist. For a fee, data firms can produce a list of competing stores in a given market. The quality of the data can vary widely by supplier and you should know the age of the information before buying it. Especially with competitive data, the only good data are the most timely.

A better, though more labor intensive, way of casing the competition requires a trip through the phone book and some old-fashioned pavement pounding. If the market area isn't too large, the researcher can visit competing stores and note the obvious signs of success such as crammed parking lots and long lines. A visit can also provide insight into how the competition handles customer service and daily operations.

Once a list of competitors is compiled, it is also a good idea to plot their locations on a map to determine where they are relative to the neighborhoods that contain the most favorable customer groups. Some of the data companies offer geographic mapping services that can plot competitors' locations relative to potential sites and customer neighborhoods.

Determine the minimum sales volume necessary for you to invest in this market. A competitive analysis may reveal that the market is already saturated. In this case, you may want to consider an area with less existing competition. But perhaps there are gaps in the competitor's product line, or you believe that a more responsive firm could edge out the competition. The market and competitive trends should be examined as objectively as possible.

8. Weigh the market growth and consumption rate against the competitive environment. The basic variables in considering any market are market growth, consumption rate, and the competitive environment. Weighing each of these factors relative to the others will help determine the viability of any given market. For example, if the market is growing quickly but the consumption rate for your product is low, it may not be prudent to invest unless the competitive environment is very favorable. By the same token, if the market is declining but consumption is growing robustly, the competitive environment will be the major determinant of whether or not an investment in this market will pay off.

A Note on Site Selection

A site selection analysis uses trade-area analysis to screen potential sites for selected criteria. Each site under consideration is ranked according to the variables that determine success, and then the results are compared to identify the site with the most favorable characteristics.

Using trade area analysis for site selection is really a process of risk analysis. The preliminary analysis is used as a means of making first, second, and final cuts on a list of potential sites. The analysis becomes ever more intensive as the list is narrowed to the five or fewer top contenders.

In the days before soaring real estate prices and interest rates, site selection wasn't such a critical function of corporate research divisions. Companies could afford to buy a piece of land and let it remain vacant until they decided what to do with it. That is no longer true. A piece of property had better become profitable quickly or it becomes a drain on company resources.

For this reason, site selection is one of the most advanced consumer information-based research activities, both in terms of technique and technology. Many data providers and research firms have intricate computer models and software products developed especially for site selection. These products can be specially designed for certain types of stores such as the groceries or those located in shopping centers.

Advanced products like these can weight the pros and cons of multiple factors for a multitude of sites all over the country. Many are so specialized that they factor in variables specific to certain industries. One product for the grocery industry is Supermarket Solutions by Market Metrics of Lancaster, Pennsylvania. The site-selection program has the ability to screen sites for physical barriers such as bridges or highway exits that would keep customers from using a store on a potential site. The program can also run different scenarios to determine what store format—super store or regular grocery—has the best chance of succeeding on the site considering the competition. One of Supermarket Solutions' databases lists dozens of physical features and competitive data for 28,000 grocery stores in the U.S.

Even for a company with a vast research department, compiling similar data would take months or years. Because using the research specialist with the best databases can save so much time and labor, it's usually well worth the expense for a research project as critical to success as site selection. An initial investment of several thousand dollars that leads a company to the best site for expansion is far cheaper in the long run than a store that fails.

Existing Site Analysis

Most businesses start operation with a major misconception: they view customers as unpredictable creatures who appear and disappear according to business cycles, price discounts, or mysterious personal whims. That belief, however, may be self-determining. If a company does nothing out of the ordinary to attract customers, why should customers bother to try the store?

Most businesses only look at ways to make a store more attractive to customers when the drop in business has already become severe enough to be a problem. That's like repairing a leak in a dam after nearly all the water has escaped. If this analysis is done on a regular basis, a business can prevent a gap from developing between the store and the customers and avoid even a short period of falling sales.

An existing site trade-area analysis can be done for any sized market area. This technique dissects the market into a series of neighborhoods. The purpose of this analysis is to identify why a store isn't generating more sales, i.e., attracting more customers. To do this we need to answer two questions:

- *Where do my customers come from?*

- *Am I operating up to my potential?*

This discussion will focus on a local retailer, but the analysis works just as well for a large company selling nationally. A manufacturer trying to increase sales of its product in certain areas may benefit from analyzing sales on a neighborhood-by-neighborhood basis. What boosts sales in one neighborhood may work in similar neighborhoods all across the country. A national manufacturer would do this analysis in several small-market test areas throughout the nation.

Purpose:	Identify if a store or outlet is performing up to its potential.
Tools:	Demographic and purchase behavior data.
Concept:	Measure the performance of a trade area by identifying where the customers are and aren't coming from. The trade area is divided into neighborhoods, customers are traced to neighborhoods of residence, and so under-performing areas are identified.
Method:	Market share usually means share of the current market—the portion of total product sales represented by company sales. But for measuring performance, we need to determine the size of the potential in each sub-group and the company's current share of each subgroup in the market.

1. Define the trade area. For the purposes of this discussion, we will define the trading area as a 1.5-mile radius around a particular store. This one happens to be a bank, which has been suffering falling deposits for 12 straight months. The enterprise under analysis could just as easily sell clothing, furniture, groceries, or any other product or service. The principle would be the same.

The primary goal of this analysis is to gather enough information about your customers to answer the question:

Where do my customers come from?

2. Get customers' names and addresses. A bank knows exactly where its customers live, but businesses that don't have such detailed address information also can get it. Names and addresses of customers can be accumulated from sales receipts. Surveys, contests, and promotior.s are other effective ways to attach an address to a customer. Most customers will provide an address if they might receive something for nothing. Getting the addresses of a few thousand customers may be well worth the purchase price of a video camera or a VCR. Free giveaways may yield results where other methods fail.

You could also get an idea of what neighborhoods attract the most customers by doing a vehicle origin survey. R. L. Polk & Co. of Detroit, Michigan, specializes in vehicle origin surveys and customer lists. The company records the license plate numbers of cars in parking lots over a certain period, then codes them by census tract or block group. Privacy laws prohibit them from providing specific addresses, but they can tell you in which general neighborhoods the cars originated.

3. Plot the addresses on a map. Once you have a list of addresses, the next step is to plot the addresses on a map of the area. This could be accomplished the old-fashioned way with push pins, or, more effectively, the data could be entered into a computer. Many of the data firms will do graphic analysis by plotting your customer list on a computer map that can also include other information such as competitors' locations and physical characteristics of the area. But there is also inexpensive and easy-to-use mapping software available for desktop computers.

Plotting the customer origins on a map of the trading area will help you determine which neighborhoods provide you with customers. By comparing the portion of customers each neighborhood provides with the portion of the trade-area total population represented by the neighborhood, you get an idea about what areas are underrepresented.

Look at the map of the trading area of the First National Bank of Anytown, USA. There are five distinct neighborhoods in the bank's immediate trading

Figure 9a: POTENTIAL *VS.* ACTUAL STORE TRADING AREA

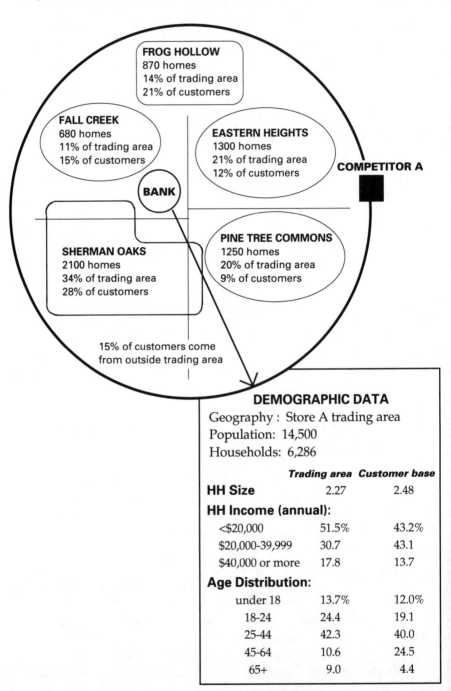

FROG HOLLOW
870 homes
14% of trading area
21% of customers

FALL CREEK
680 homes
11% of trading area
15% of customers

EASTERN HEIGHTS
1300 homes
21% of trading area
12% of customers

COMPETITOR A

BANK

SHERMAN OAKS
2100 homes
34% of trading area
28% of customers

PINE TREE COMMONS
1250 homes
20% of trading area
9% of customers

15% of customers come
from outside trading area

DEMOGRAPHIC DATA

Geography : Store A trading area
Population: 14,500
Households: 6,286

	Trading area	Customer base
HH Size	2.27	2.48
HH Income (annual):		
<$20,000	51.5%	43.2%
$20,000-39,999	30.7	43.1
$40,000 or more	17.8	13.7
Age Distribution:		
under 18	13.7%	12.0%
18-24	24.4	19.1
25-44	42.3	40.0
45-64	10.6	24.5
65+	9.0	4.4

SOURCE: © 1988, American Demographics, Inc.

area containing an estimated 6,200 households. The address records and a simple customer origin survey have revealed that the Frog Hollow and the Fall Creek neighborhoods are the only ones performing beyond their potential.

4. Determine the demographic differences of each neighborhood. The next step will use demographics and lifestyle characteristics to determine why these two areas produce so many customers.

Each bank, store, or service business has a character, which consists of many factors. The image a store presents, its employees, its style of customer service, and its line of products all go into forming the character of the store. This character determines what type of customer is most likely to use the business.

Look at the areas where you are most successful to determine what you do best. In the case of our bank, we look at who lives in Frog Hollow and Fall Creek. Both of these neighborhoods have a higher than usual proportion of residents in the 45 to 64 age groups with incomes of $20,000 to $39,999. Look at the demographic data attached to the map. They show us that our customer base is more likely to have these two characteristics than are the rest of the people in the trading area.

Our bank was one of the first in the area and has always prided itself on its conservative image. As we've seen by comparing the characteristics of our customers with those of the whole trading area, our customers tend to be older with higher incomes. These are the people to whom the conservative image is most appealing.

Now let's look at where we are doing poorly to find out who our customers aren't. Examine the characteristics of the underrepresented neighborhoods. Pine Tree Commons and Eastern Heights both have more households than the ones in which we are doing well. Let's say Pine Tree Commons has a younger, blue-collar makeup and Eastern Commons is composed mainly of young professionals who are making $40,000 or more. For different reasons, our bank is failing to appeal to each of these groups.

Sherman Oaks is not doing as poorly, but it could do better. Because it has the most households of any neighborhood, it holds a lot of potential. In analyzing this neighborhood, we find out that many of the residents fit our emerging customer profile, but there are also many younger, middle-income families moving into the neighborhood.

5. Figure in the competition. Next plot the locations of the major competing banks and branches. This will provide the first indication of why some neighborhoods are producing fewer customers than others. When we do this, we find out that our major competitor is situated more conveniently for people in Eastern Heights and Pine Tree Commons, especially for those who go to work by driving east.

Learning the reason for the competition's edge in certain areas may be a matter of common sense, depending upon the business. Consumers make many of their patronage choices based on convenience—how close the store or branch is to where they live or work. By examining the neighborhoods in the trading area in terms of where the competition is, we can see that the weakest neighborhoods are the ones nearest the competition.

People will rarely travel out of their way to shop at one grocery store when there's another close at hand, unless the other store has a special format or something else that is worth traveling for. Banks are in a similar situation. If all banks have comparable reputations for security and offer relatively competitive interest rates, most people will choose a convenient bank.

Another method of analyzing the competition is to study what competitors are doing differently in product offerings and customer service. Perhaps in addition to being more conveniently located, our major competitor is also offering what the customers who live in Eastern Heights and Pine Tree Commons want most—investment services that promise high returns and easy, cheap credit.

Our bank, on the other hand, is a safe, predictable place for pre-retirees and older residents to keep their savings. The interest rates we offer are only very good on long-term securities, but our customers don't seem to mind. They like the idea that our bank has been around since before they were born.

Our bank now has to make a crucial decision. Since the reason for undertaking the analysis in the first place was falling deposits, our goal here is finding the most logical and possible way to increase deposits. This requires an objective look at three factors: the character of the bank, the character of the potential target areas, and how much we are willing and able to alter our image or product offerings to win more customers.

Even if our board of trustees was willing to go for a more modern, exciting image, it is not very likely such a firmly established conservative image could be changed easily. It is easier to change the product offering slightly to appeal to one or two target groups.

The next essential problem looks at the bank's performance relative to the potential that exists in the trade area. Look at the areas producing the most customers and the areas producing the fewest and find out whether either situation can be improved to answer the question:

Am I operating up to my potential?

6. Determine which areas hold the most and least potential. The Sherman Oaks neighborhood looks good. Considering the customer profile, we should be doing more business there. Why aren't we? Maybe they don't know about us. Examine what services would best meet the needs of the young families who are moving in. Like most parents, they are concerned about being able to pay for college. Perhaps a certificate of deposit linked to college tuition rates and more financial planning services would draw them in. Perhaps all it will take is some specially designed promotional literature and some new blood in the bank's investment services department.

What becomes clear with an existing market analysis is that sometimes businesses have to adjust their expectations. Given the character of Pine Tree Commons, our bank may never draw any more customers from that neighborhood. Those customers want free checking and easy credit. Our bank can't be all things to all people. We have to realize that ad spending in that area will probably be a waste of money.

Ads on TV, radio, or in newspapers that blanket the whole area also will be a waste of money because they will reach current customers and the people who will probably never be our customers. It would be far more efficient to concentrate on the area where we have the most chance of improving our drawing power—the Sherman Oaks area. By sending discount offers or special brochures to each household in the neighborhood, we could shape a special appeal to the households most likely to try our bank. Ads and promotions targeted specifically to Sherman Oaks will be the most cost-effective.

Market Potential or Territory Analysis

We've examined trade-area analysis for retail purposes. Now let's look at how the analysis works for a manufacturer or a distributor who must depend on a third party to get the goods out to the public.

It is not necessarily true that the most productive market or territory is the one with the most potential. This analysis is designed to answer the questions:

• *Which markets or territories are performing up to their potential?*

• *In which markets or territories will increased effort produce more sales?*

Purpose: Determine whether each market or territory is producing up to its potential.

Tools: Demographic and purchase behavior data

Concept: Territory analysis examines each territory separately and compares them to determine potential sales. The performance in each site is evaluated relative to total performance, and resources are allocated according to potential.

Formula: Actual sales ÷ by potential sales = performance index.

Figure 9b: CHARACTERISTICS OF THE CLASSICAL MUSIC MARKET

Market Potential—*Classical Record or Tape Buyers*

	% of Adults	% of Buyers	Index
All Adults	100.0%	100.0%	100
Education			
College	17.5	32.8	188
Attended college	18.1	25.2	139
Graduated H.S.	38.9	26.3	67
Not H.S. grad	25.5	15.7	62
Age			
18 - 24	15.8	18.4	116
25 - 34	23.9	23.8	100
35 - 44	18.5	26.0	142
45 - 54	13.1	12.5	96
55 - 64	13.0	12.2	93
65+	15.7	7.1	45
Occupation			
Professional	8.1	15.8	195
Admin./Mangr.	7.4	10.4	140
Clerical/Sales	19.2	22.8	119
Craft/Repair	7.8	7.0	91
Other employed	19.5	13.2	68
Not employed	38.0	30.8	81
Income			
$50,000+	20.9	34.2	163
$35,000-$50,000	22.3	25.2	113
$25,000-$35,000	18.7	19.2	103
under $25,000	38.1	21.4	56

SOURCE: © 1988, American Demographics , Inc.

Method: Examine whether certain demographic characteristics predetermine demand for the product and prioritize each demographic characteristic relevant to demand. Evaluate each territory in terms of the presence of each demographic group and create a matrix that represents the proportion of each segment in each territory. Calculate the potential for each territory and compare it with actual sales to get the performance index for each area.

1. Identify demographic determinants of product demand. Every product has a slightly different demographic demand profile. For some products, age will be the primary factor; for others, income or another factor will be most important. Analyze your customers and determine what demographic characteristics they share and which are the most important. For this discussion we will examine a product—classical music—for which education is the key determinant of demand. This report was produced for a company that distributes classical records and tapes to record stores throughout the nation. The information comes from Mediamark Research Inc.

2. Rank order the demographic determinants. In the example, we see that four characteristics are important in the classical music market. They are education, age, occupation, and income. The goal here is to rank the demographic characteristics of your customers in order of importance. Primary data from your own customer survey are the best source of ranking criteria; they can tell you the relative significance of each characteristic. Lacking this information, you can use what you know about your customers along with indexes in reports like this one from Mediamark to establish an "eye-ball" ranking.

The Mediamark report shows that about 58 percent of the people who buy classical records or tapes have either attended college or graduated. Because educational attainment is such a crucial factor in the demand for this product and you know that most of your customers are highly educated, you might call it factor number one.

Factor number two might be age since half of the people in the report who buy classical records or tapes are between the ages of 25 and 44 and this is consistent with your customer profile.

3. Use a matrix to evaluate each territory by demographics. Once we have defined the market, we weigh each area where we do business or are considering doing business for each of these variables. For example, look at the percentage of total college graduates in your sales territories who live in territory one and so on. Remember, you can break the markets into any geographic configuration you choose, but for this case let's use metropolitan statistical areas (MSAs).

121

One simple way to proceed is to draw a basic matrix, putting the four demographic factors across the top of the page and the markets being considered down the left side. Start by determining what percentage of all the college graduates in your entire market (all trading areas combined) live in each MSA. Let's suppose that 7 percent of college graduates you can reach live in MSA#1. Now look at the second factor, age. You find that 14 percent of people aged 25 to 44 live in MSA #1. Keep filling out the matrix until the percentages of the total market are listed for each factor in each market (*see below*).

4. Consider whether one of the factors is more important. If you think all factors have equal value, simply add up the percentages for each MSA and divide by four to get the average potential you can expect for each market. If one factor, such as income, is determined to be more important, increase the value by weighting the income numbers. This can be done by doubling the income numbers, adding them along with the rest of the numbers, and dividing the total by five. Such a matrix might look like this:

Figure 9c: MARKET POTENTIAL MATRIX

	Education College	Age 25-44	Occupation Mngr/Prof	Income $35,000+	Average Potential	Actual Sales	Performance Index
MSA #1	7	14	20	20	15.2%	11.5%	76
MSA #2	20	16	18	6	15	18.5	122
MSA #3	31	25	22	21	24.5	29	118
MSA #4	11	27	31	28	24.2	11	45
MSA #5	32	28	29	25	28.5	30	105
Total %	100	100	100	100		100	

SOURCE: © 1990, American Demographics, Inc.

This is just a hypothetical exercise, and the important factors for your own business might be completely different. Demand for your product could be driven by household size, ethnic origin, or even psychographic attributes such as the willingness to take risks. But whatever factors you choose, the important thing is to determine what percentage of your customers come from each segment of your total market.

To answer the main questions of a territory analysis, we have to look at how well each territory is performing. A simple performance index will answer the question:

Which territories are performing up to their potential?

5. Calculate the performance index for each territory. The matrix reveals the average potential of each territory. Now compare the potential with actual sales. We see from the matrix above that MSA #2 contains 15 percent of our potential customers. Therefore, we have every right to expect this market to account for 15 percent of sales. If this isn't the case, we know there is unmet potential in this market. Divide the potential by the actual sales, and we can get a performance index for each market. The index reveals how well each of our markets is performing.

For example, let's say that a higher share (18.5 percent) of our total sales came from MSA #1. Divide the actual sales by the potential sales, and we get 1.22 percent, which translates into a performance index of 122. This means we're selling 22 percent above our potential in MSA #1.

That may be good news for the sales people in MSA #2, but it means that one or more of our other markets is performing below potential. This analysis is useful in helping to adjust the company's expectations and answer the question:

In which territories will increased effort produce more sales?

6. Review expectations for each territory in terms of potential. A territory that produces fewer sales than the others may not be a failure. By the same token, a super performing territory may not be a success. It all depends on the potential that exists in each territory.

Look again at the market potential matrix. Three of the five areas are performing at or above potential, but two areas, MSA #1 and #4, are performing poorly. With this information, we can begin to allocate our resources—sales people, advertising, etc.—differently to correct the deficient territories.

We can see the value of the performance index. If we were only looking at actual sales, we might think that MSA #2, which only accounts for 18.5 percent of sales, was also underperforming. But looking at the potential, we see this territory is actually exceeding its potential, and so we can concentrate our efforts on MSAs #1 and #4, which need the most attention.

Now the question arises: Why are some markets underperforming? The reason can involve all the variables that affect your markets and it may be hard to pinpoint a single culprit. If the underperforming areas are far from distribution points, maybe your product isn't readily available to the best customers. The problem may lie with the type of store or outlet offering your product. Perhaps the store is situated in an inconvenient neighborhood for your frequent buyers. You might consider changing locations or increasing the number of outlets.

A more in-depth look at the markets that are underperforming is necessary to determine the exact nature of the problem. If it isn't a distribution problem, the problem could be the product. To find out why the product is missing its mark with certain groups, continue the investigation with primary research in the form of surveys or focus groups. This will be discussed in more depth in the next chapter on product analysis.

Data Products

An increasing number of American companies are conducting a variety of market analyses. Because the number of databases containing potentially relevant information are so varied and diverse, firms often find it cost effective to hire a data specialist to gather and repackage the data for them in an accessible form.

Market research consultants and firms specializing in data products for target marketing are changing from data specialists to experts in problem solving. They can guide clients through every step of the analysis, and then produce reports and make recommendations based on their findings. As clients' needs for data grow more complex, the marketing information industry is becoming more sophisticated.

The next problem-solving area is product analysis. We will look at techniques for determining how products or services perform in the marketplace and how well they meet the target markets' needs. In chapter 11, we explore advertising and promotion analysis. Each of these is a critical next step in optimizing the efficiency of target marketing.

CHAPTER TEN

Product or Service Analysis

CUSTOMERS are central to product or service analysis, just as they are to market analysis. The focus of this analysis, however, shifts from concern about the geographic locations of customer groups to their behavior and attitudes relative to the product or service. A market analysis uses demographic and purchase behavior to examine the characteristics and business potential of a market. The product and service analysis uses demographics, purchase behavior, and psychographic research to focus more intensely on which customers do or don't buy your product or service.

Thousands of new products will be launched in the U.S. this year, and the vast majority will sink without a trace in the sea of other products. Many of these products will die because they were not targeted to the right customers. Others will fail because customers don't see anything special about them. Pitfalls can develop at any step in the complicated process of bringing a new product to market.

This discussion presumes that the product being analyzed has been correctly conceived. That is, it started with a good idea, which was then analyzed for its marketability. Then it was market tested and finally, to grand fanfare, the product was introduced. Once it was introduced, it was analyzed further, and any remaining bugs in either production, distribution, or consumer acceptance were worked out.

At this point, we begin our product or service analysis. This discussion is not concerned with new product development. It is concerned with the performance of an existing product. The purpose of the analysis is to give businesses a clearer picture of their customers and how the product is performing with those customers. It helps to uncover potential trouble spots before they result in falling sales. A vigilant firm will do such an analysis annually or as frequently as necessary to keep the product on target. The process is applicable to both products and services.

Product and service analysis consists of segment evaluation and product/service performance analysis. It reveals:

- *Who are the primary and secondary customers?*
- *How much and how often do they buy?*
- *What are their needs for the product/service?*
- *What are the characteristics of the product/service?*
- *How does the product/service meet the needs of each group?*
- *How are the customers changing?*
- *How are their needs for the product/service changing?*
- *Can I alter the product/service to better meet their needs?*

Purpose: Identify mismatches between customers' needs and product's/service's attributes or presentation.

Tools: Demographic, purchase behavior, and psychographic data.

Concept: Examine the characteristics and needs of the people who most often buy the product or service. Then analyze how well the product is meeting the needs of each customer segment. In the final phase of the analysis, psychographic research can be used to assess customers' changing needs and identify ways product or service alterations could increase sales.

Method: Product and service analysis has three essential parts. First, the researcher uses demographics and purchase behavior data to identify all users of the product or service, what each customer segment spends on the product, and their needs for the product. The second part focuses on the product: what are its unique characteristics, and how does it meet the needs of each segment? Then using demographic trends and psychographic research, look at how either the customers or their needs are changing and assess how well the product is performing and can be expected to perform in the future.

Who are the primary, secondary, and tertiary customers?

1. Identify all significant customer segments. Most products and services have primary, secondary and perhaps tertiary customers. Some customers buy the product regularly and other customers buy it only occasionally. Companies probably have a good idea who their primary customers are, but may not know much about the others.

The Stouffer Corporation found this out when they introduced their successful line of Lean Cuisine low-calorie frozen dinners. The company's market research determined that a line of low-calorie convenience foods would be especially attractive to young and middle-aged working women. But after the product was introduced the company was surprised to find that a lot of Lean Cuisine was being bought by women older than 55. Without trying, the company had created a low-calorie, low-salt product ideal for the dietary needs of older women. The company has since capitalized on that success by targeting ads at all three age groups.

To categorize various customer groups as primary, secondary, or lesser users of the product, we need to look at the next question:

How much and how often do they buy?

To get the most accurate breakdown of our customers by quantity of product or service consumed, we need purchase data linked to demographics, and the greater the detail the better. As mentioned in previous chapters, there are several sources of this data, ranging from data firms to syndicated surveys. The rule of thumb here is that the most valuable data are the most specific to your product.

Look Inside

The best source for specific product information is actual sales records. In the ideal case scenario, a business could access in-house records to find out exactly who was buying its product, how much each demographic segment was buying, and how often. Unfortunately, the real world is seldom ideal and the sales records of most firms usually are little more than a transaction record. But more and more companies are building databases with sales records or product registration cards.

If in-house sales records are limited, the best way to attach demographics to them is through primary research such as surveys or exit interviews. Some businesses collect basic customer information (name, address, sex) at the point of sale by filling out detailed sales receipts. For example, an alert salesperson could also record approximate age. But what companies really need at this stage is the customers' exact demographics, such as age, marital status, education, income, and whether or not they have children. Few customers, however, would stand there complacently and give away such personal information.

As more companies recognize the importance of knowing their customers, finding out who is doing the buying is becoming a greater concern, and firms are finding innovative ways to attach demographics to their in-house purchase records. Some are getting information from their customers through the following methods:

Exit interviews: Samples of customers are asked what they bought that day, how much they spent, how often they buy, and their demographics.

Check surveys: Questionnaires are sent to the addresses on checks cashed or to check-cashing cardholders to determine usage patterns and demographics.

Credit-card surveys: Companies with their own credit cards are favored. They have access to direct purchase knowledge for at least a portion of their customers. Once the company gets to know its cardholders, it can go on to do in-store surveys and find out about the non-credit-card customers.

Product registration cards: Companies that can include surveys with their products or mailings to customers use this information to profile customers and track retail sales activity. Surveys can include questions about demographics, lifestyles, media and product preferences

Scanner Data

The next best option is scanner data. Large chains equipped with scanners have access to data that tell them immediately how much of a product they carry is sold. The disadvantages of scanner data are that often they are just records, albeit very detailed ones, that purchases have occurred.

The advantages of scanner data are that they are based on actual sales and so they are much more accurate than a syndicated survey based on a customer's recollection of purchases in the last 12 months. And when demographics are available either through customer check-cashing cards or through household panels, scanner data can tell exactly who buys what in a given market.

SCANTRACK, Behaviorscan, and some other scanner-based products can provide detailed customer profiles of heavy, medium, and light users of a given product.

Figure 10a. shows just a small portion of the brand data that scanning services can provide. It compares the demographic makeup of heavy buyers of brands A, B, and C. You can do extensive analyses of the brands that scanner data track. For example, a manufacturer can find out relative market share and how it changes per market and per deal, buying rates, purchase frequency, brand-loyal buyers, which buyers shift brands, how their brand does by outlet or when a new product is introduced, and the performance in each market. Scanner data also show which buyers try a product when it's featured in any deal, coupon, or promotion and the overall source of the brand's business.

Nielsen and IRI already have sophisticated products in place that can give manufacturers and grocery retailers detailed purchase information. Arbitron is developing its ScanAmerica into a national program. In addition, increasing numbers of smaller companies are developing products that use scanner

Figure 10a: SCANTRACK'S DEMOGRAPHIC PROFILES OF BRAND BUYERS

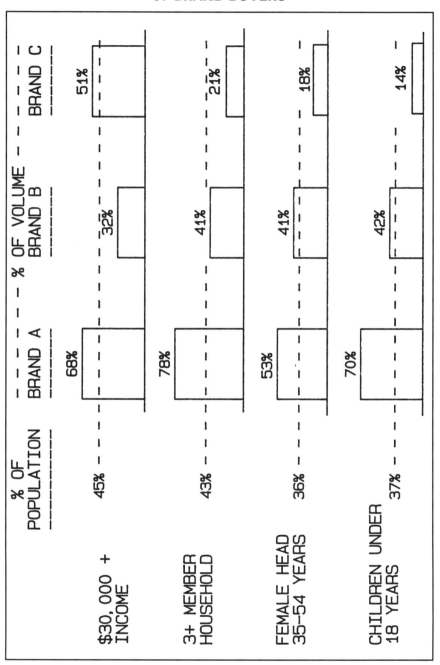

SOURCE: © 1989, *Introduction to Nielsen's Household Panel Analyses*, NPD/Nielsen, Inc.

data to provide detailed brand purchase data. Spectra Advantage, a Chicago-based firm, links Claritas' PRIZM cluster analysis system to the purchase data from IRI's household panel.

The example of Spectra Advantage's brand-use report segments PRIZM's 40 cluster groups into seven subgroups by four demographic traits—whether they live in urban or suburban areas, their economic status (upscale, blue-collar, middle, downscale), their age, and whether or not they have children.

This report has been done to show what quantities of brands A, B, and C are purchased by each of these seven different groups. The report shows the total number of households in each group, the share of total households held by each group, and the percent of sales volume going to each. It includes a consumption index that shows how likely each group is to buy each brand. Other parts of the report tell us whether each group's sales volume changes if the item is discounted, or if it's featured in a newspaper advertisement, an in-store display, or with a coupon.

Because this report is based on the PRIZM clustering system, the researcher could also order another report to locate the neighborhoods all over the country where each consumer group lives. Once one group is shown to buy more of the product, the clustering system can match those demographic characteristics to all neighborhoods in the U.S. and find out where most of those customers are concentrated.

The consumption index on this report tells us that upscale, urban/suburban people aged 55 and older are the best customers for brand A, and upscale suburban people younger than age 54 with children are the secondary customers. Compare the customer segments of all three brands, and you can begin to see which factors influence demand for each brand.

Is That All There Is?

If both scanner and primary data are not available to you, there are other ways to identify primary, secondary, and tertiary customers. The following databases provide profiles of customers for various products on a national basis. One of the major advantages of these national databases is that they give some idea of the product's penetration of the national market. The national data can be used in two ways for product analysis: 1) If you have no other indication of who buys the most of your product, use the national average as a guideline; 2) if you have a specific profile of your customers, use the national data as a benchmark to find out how your customers compare with the national average.

Syndicated Surveys

Syndicated surveys are especially useful in identifying the heavy, me-

Figure 10b: SPECTRA ADVANTAGE'S BRAND-USE REPORT

Retail Consumer Targets Supermarket Sales Total U.S.
TOTAL MANUFACTURER

Consumer Target	Product	HH	% HH	% Vol.	Vol./100 HHs	Cons. Index	Vol. Share	Pene./100 HHs	% Vol. any Deal	% Vol. Feature	% Vol. Display	% Vol. Feature & Display	% Vol. Coupon
UPSC SUB <54 KDS	Brand A	13,264,767	14.5	19.7	12.89	136	27.1	N/A	43.72	15.15	5.11	2.25	17.96
UPSC URB <54 NOKIDS		10,696,489	11.7	14.3	11.61	122	24.5	N/A	36.28	13.44	6.35	4.07	13.57
BLUE COL FAM <54		9,244,933	10.1	7.3	6.83	72	17.1	N/A	33.42	12.12	8.44	3.97	10.60
DNSC RURAL 18–54		13,121,092	14.3	9.1	6.05	64	19.3	N/A	33.55	11.63	6.79	2.15	13.04
MID–DNSC URB <54		13,186,123	14.4	12.7	8.39	88	22.0	N/A	46.28	23.11	11.97	7.59	14.42
UPSC URB/SUB 55+		11,592,566	12.6	20.5	15.39	162	33.9	N/A	44.11	18.36	7.41	4.36	15.71
DNSC URB/RUR 55+		20,614,601	22.5	16.5	6.95	73	24.6	N/A	37.99	14.38	7.42	4.39	13.53
ALL TARGETS COMB	Brand A	91,720,571	100.0	100.0	9.49	100	24.7	N/A	40.44	15.91	7.41	4.09	14.71
UPSC SUB <54 KDS	Brand B	13,264,767	14.5	16.2	2.32	112	4.9	N/A	26.24	10.23	4.08	2.11	5.42
UPSC URB <54 NOKIDS		10,696,489	11.7	9.3	1.65	80	3.5	N/A	33.66	11.67	2.65	1.68	4.71
BLUE COL FAM <54		9,244,933	10.1	8.2	1.68	81	4.2	N/A	23.24	9.80	4.29	2.61	2.65
DNSC RURAL 18–54		13,121,092	14.3	9.4	1.35	65	4.3	N/A	32.00	10.47	1.57	0.99	8.98
MID–DNSC URB <54		13,186,123	14.4	14.5	2.09	101	5.5	N/A	34.19	14.06	6.57	2.14	5.80
UPSC URB/SUB 55+		11,592,566	12.6	17.4	2.84	137	6.3	N/A	25.38	11.42	4.95	2.81	4.99
DNSC URB/RUR 55+		20,614,601	22.5	25.0	2.30	111	8.1	N/A	26.79	11.60	4.13	2.56	5.29
ALL TARGETS COMB	Brand B	91,720,571	100.0	100.0	2.07	100	5.4	N/A	28.37	11.46	4.26	2.24	5.41
UPSC SUB <54 KDS	Brand C	13,264,767	14.5	23.2	4.89	161	10.3	N/A	33.02	9.75	1.87	0.61	16.92
UPSC URB <54 NOKIDS		10,696,489	11.7	13.1	3.41	112	7.2	N/A	33.27	5.12	1.03	0.01	20.58
BLUE COL FAM <54		9,244,933	10.1	9.0	2.71	89	6.8	N/A	32.28	4.07	1.08	0.00	16.15
DNSC RURAL 18–54		13,121,092	14.3	16.6	3.54	116	11.3	N/A	31.10	1.80	1.27	0.39	18.36
MID–DNSC URB <54		13,186,123	14.4	14.7	3.10	102	8.1	N/A	33.48	6.26	0.47	0.19	15.51
UPSC URB/SUB 55+		11,592,566	12.6	11.2	2.71	89	6.0	N/A	29.89	6.53	1.72	0.53	15.37
DNSC URB/RUR 55+		20,614,601	22.5	12.2	1.65	54	5.8	N/A	31.03	4.95	1.20	0.52	17.69
ALL TARGETS COMB	Brand C	91,720,571	100.0	100.0	3.04	100	7.9	N/A	32.14	5.85	1.28	0.36	17.28

SOURCE: © 1989, Spectra Advantage.

131

Figure 10c: LIGHT MEDIUM & HEAVY USERS

Base: Women*		Lipstick and Lip Gloss Usage		
		Heavy Users Index	Medium Users Index	Light Users Index
Age:	18 - 34	67	89	120
	35 - 44	122	99	94
	45 - 54	141	121	76
	55 - 64	136	101	89
	65 or over	94	109	87
Employment:				
	Professional	118	109	81
	Executive, Administrative, Managerial	148	109	65
	Clerical, Sales, Technical	133	104	81
	Precision, Crafts	128	63	79
	Other employed	84	100	110
Household Income:				
	$50,000 or more	134	112	84
	$40,000-$49.9	130	102	77
	$35,000-$39.9	123	98	90
	$25,000-$34.9	95	103	107
	$15,000-$24.9	87	105	108
	Less than $15,000	67	85	115

dium, and light buyers of specific products and brands.

The syndicated surveys can give a breakdown of the primary, secondary, and tertiary customers in the national market. If there were no company-specific demographics available, this segmentation could be used for product analysis. A company looking for information on lipstick users, for example, could look through Mediamark's or Simmons' database and find demographic profiles of light, medium, and heavy users (*see figure 10c.*).

Survey data may not be available for your category of product or service or your particular brand. But most syndicated survey firms will do customized research for reasonable prices. Simmons Custom Studies division, for example, will include specific questions on a nationally representative survey for about $1,000 per single response question and $1,500 per open-ended question. The results can then be linked with Simmons Study of Media and Markets database to greatly enhance their analytical and profiling capabilities.

The Consumer Expenditure Survey

The CEX, like syndicated surveys, can provide specific purchase data on numerous product categories.

Let's suppose that we are a company that manufactures window coverings—drapes, blinds, and curtains. By looking at the CEX, we find the following age groups buy the most of the product every year:

Age Group	Ave. Exp.	x	Size of Group (in millions)	=	Aggr. Exp. (in millions)	% of Total
under 25	$2.34		7.8		$18.3 million	1.5%
25 - 34	17.16		21.3		366.3 million	26.6
35 - 44	24.65		18.7		462.1 million	33.5
45 - 54	11.46		13.4		153.5 million	11.2
55 - 64	11.36		13.11		48.6 million	10.8
65 - 74	14.79		11.61		71.2 million	12.4
75 & older	6.92		8.2		56.7 million	4

SOURCE: *Consumer Expenditure Survey, Bureau of Labor Statistics*

The above information gives us a general idea of the total market for window coverings. The members of each age group are all heads of households. By multiplying the average annual expenditure of each age group by the total number of households in each age group, we arrive at the amount spent annually by the age group on window coverings. Then we add up the aggregate expenditures for all the age groups and get the total annual expenditures on window coverings. By figuring out what proportion the expendi-

133

tures of each age group represent of the total, we can measure the relative importance of each.

As we mentioned above, these figures can be useful either as a general guideline on who purchases your product (if no company-specific data exist), or as a benchmark against which to compare your product's performance. Let's suppose that a company that manufactures and distributes window coverings in one state has sales record data on its customers' ages. By calculating the average expenditure for each age group and then comparing with the national average, the company can get an idea of how the product is failing or exceeding its potential, and efforts can be made to attract customers in underrepresented age groups.

Extending the analysis, the company could determine the size of the potential market by multiplying the average sales per age group by the number of people in each age group. Then the firm could compare its sales per age group with the potential to determine if there is a problem and which age groups should be targeted.

Reviewing the sources for purchase data linked to demographics:
- In-house records backed by primary research
- Scanner data firms
- Syndicated surveys
- The Consumer Expenditure Survey

Once a researcher understands who buys the product or service and whether they are heavy, medium, and light buyers, the next step is to answer the question:

What are their needs for the product?

2. Why do they buy it? Identify the heavy, medium, and light buyers of a product category. Then examine the customers more closely to find out why they buy more or less of the product.

There is only one way to determine the customers' needs. You have to ask them. If you're lucky, an industry trade association may have already asked. Many trade and industry associations survey consumers of their products about their purchase behavior.

If no survey is available through a trade association, you probably have to ask them yourself or hire a research firm to do it. Ask them through the mail, over the telephone, or face-to-face. You can use exit interviews or hire a firm to interview shoppers in malls. But the only accurate way to find out why customers buy what you sell in the quantities they do is to ask them through a survey or a focus group.

The important thing to discover here is when they use the product or service and what they use it for. Sometimes this step of the analysis reveals that some customers are buying the product for entirely different reasons than had been previously thought.

Look at the customers' motivations. Do they buy the product for prestige, quality, utility, price, convenience, or some special product aspect? Find out what prevents them from buying more or why they buy in large quantities.

The second part of this is to ask the customers specific questions about the product to find out:

How does the product/service meet the needs of each group?

3. What do the customers think/feel about the product? The next step is to look at the product and determine how well it meets the needs of the various customer segments. The reasons one group buys the product may differ significantly from the reasons other groups buy it. Again, you'll need psychographic or attitude research to find out how customers regard your product or service. The primary goal is to discover how customers' differences translate into different ways of using your product.

A creative researcher may also use this opportunity to develop additional uses for the product. Someone working for Arm & Hammer Baking Soda did a little creative thinking and realized that baking soda had long been used to brush teeth and deodorize small spaces. Ads that emphasized these "new" uses for an old product helped many customers think about baking soda in a new way, and also increased sales.

Once you understand the customer groups involved, take a fresh look at the product to determine:

What are the unique characteristics of the product/service?

4. Are there better ways to present the unique characteristics of the product or service? Take a fresh look at the product in light of survey or focus group results. Each product and service has individual characteristics that determine what types of customers will buy the product or service.

In some cases, products and services are marketed strictly by their characteristics and what benefits they offer customers. A shampoo is not merely something that will clean hair; it becomes a luxurious liquid that produces shine, manageability, and body.

The same is true for services. What is it that AT&T, MCI, and the rest offer, if not a network of wires? That reality, however, won't convince many customers to sign up. To compete, phone companies have learned to distinguish themselves as service providers—a reliable group of communications specialists with state-of-the-art technology and a desire to give their customers simple and efficient phone service.

This illustrates an important lesson in product or service analysis. With consumer products as well as with services, one crucial variable in sales success is the ability to distinguish your product from the rest of the pack. This should have been done during the product development phase. But perhaps something about the marketplace or the product has changed. Take a fresh look at your product.

Assess the benefits of the product or service to the customers. Is there a feature of the product that is special but hasn't yet been publicized? Is there a new angle to an old characteristic?

Often the only way to distinguish a product from the competition is to find a way to distinguish the company in the mind of consumers. Is there something special about the company that will appeal to the targeted customers?

In the competitive race between Sears, K mart and Wal-Mart—the largest general merchandise stores in the U.S.—Sears' sales have lagged behind because the company has failed to capture the attention of the American public. Sears' "everyday low prices" campaign bombed despite the suspense behind the national rollout. It didn't work because it only offered what K mart and Wal-Mart already had.

Wal-Mart, however, has shown a stronger creative force in its marketing campaign. In August 1989, Wal-Mart announced it would give special support to companies that made packaging improvements preventing lasting environmental problems. Shortly afterward, K mart announced that it too would help promote packaging improvements and that it would soon be using photodegradable plastic bags in its Florida stores. Wal-Mart representatives said they were glad K mart followed suit. That's what the company had intended when it made its announcement a month before.

Wal-Mart stays on top of consumer trends. A Gallup poll in 1989 found that 92 percent of men and 96 percent of women said they would make a special effort to buy products from companies trying to protect the environment. Wal-Mart recognized this trend of growing environmental concern and acted on it. By the end of the year Wal-Mart sales were up significantly, while Sears sales were still in a slump. Wal-Mart's sales were already doing well, but there's no doubt it gained an immeasurable amount of good will by being first to champion package improvements.

This example shows the potential of creative thinking. A slight twist on a popular theme can work to distinguish companies with very similar product offerings.

Next, we have to compare the customers' needs to the product's characteristics to answer the question:

How are my customers changing?

5. Examine customer demographics over time. We know what our customer breakdown is now, but what happened to the heavy, medium, and light users in the last five years? The last ten years? A look at the trends will give you an idea of how product demand changes over time. For this you could analyze past issues of the CEX or look back through the Mediamark or Simmons databases or your customer database if you have invested in developing one.

The syndicated surveys could show you something like figure 10d, on the next page. From these data, we see that the demographic profile of lip-balm users is relatively stable. The profile shows that single women are more likely to use lip balm, and most users are in the 18-to-24 age group. Income doesn't affect usage, but slightly more users are in the western states, while the Northeast is still underrepresented. This profile hasn't changed much in the time period studied.

But suppose it had changed. The differences would tell you whether the average user was more likely to be male or female. By projecting trends into the future, you could get a better idea of what to expect and who to target next year and beyond.

Look at the demographic projections. Suppose you know that women aged 35 to 44 with incomes of $35,000 or more are the heaviest buyers of your product. Demographic projections for women in that age group show more of them entering the work force and their incomes increasing. And the number of women in this market will be increasing sharply in the next decade. If you understand the trends, you are better positioned to form a strategy to sell your product to this age group in the coming years.

Also consider: Does the product appeal to a specific group of people or is it useful only to one age segment? This determines what reactions you'll have to monitor.

Levi Strauss, for example, found their product appealed to a particular group of people—the baby boomers. That knowledge allowed them to monitor the changing needs of this group as they aged and alter its product accordingly to continue selling to this group.

However, other products are only used by people of a certain age segment, and after they age out of the segment, they stop using the product. In this case, the manufacturer has to monitor the changing needs of the new generation entering the age segment and fit the product to the new customers.

Consider all the demographic and lifestyle changes that could affect product demand. Each customer has different attitudes about the product and how it meets or fails to meet his needs. Find out customers' attitudes toward the product either by conducting a focus group, or by surveying customers.

A survey or analysis of your customer database is also the way to find out

Figure 10d: DEMOGRAPHICS OF THE LIP BALM USER, 1982 TO 1986

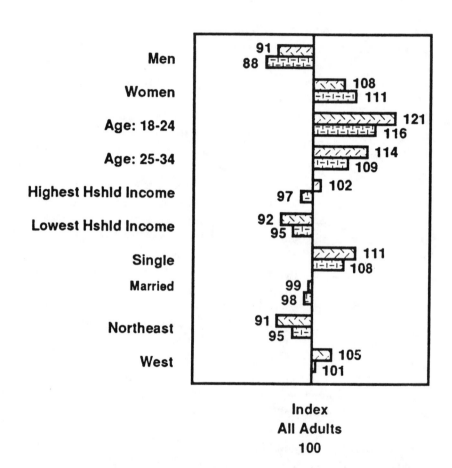

Men 91 / 88
Women 108 / 111
Age: 18-24 121 / 116
Age: 25-34 114 / 109
Highest Hshld Income 102 / 97
Lowest Hshld Income 92 / 95
Single 111 / 108
Married 99 / 98
Northeast 91 / 95
West 105 / 101

Index
All Adults
100

Spring 1982
Spring 1986

how customers' lifestyles are changing. You may be able to figure out some general changes your customers are going through from your primary and secondary customer research.

Once you understand the changing needs and attitudes of your customers, you can begin to answer the final question:

Will product/service alterations better meet their needs?

6. How can we increase sales? Sales problems can often be traced to changes in the customers' lifestyles or perceptions that induce them to buy a competing product. A company faced with such a problem has at least three options: 1) change the product to meet the new needs; 2) pitch the product differently to play up a feature not before noted; 3) or forget about that customer group and try to get other groups to buy more. Change the product, change the image, or change the target.

The option chosen will be the one that offers the most potential sales for the lowest cost. To determine this the company must enter a whole new phase of product analysis, which employs much the same intensive review as new product development. The market, the customer segments, the company's production capabilities, and the relative strength of the competition and other operational factors must all be considered in this final phase of product analysis. Ultimately, the company has to determine the costs of each option relative to the number of new customers gained because of the changes.

Hypothetical Case Study

To better understand how product and service analysis can be applied to a particular product, let's look at how one hypothetical company uses it. A sporting goods company named Outdoors Inc. has become concerned about declining backpack sales. Currently, it has 45 percent of the total market, down from 50 percent last year.

Researchers look at company records and warranty cards and at Mediamark's survey and determine that most of what they sell is bought by single 18-to-34-year-olds, slightly more men than women. The data show that they read *Ski*, *Sports Afield*, and the *New York Times*.

They also identify an important secondary market of 35-to-44-year-olds who are married and may have children aged two or older. Plus, there is another smaller group of backpack users who rent packs from universities or sports stores rather than buy.

Even before doing a survey, researchers can make certain assumptions about the customers. The very nature of the product tells them the customers are physically active. They also read *Hunting* and *Car Craft* magazines.

They are very probably outdoor buffs and risk takers. Some of these assumptions are intuitively obvious, but it is still useful to articulate them and then test them against survey results.

The company uses product registration, or warranty, cards to gather information on their customers, and mails surveys to existing customers to find out that the reasons the primary group buys backpacks are much different than why the secondary group buys. Some of the younger group bought their first backpacks to travel while in college. They needed rugged but light equipment that would endure hard use for a number of months. Most of these packs wore out after the excursion, and many of the customers never bought another one. Many of the younger group are hiking hobbyists who hike regularly. They buy backpacks for longer hikes and camping expeditions that require sturdy lightness.

A majority of the 35-to-44-year-olds used to do a lot more hiking and camping than they do now, but they try to get a trip in whenever time permits. They are likely to have already bought two or more backpacks. Now they have young children, so when they can get out with their backpacks, it's usually for only a weekend and they often take the kids along. Their demands on the equipment are not as great as younger users. In fact, by surveying these customers, you find that the packs are often too big for their new needs.

Up until now, Outdoors Inc. sold three different models of backpacks—a large, rugged one for heavy use, a medium-sized one, and a day pack. Each has a number of outside zippered pockets of various sizes to fit water bottles and other gear. The seams are double stitched and the company uses only the highest quality materials. It also offers a one-year warranty against manufacturer defects. Outdoors Inc. emphasizes ruggedness, durability, and lightness in their promotional literature.

In looking carefully at its customers' changing needs, Outdoors Inc. finds out that some of its original customers are now in their late 30s and 40s, with children. These two facts alone suggest that their trips will be shorter, and they may not need the large pack. The initial survey results support this assumption. The company decides to take a more in-depth survey of these customers. They ask older customers what they like best and least about the product and what improvements they would like to see. They also ask younger customers about their intentions to continue backpacking when they marry and have children.

The results of the survey are very illuminating. They show that 79 percent of women and 95 percent of men younger than 35 say they will continue backpacking and hiking when they have children. The majority also say that they will take the children along whenever possible. These customers say they will continue to buy Outdoors Inc.'s products because they are rugged and high-quality and have specialized pockets that the competition lacks.

Next, the company looks at what the older customers say about the product. Falling sales among this group turn out to be the source of the company's market share erosion. Nearly 50 percent of the older customers say they recently bought additional backpacks for their family members from other companies because they couldn't find the right size packs among the company's products. The needs of women and older children fall somewhere between the medium-sized pack and the large pack. Younger children want something lighter and smaller than the mid-sized pack, but more sturdy than the day pack.

Outdoors Inc. knows their products have a long life span. One backpack can last between two and 20 years depending upon its use. Generally, the company's customers buy one backpack that lasts them for as long as they need it. A minority of the customers, who are hard travelers or real hiking and camping enthusiasts, have to buy two or more during their lifetimes. The company reviewed the situation and decided that, because there was a limited market, it would either need to sell auxiliary products, find additional ways to reach more hikers and campers, or invent new uses for the product to boost sales.

Sales of Outdoors Inc.'s backpacks were still strong among the younger crowd. But company decision makers knew that the upsurge in hiking popularity had begun with the baby boomers. Now they worried, if they were losing their original customers, what would happen when this young group moved into its 30s and 40s? Outdoors Inc. reviewed its choices and decided it couldn't afford to lose two generations of 35-to-44-year-olds. Clearly, the company had to look into product alterations.

Alter the Products

Company officials further agreed that the severity of the sales loss justified immediate product improvements. Managers decided they needed to alter the products so they would be more in line with the needs of the 35-to-44-year-old customers with children who were dissatisfied with the product. Those customers needed more flexibility and variety in backpack capacities, as well as ruggedness, lightness, and durability. After analyzing the product and the plant capacity, company officials determined that they could offer three additional expandable backpacks without incurring prohibitive costs.

One of the new products will be a smaller expandable pack perfect for shorter hikes or for older children. But as the customers' needs and uses grow, they can buy additional sections that zip on and attach to the frame with heavy-duty space-age snaps. The company also plans to build a child-sized pack that can be altered for use as a more structured day pack as the child grows older. Additional sections can be added onto this pack.

The company is especially excited about its third new product. This is an expandable backpack a little larger than the existing mid-sized model with the option of adding extra sections until it has more capacity than the largest existing model. An added selling feature is that when the frame is removed from this pack, it can be converted into a large, softsided piece of luggage. Not only can it carry everything needed on the trail, it can also become a large suitcase.

The company believes these new products will exactly meet the changing needs of its customers. Flexible design will give the company an edge on the competition, and the fact that the largest backpack also converts into a large suitcase might just convince some of the occasional users to buy a backpack instead of renting one.

For Outdoors Inc. product analysis resulted in a happy ending. One year after the new products were introduced, accompanied by special discounted announcements mailed directly to customers in the older groups who had returned warranty cards, the company's backpacks again claim a 50 percent market share.

The analysis works smoothly in the hypothetical world. But how does it fare in the real world? The following section examines a real world problem that databases helped to solve

Case Study: Selling Lexus

Equifax Marketing Decision Systems (formerly National Decision Systems) is a marketing information company based in Encinitas, California. It provides a wide range of products including VISION geodemographic segmentation system and Infomark, an integrated desktop marketing information system. Its research specialists provided the following product-related case study.

In 1986, Toyota Motors Company decided to develop Lexus, a luxury car. Late that year, they approached Equifax to help them solve two problems. Toyota wanted to find out who would buy Lexus cars and where to locate its dealerships. Equifax's first task was to identify the market for Japanese luxury cars. The problem was that since there had been only two Japanese luxury cars, the Toyota Cressida and the Nissan Maxima, selling in the American market for a limited time, there were few sales records on which to base a potential customer profile.

Equifax gathered data from various databases to form a composite profile of potential buyers for Toyota's new Lexus division. They used R. L. Polk's vehicle registration data to form a profile of people who currently own luxury cars, including American makes, Mercedes, and BMW, and they formed a profile of buyers of existing Japanese luxury cars made by Toyota and Nissan. By combining the two profiles, they formed a composite luxury car-buyer profile.

Then they used Allison-Fisher syndicated survey data on car buying intentions to determine what type of people intended to buy a Japanese luxury car and where these customers were located. Because the Allison-Fisher data are also coded to VISION geodemographic segmentation system, Equifax could determine which VISION segments were most likely to become Lexus buyers.

By analyzing all the data, Equifax was able to identify, out of a total of 48 segments, the VISION segments that would go for three separate luxury car types:

Product category	Price Range	Similar Product	Lexus Product
Japanese Luxury Sedan	$35K to 75K	BMW 500 & 700	Lexus LS400
Japanese Luxury Sports Coupe	—	BMW 325 series	none yet
Japanese Near-Luxury Sedan	$25K to 30K	BMW 325	Lexus ES250

VISION segments in Category 1

1. Suburban Gentry	6. High Tech Frontiers
2. Nouveau Riche	7. Condos & Palms
3. Tuition & Braces	8. Comfortable Suburbanites
4. The Good Life	9. Leave It to Beaver
5. Suburban Up & Comers	10. Porch Swings & Apple Pies

Equifax predicted that the top three segments in this category would account for slightly more than one-quarter of all LS400 buyers. The Suburban Gentry segment (the wealthiest of all households) had a usage index of 640, meaning they were six and a half times more likely than average to be LS400 buyers.

No.	Segment	% of Customers	% of Households	VISION Index
1	Suburban Gentry	11.7%	1.8%	640
2	Nouveau Riche	7.5	2.6	286
9	The Good Life	7.2	1.9	375

Equifax did a VISION Profile Report that included similar breakdowns for each of the 48 VISION segments.

VISION Segments in Category 3

1. Suburban Gentry	6. Comfortable Suburbanites
2. Nouveau Riche	7. High Tech Frontiers
3. Tuition & Braces	8. Leave It to Beaver
4. Suburban Up & Comers	9. Porch Swings & Apple Pies
5. The Good Life	10. Condos & Palms

Next Equifax developed a VISION Market Index (VMI) and Customer Household Count (CHH) to identify the markets containing the highest concentration of the targeted VISION segments:

VISION Market Index = index of use per segment **x** incidence of segment households in area.

This results in a measurement of the potential in each market.

Customer Household Count = number of households in target VISION segments in geography.

This is a way of calculating the attractiveness of each market.

Using the above techniques, Equifax predicted the number of potential sales of Japanese Sedans and Near Luxury Sedans Lexus could expect for every metropolitan area in the country. Then Equifax ranked the top ten markets in the country by potential sales:

1. Los Angeles	6. Nassau-Suffolk
2. Washington, D.C.	7. Houston
3. Chicago	8. Philadelphia
4. Anaheim-Santa Ana, CA	9. Boston
5. New York	10. Oakland

Using the same method, Equifax also determined the ten worst areas for Lexus sales. Among them were Lewiston-Auburn, Maine; Danville, Virginia; and Sheboygan, Wisconsin.

Lexus used the Equifax results to determine which geographies had the sales necessary to support dealerships. The VISION segmentation profiles also became the basis for the company's marketing plans and dealer development programs.

After Lexus began selling cars in late 1989, Equifax went back and did a follow-up analysis to determine how their initial profiles compared with actual customers. After analyzing 8,204 buyers from registration data, and allowing again for VISION segmentation, Equifax found that there was a .91

correlation (1.00 is perfect correlation) between the Luxury Sedan buyer estimates and the actual customer profile for the Lexus LS400. There was a .97 correlation between the Near-Luxury buyer profile and the actual customers for the Lexus ES250.

When looking for potential Japanese Luxury Sedan buyers, Equifax had overlooked the Fixed Income Blues segment. Equifax also omitted the Sun City segment from its Near-Luxury Sedan buyer profile. But these segments were included among actual buyers of the Lexus cars. In both cases, the Porch Swings & Apple Pies segment was the one that didn't show up in actual buyers.

"We hadn't included these groups initially because their incomes weren't high enough. Both segments are made up of retirees who don't have very high incomes, but have significant accumulated wealth," said Steve Heffernan, Equifax researcher who handled the analysis. "Obviously, these groups like the product well enough to pay cash. They're cashing in their certificates of deposit or whatever to buy the cars."

The new data won't have much effect on Lexus strategy, since the original research turned out to be so close to reality. The Equifax follow-up study identified "early adoptors," those people who bought the car in the few months it was available. Lexus representatives said they would probably repeat the analysis periodically to see if the customer segments change as the product gains market acceptance.

The case study illustrates the use of geodemographic segmentation in product or service analysis. The advantage of geodemographics is that the geographic component allows the analyst to identify the potential of each customer segment per market area. Combining the most valuable aspects of geographic market analysis with product analysis produces a powerful technique for identifying, locating, and capturing customers.

CHAPTER ELEVEN

Advertising & Promotion Analysis

GETTING A message through the media maze to a target market is now the most challenging task that businesses face. Networks, independent stations, cable television, radio, newspapers, magazines, direct mail, promotions, point-of-purchase advertising, outdoor advertising, and even event marketing all compete for advertising dollars. But who exactly is watching, reading, or listening? Increasingly, advertisers are demanding to know.

Reach and frequency are still the way most agencies make decisions about buying national television time. An advertiser can decide to go for reach and place an ad during the Super Bowl when the maximum number of people will be watching. Or the advertiser could go for frequency and bombard the audience of less expensive programs with numerous ads over a longer period of time. Either way, the audience is a large, faceless mass.

Most national spot advertising is still purchased by cost per thousand to deliver a broad demographic, such as everyone between the ages of 18 and 34. Using a demographic this broad is like trying to hit a bulls-eye with a wrecking ball. You not only get the bulls-eye, but in the process you obliterate the entire target. Put another way, there are 70.5 million Americans in the 18-to-34-year-old age group. Let's say only 10 percent of them would even consider buying the product being advertised. Suppose the advertiser spends enough money to reach 7.5 million consumers aged 18 to 34. Most of that money will be wasted. The ads will reach 10 percent of the total market, but they might not reach the 10 percent who would actually buy the product.

This is not to suggest that anyone should abandon national advertising. Rather, for some products, attention needs to be diverted to distinct target markets. As the fragmenting of America continues, companies that tailor their approaches and messages to specific markets can communicate effectively with the right people and optimize their sales.

Effective advertising is focused advertising, the kind that speaks directly to your best customers and moves your product. The purpose of undertaking an advertising and promotional analysis is to find the optimal media and message to communicate most effectively with those customers.

Advertising analysis consists of: 1) media evaluation; 2) media and promotion planning; and 3) message design. It reveals:

- **What media can best reach my customers?**
- **Will a combination of media optimize sales?**
- **What formats and programs reach my customers?**
- **What messages will induce them to buy?**
- **What ads or promotions get results?**

Purpose: Find the optimal mix of media and message to reach the most customers.

Tools: Demographic, psychographic, purchase behavior, and media preference data.

Concept: Select the most cost-effective media (TV, radio, print, direct mail) among competing broadcasters or publishers and develop a message specially designed to get the customers' attention and induce them to buy.

Method: Demographics and media preference data are used to identify the target groups and the type of media they watch, listen to, or read most frequently. Then data on purchase behavior are added in to find out what media the heavy, medium, and light buyers of the product use and what programs, formats, or topics appeal to them. The next step is to craft a message that will appeal to each consuming group, and for this psychographic data are most useful. Once the media have been selected, the mix has been determined, and the message designed, the last step is measuring the effectiveness of the resulting advertising and/or promotional campaign using more purchase behavior data.

The analysis detailed here is intended for ads and promotions of a local or regional nature. Some of the same principles apply to a major national campaign, but the analysis becomes more complex as the number of markets increases. Our purpose here is to suggest a basic outline for using consumer databases to craft better ads and promotions. This analysis is useful both for companies with and without advertising agencies.

1. Identify the target. Again, the first step of the analysis is to get a clear picture of exactly who we want to attract—a customer profile. The analysis will be market-based (such as for a small retailer in one location) or product-based (such as for a large manufacturer). The more detailed your demographic and purchase behavior information, the better. How to establish a customer profile is described in detail in the previous chapter on product and service analysis.

Now focus on the media choices of the customers you want to reach and answer the question:

What media can best reach my customers?

2. Identify the type of media each group prefers. Media usage can vary greatly according to demographics and purchase behavior differences. For the most accurate determination of media preference, cross-tabulate media preferences by both demographics and purchase behavior if the data are available. For this you could go to any of the media preference sources given in chapter 7.

You must then determine whether a promotion should be done either alone or in concert with the advertising campaign. To do this, get data on how product sales are affected by any kind of deal—sales, discounts, coupons, or in-store promotions. The scanner data firms can provide detailed information on volume of sales in any deal. The sample report from Spectra Advantage in Chapter 10 illustrates how these data might look. Other sources would be in-house sales records, product registration cards, or syndicated surveys. Next we must consider the media strengths and limitations in the individual market.

Will a combination of media optimize sales?

3. Evaluate the media choices in the market. Perhaps in the local market a television station, a radio station, and the Sunday paper are all very strong media choices for your customers. The ideal campaign should include each medium that shows it can deliver. To find out, first look at the area you want to cover and get an idea about the relative competitive positions of each medium in the market. What radio or TV station is first, second, or third? What is the circulation of the daily newspaper? What is the penetration of each medium in the segments you want to reach? Look at the market by geographic segments.

To determine the best media choices, you need reach and penetration data as well as knowledge about the demographic make-up of the respective audiences. The ratings data of Nielsen, Arbitron, and Birch/Scarborough will tell you the reach and frequency and something about each station's audience. Now you know how much of the total market each medium reaches. Next consider the relative composition of each audience to establish exactly who each medium reaches and when.

Ratings data are limited because they often only segment the audience by broad demographics such as age and sex. If one station reports the largest audience of men aged 35 to 54, that shouldn't be enough to convince you to buy time on that station. There can be vast differences between all men aged

35 to 54 and the men in that age group who happen to be your best customers. Maybe the particular group you seek is instead included in the smaller audience of another station. Identifying those differences may require additional data. The primary goal here is to get a detailed demographic profile of audiences of each medium and to match that to your own customer profile.

An important source of media preference is the actual media—the stations and publications selling time and space. In competitive markets, the media should be able to tell advertisers exactly who their customers are. Sophisticated stations and newspapers will be able to provide data showing, for example, that in addition to attracting the most men aged 35 to 54 with incomes of more than $30,000, the station attracts the most people who report using your product.

As the demand for detailed media data increases, media have to provide more than ratings data to their advertisers to remain competitive. A station may lead in a particular market, but it may not attract the biggest audience of a particular group of customers. So, many stations and newspapers hire research specialists to profile the local media market. Two firms that specialize in surveying broadcast audiences in local markets are Marshall Marketing & Communications of Pittsburgh, and Leigh Stowell & Company of Seattle. Leigh Stowell has produced psychographic profiles for 70 markets, and Marshall Marketing has surveyed more than 59 markets in the country for client broadcasting firms. Their data are based on randomly generated telephone surveys of at least 1,000 people in each market. Marshall uses the VALS psychographic segmentation system, whereas Stowell creates individual typologies for each market.

These surveys are then used by the client stations to generate advertising from area businesses. Because the surveys usually include questions about purchase behavior, media preferences, psychographics, and demographics, they are also valuable sources of information for local advertisers. Although the surveys vary according to the needs of the client station, they frequently include questions about clothing, department store, automobile, and new home purchases—basically any purchase behavior the station's advertisers would be interested in.

For example, suppose that a local Safeway grocery store wanted to find out what images appeal to its customers. If a station in the area had bought a Leigh Stowell survey, the store could find out that Safeway shoppers fit into two of the five psychographic types found in the market. Let's say one type of Safeway customer responded to images of women and men in nontraditional roles, and the other was an older segment that liked images of days gone by. The images could be used to build advertising campaigns. The same analysis could be done to find out how Safeway could attract non-customers too—those who said they did their grocery shopping at other stores.

Data are also available for some newspaper and radio markets. Market Opinion Research of Detroit, and VNU subsidiary, Belden Associates, of Dallas, conduct surveys of newspaper markets. Ask local newspapers what circulation, readership (per section and day), and demographic (who reads which section most and when) data they can supply to help you understand who they reach and when.

The Birch Radio Quarterly Summary Reports include various consumer attribute data. Birch regularly questions the respondents of its radio surveys in certain markets about a wide range of purchase-related topics. The results give advertisers a precise breakdown of listening habits by purchase behavior. A recent quarterly report included the following topics:

- newspaper and TV usage
- airline travel
- plans to purchase a new car
- use of banking services
- beer and soft-drink consumption

- convenience-store usage
- fast-food restaurant usage
- home furniture purchases
- movie theater usage
- house purchases

Figure 11a. shows weekly audiences aged 18 and older of stations in the market who 1) have no plan to buy a house in the next year, 2) plan to purchase a single-family home in the next year, and 3) plan to purchase an apartment or a condo in the next year. Two stations stand out as having a higher index of listeners planning to buy a house. Look at the fifth column from the left, and it's clear WFME-FM has an index of 404 and WNYC-FM has an index of 274, meaning their listeners are 304 percent and 174 percent more likely to buy a home in the next year than are listeners in the general market. The next two pages of the report also break down the audience by sex to provide additional information on future home buyers.

A report like this can be useful for real estate agents or other new-home service providers trying to find the radio stations that can reach the most potential customers in this market. The value of these data is that they not only reveal reach and frequency, but consumer purchase behavior as well.

Once we have identified the types of media our customers prefer and the best providers in the market, the next thing to consider is time of day and program type.

What formats and programs reach my customers?

4. Identify the programs, formats, or sections to use. Demographics and purchase behavior can be used to help determine what kind of programs, music, and topics interest different people. One of the best sources for

Figure 11 a: SAMPLE PAGE FROM BIRCH RADIO REPORT

| | TOTAL WEEKLY AUDIENCE | | COMPARATIVE VALUES - READ DOWN | | | | | |
| | | | NO PLAN | | HOUSE | | APT/CONDO | |
	AQH	CUME	% IND	% PEN	% IND	% PEN	% IND	% PEN
WABC	402	4681	102	7.5	110	8.0	53	3.8
WADO +	154	1663	111	2.9			94	2.4
WALK		27	*	*	*	*	*	*
WALK-FM	120	1381	105	2.3	69	1.5	78	1.7
WBAB-FM	182	1757	102	2.8	115	3.1	49	1.3
WBGO-FM	110	1347	96	2.0	123	2.6	122	2.5
WBLI-FM	67	1082	91	1.5	160	2.7	136	2.3
WBLS-FM	507	6370	90	9.0	119	11.7	214	21.2
WCBS	351	7862	104	12.8	66	8.1	91	11.1
WCBS-FM	501	6850	106	11.4	86	9.1	26	2.8
WDHA-FM	59	1083	94	1.6	74	1.2	229	3.9
WDRE-FM	110	1644	85	2.2	193	4.9	182	4.7
WEZN-FM	53	1634	104	2.7	19	0.5	163	4.1
WFAN	554	8365	97	12.7	81	10.6	167	21.8
WFME-FM	60	717	75	0.8	404	4.5		
WHTZ-FM	429	6335	97	9.6	103	10.1	144	14.2
WINS	520	11204	98	17.0	105	18.2	130	22.6
WKDM +	74	720	110	1.2			102	1.1
WKJY-FM	51	565	99	0.9	59	0.5	185	1.6
WLIB*	252	1793	94	2.6	124	3.5	153	4.3
WLTW-FM	382	4761	98	7.3	82	6.1	159	11.8
WMCA	23	710	79	0.9	173	1.9	306	3.4
WNCN-FM	129	2227	101	3.5	71	2.4	125	4.3
WNEW	184	2492	108	4.2	41	1.6	69	2.7
WNEW-FM	865	9283	102	14.8	87	12.6	85	12.3
WNSR-FM	318	3950	104	6.4	54	3.3	114	7.0
WNYC-FM	64	1611	89	2.2	274	6.9		
WOR	208	3111	105	5.1	81	3.9	50	2.4
WPAT	106	1220	110	2.1			110	2.1
WPAT-FM	250	3746	107	6.3	67	3.9	44	2.6
WPLJ-FM	236	5703	97	8.6	74	6.5	191	16.9
WQCD-FM	475	4895	88	6.7	166	12.6	175	13.4
WQHT-FM	476	5032	98	7.7	72	5.7	173	13.5
WQXR	7	274	*	*	*	*	*	*
WQXR-FM	186	3209	99	5.0	87	4.4	129	6.5
WRKS-FM	605	6787	91	9.6	123	13.0	202	21.4
WSKQ +	55	572	108	1.0	87	0.8		
WSKQ-F+	139	1462	100	2.3	117	2.7	75	1.7
WWRL	43	1040	84	1.4	·226	3.7	147	2.4
WXRK-FM	577	8110	97	12.3	120	15.1	108	13.6
WYNY-FM	239	2620	101	4.1	128	5.2	46	1.9
WPLR-FM	79	769	100	1.2	136	1.6	40	0.5
PUR	11835	61767	100	96.3	100	96.0	100	96.2

+ DENOTES SPANISH STATION. SEE ADVISORY, PAGE IV.

information on what general programs and formats appeal to your customers is syndicated surveys. These large national surveys can reveal customer preferences for magazines, television networks and cable channels, and radio formats. Customers can be segmented by selected demographics or by the types of products or brands they purchase.

Figure 11b. shows clearly the media choices of men who buy designer jeans (compared with all men). This information is also available for women customers. The data show the following media information about men who buy designer jeans:

Radio

- They are 23 percent more likely to listen to the radio between 10 a.m. and 3 p.m.
- They are 18 percent more likely to listen to the radio between 7 p.m. and midnight.
- They are 146 percent more likely to listen to urban contemporary formats, and 75 percent more likely to listen to black music stations.
- To lesser degrees they listen to rock, album-oriented rock, all news, and golden oldies formats.
- They don't like country, easy listening, or nostalgia formats.
- They get above-average exposure to the following radio networks— NBN, Concert Music Network, ABC FM, ABC Contemporary, and The Source.

Television

- They are slightly above average in their TV viewing between 11 and 11:30 p.m.
- They are 14 percent below average in their viewing between 8 and 11 p.m.
- They are 41 percent more likely than average to watch prime-time feature films and 40 percent more likely to watch early morning talk shows.
- They are below average in exposure to daytime dramas and game shows.

Cable

- If they subscribe to cable, they are slightly more likely to take one of the pay channels, but they are not likely to be heavy cable viewers.
- They like the music channels. They are 75 percent more likely to see VH1 and 26 percent more likely to see MTV than average.
- They watch the Arts & Entertainment channel, the Christian Broadcasting Network and the Learning Channel the least.

Figure 11b: MEDIA PREFERENCES OF DESIGNER JEANS BUYERS

MEN'S CLOTHING: PURCHASED PAST 12 MONTHS

BASE: MEN	TOTAL U.S. '000	SLACKS A '000	B % DOWN	C % ACROSS	D INDEX	DESIGNER JEANS A '000	B % DOWN	C % ACROSS	D INDEX	JEANS A '000	B % DOWN	C % ACROSS	D INDEX	SWEATER A '000	B % DOWN	C % ACROSS	D INDEX
ALL MEN	83367	25262	100.0	30.3	100	4957	100.0	5.9	100	27269	100.0	32.7	100	12808	100.0	15.4	100
RADIO WKDAY: 6-10:00 AM CUME	49581	16326	64.6	32.9	109	3117	62.9	6.3	106	16796	61.6	33.9	104	7938	62.0	16.0	104
10:00 AM - 3:00 PM	30609	9798	38.8	32.0	106	2246	45.3	7.3	123	11025	40.4	36.0	110	5104	39.9	16.7	109
3:00 PM - 7:00 PM	36940	12107	47.9	32.8	108	2198	44.3	6.0	100	13134	48.2	35.6	109	5851	45.7	15.8	103
7:00 PM - MIDNIGHT	18500	5141	20.4	27.8	92	1301	26.2	7.0	118	6815	25.0	36.8	113	2959	23.1	16.0	104
RADIO AVERAGE WEEKDAY CUME	68339	21582	85.4	31.6	104	4402	88.8	6.4	108	23461	86.0	34.3	105	10906	85.1	16.0	104
RADIO AVG. WEEKEND DAY CUME	55856	17122	67.8	30.7	101	3570	72.0	6.4	107	19358	71.0	34.7	106	9384	73.3	16.8	109
RADIO FORMATS: ADULT CONTEMP	21084	7155	28.3	33.9	112	1413	28.5	6.7	113	7233	26.5	34.3	105	3602	28.1	17.1	111
ALBUM ORIENTED ROCK (AOR)	13684	4381	17.3	32.0	106	1104	22.3	8.1	136	5791	21.2	42.3	129	2780	21.7	20.3	132
ALL NEWS	4215	1764	7.0	41.9	138	331	6.7	7.9	132	1056	3.9	25.1	77	868	6.8	20.6	134
BLACK	2251	*622	2.5	27.6	91	*234	4.7	10.4	175	578	2.1	25.7	79	*408	3.2	18.1	118
CLASSICAL	2844	1267	5.0	44.5	147	*205	4.1	7.2	121	969	3.6	34.1	104	685	5.3	24.1	157
CHR/ROCK	15733	4961	19.6	31.5	104	1301	26.2	8.3	139	6342	23.3	40.3	123	3143	24.5	20.0	130
COUNTRY	16614	4270	16.9	25.7	85	678	13.7	4.1	69	6142	22.5	37.0	113	2085	16.3	12.5	82
EASY LISTENING	5805	2051	8.1	35.3	117	*206	4.2	3.5	60	1565	5.7	27.0	82	941	7.3	16.2	106
GOLDEN OLDIES	3166	1086	4.3	34.3	113	*227	4.6	7.2	121	1010	3.7	31.9	98	641	5.0	20.2	132
MOR/NOSTALGIA	4662	1553	6.1	33.3	110	*151	3.0	3.2	54	1232	4.5	26.4	81	650	5.1	13.9	91
NEWS/TALK	7114	2729	10.8	38.4	127	422	8.5	5.9	100	1789	6.6	25.1	77	1180	9.2	16.6	108
URBAN CONTEMPORARY	3215	1105	4.4	34.4	113	*470	9.5	14.6	246	1077	3.9	33.5	102	702	5.5	21.8	142
RADIO NETWORKS: ABC CONTEMP	5368	1686	6.7	31.4	104	*531	10.7	9.9	166	2036	7.5	37.9	116	1069	8.3	19.9	130
ABC DIRECTION	4547	1369	5.4	30.1	99	*208	4.2	4.6	77	1471	5.4	32.4	99	666	5.2	14.6	95
ABC ENTERTAINMENT	5219	1558	6.2	29.9	99	*192	3.9	3.7	62	1544	5.7	29.6	90	665	5.2	12.7	83
ABC FM	3816	1351	5.3	35.4	117	*420	8.5	11.0	185	1686	6.2	44.2	135	742	5.8	19.4	127
ABC INFORMATION	9465	3506	13.9	37.0	122	378	7.6	4.0	67	2672	9.8	28.2	86	1547	12.1	16.3	106
ABC ROCK	5899	1951	7.7	33.1	109	562	11.3	9.5	160	2595	9.5	44.0	134	1278	10.0	21.7	141
CBS	8020	2810	11.1	35.0	116	339	6.8	4.2	71	2179	8.0	27.2	83	1357	10.6	16.9	110
CONCERT MUSIC NETWORK	1214	517	2.0	42.6	141	*138	2.8	11.4	191	443	1.6	36.5	112	234	1.8	19.3	125
INTERNET	27091	9178	36.3	33.9	112	2183	44.0	8.1	136	9921	36.4	36.6	112	5052	39.4	18.6	121
KATZ RADIO GROUP	28995	9853	39.0	34.0	112	1893	38.2	6.5	110	9452	34.7	32.6	100	4975	38.8	17.2	112
MUTUAL	9058	2859	11.3	31.6	104	541	10.9	6.0	100	3039	11.1	33.6	103	1480	11.6	16.3	106
NBC	5755	2104	8.3	36.6	121	*399	8.0	6.9	117	1641	6.0	28.5	87	933	7.3	16.2	106
NBN	1058	*286	1.1	27.0	89	*150	3.0	14.2	238	*310	1.1	29.3	90	*258	2.0	24.4	159
RADIORADIO	3783	1200	4.8	31.7	105	*249	5.0	6.6	111	1514	5.6	40.0	122	719	5.6	19.0	124
SATELLITE MUSIC NETWORK	4340	1117	4.4	25.7	85	*327	6.6	7.5	127	1474	5.4	34.0	104	598	4.7	13.8	90
SHERIDAN	1652	437	1.7	26.5	87	*141	2.8	8.5	144	*380	1.4	23.0	70	*185	1.4	11.2	73
THE SOURCE	5995	1894	7.5	31.6	104	520	10.5	8.7	146	2386	8.7	39.8	122	1279	10.0	21.3	139
SUPERNET	21241	6945	27.5	32.7	108	1328	26.8	6.3	105	7766	28.5	36.6	112	3804	29.7	17.9	117
TRANSTAR	4500	1551	6.1	34.5	114	*254	5.1	5.6	95	1431	5.2	31.8	97	782	6.1	17.4	113
US1	5705	1884	7.5	33.0	109	488	9.8	8.6	144	2125	7.8	37.2	114	1142	8.9	20.0	130
US2	4408	1455	5.8	33.0	109	*285	5.7	6.5	109	1291	4.7	29.3	90	687	5.4	15.6	101
WALL STREET JOURNAL NETWORK	4790	1972	7.8	41.2	136	355	7.2	7.4	125	1288	4.7	26.9	82	899	7.0	18.8	122
TV WKDAY AV 1/2 HR:7-10:00AM	3707	1053	4.2	28.4	94	*190	3.8	5.1	86	916	3.4	24.7	76	*342	2.7	9.2	60
10:00 AM - 4:30 PM	6508	1619	6.4	24.9	82	*371	7.5	5.7	96	1677	6.1	25.8	79	719	5.6	11.0	72
4:30 PM - 7:30 PM	16995	4785	18.9	28.2	93	882	17.8	5.2	87	4563	16.7	26.8	82	2579	20.1	15.2	99
7:30 PM - 8:00 PM	28436	8170	32.3	28.7	95	1694	34.2	6.0	100	8152	29.9	28.7	88	4285	33.5	15.1	98
8:00 PM - 11:00 PM	35411	10679	42.3	30.2	100	1809	36.5	5.1	86	10832	39.7	30.6	94	5532	43.2	15.6	102
11:00 PM - 11:30 PM	25526	8177	32.4	32.0	106	1646	33.2	6.4	108	8216	30.1	32.2	98	4134	32.3	16.2	105
11:30 PM - 1:00 AM	8326	2545	10.1	30.6	101	502	10.1	6.0	101	2734	10.0	32.8	100	1382	10.8	16.6	108
TV PRIME TIME CUME	62410	19289	76.4	30.9	102	3576	72.1	5.7	96	19751	72.4	31.6	97	9822	76.7	15.7	102
PROGRAM-TYPES:DAYTIME DRAMAS	3438	818	3.2	23.8	79	*193	3.9	5.6	94	1108	4.1	32.2	99	513	4.0	14.9	97
DAYTIME GAME SHOWS	2177	494	2.0	22.7	75	*121	2.4	5.6	93	600	2.2	27.6	84	*215	1.7	9.9	64
EARLY MORNING TALK/INFO/NEWS	4498	1672	6.6	37.2	123	*375	7.6	8.3	140	1471	5.4	32.7	100	980	7.7	21.8	142
EARLY EVE. NETWK NEWS - M-F	12163	4173	16.5	34.3	113	772	15.6	6.3	107	3857	14.1	31.7	97	2175	17.0	17.9	116
FEATURE FILMS - PRIME	9366	3086	12.2	32.9	109	787	15.9	8.4	141	3466	12.7	37.0	113	1579	12.3	16.9	110
GENERAL DRAMA - PRIME	7806	2546	10.1	32.6	108	452	9.1	5.8	97	2231	8.2	28.6	87	1437	11.2	18.4	120
PVT DET/SUSP/MYST/POL-PRIME	11564	3554	14.1	30.7	101	849	17.1	7.3	123	4027	14.8	34.8	106	1853	14.5	16.0	104
SITUATION COMEDIES - PRIME	7837	2428	9.6	31.0	102	517	10.4	6.6	111	2952	10.8	37.7	115	1195	9.3	15.2	99
CABLE TV	42380	13469	53.3	31.8	105	2518	50.8	5.9	100	13871	50.9	32.7	100	6436	50.2	15.2	99
PAY TV	24707	7936	31.4	32.1	106	1541	31.1	6.2	105	8647	31.7	35.0	107	3768	29.4	15.3	99
HEAVY CABLE VIEWING (15+ HR)	18192	5285	20.9	29.1	96	834	16.8	4.6	77	6078	22.3	33.4	102	2401	18.7	13.2	86
CABLE NETWORKS: A&E	5851	2016	8.0	34.5	114	*179	3.6	3.1	51	2095	7.7	35.8	109	915	7.1	15.6	102
BET (BLACK ENTERTAINMENT TV)	1479	*291	1.2	19.7	65	*92	1.9	6.2	105	*447	1.6	30.2	92	*187	1.5	12.6	82
CNN (CABLE NEWS NETWORK)	19059	6590	26.1	34.6	114	1170	23.6	6.1	103	5962	21.9	31.3	96	2955	23.1	15.5	101
CNN HEADLINE NEWS	13622	4372	17.3	32.1	106	818	16.5	6.0	101	4230	15.5	31.1	95	2088	16.3	15.3	100
CBN CABLE NETWORK	7629	2099	8.3	27.5	91	*266	5.4	3.5	59	2537	9.3	33.3	102	847	6.6	11.1	72
THE DISCOVERY CHANNEL	6500	2174	8.6	33.4	110	*405	8.2	6.2	105	2507	9.2	38.6	118	926	7.2	14.2	93
ESPN	24451	7783	30.8	31.8	105	1225	24.7	5.0	84	8088	29.7	33.1	101	3786	29.6	15.5	101
FNN (FINANCIAL NEWS NETW'K)	1353	587	2.3	43.4	143	*85	1.7	6.3	106	289	1.1	21.4	65	281	2.2	20.8	135
THE LEARNING CHANNEL	857	*283	1.1	33.0	109	*29	.6	3.4	57	*278	1.0	32.4	99	*205	1.6	23.9	156
LIFETIME	5165	1498	5.9	29.0	96	*191	3.9	3.7	62	1895	6.9	36.7	112	790	6.2	15.3	100
MTV	10833	3056	12.1	28.2	93	814	16.4	7.5	126	4651	17.1	42.9	131	1959	15.3	18.1	118
THE NASHVILLE NETWORK	9053	2331	9.2	25.7	85	*410	8.3	4.5	76	3322	12.2	36.7	112	888	6.9	9.8	64
NICK AT NITE	4473	1422	5.6	31.8	105	*176	3.6	3.9	66	1544	5.7	34.5	106	667	5.2	14.9	97
NICKELODEON	5757	1698	6.7	29.5	97	*276	5.6	4.8	81	2031	7.4	35.3	108	969	7.6	16.8	110
TNT NETWORK	12354	3996	15.8	32.3	107	581	11.7	4.7	79	4481	16.4	36.3	111	1703	13.3	13.8	90
VH-1 (VIDEO HITS ONE)	3254	1020	4.0	31.3	103	*339	6.8	10.4	175	1324	4.9	40.7	124	761	5.9	23.4	152
THE WEATHER CHANNEL	11686	3914	15.5	33.5	111	738	14.9	6.3	106	3706	13.6	31.7	97	1891	14.8	16.2	105
WTBS	19933	5937	23.5	29.8	98	951	19.2	4.8	80	6732	24.7	33.8	103	2687	21.0	13.5	88

153

This report gives the researcher a relatively thorough media profile of male designer jeans customers. With the above data and the media usage quintiles explained in chapter 7, we can begin to make some decisions about where and when to run our advertising messages. Next we must determine what we should say.

What messages will induce them to buy?

5. Segment your customers by psychographics. Psychographic, or lifestyle, analysis reveals what messages, images and key words appeal most to your customers and allow you to design messages that get results. Fortunately, a growing number of companies offer psychographic tools.

Some psychographic tools are syndicated, meaning you have to pay the companies that do the studies to get you the results. Two examples of this are the syndicated surveys of Mediamark and Simmons. Some of the information you can get on the customers of toothpaste, for example, are additional breakdowns by VALS 2 type. (See chapter 5 for details on syndicated psychographic studies.)

Proprietary Studies

Psychographic data come from the proprietary studies done by local media companies. If you do business in one of the markets covered by Marshall Marketing & Communications or Leigh Stowell & Company, you can probably get local psychographic data free from the station that paid for the study. Belden Associates of Dallas also has similar data for newspapers in many markets. Since generating advertising is often the major reason these studies are done, the TV stations or newspapers will be more than happy to make the information available free to major advertisers or prospective advertisers.

A large department store, for example, may find that the local TV station already knows the psychographic profile of the store's best customers. Or if the survey didn't ask which department store the respondents use most often, the survey firm can go back and pose that question or others to their survey participants for an additional charge. Then a researcher could delve into the existing database to find out the most prevalent psychographic types who reported shopping at the client store.

Leigh Stowell & Company, however, has developed its own segmentation system based on the results of individual surveys. The size of the surveys can range from slightly less than 1,000 in very small markets to about 2,500 in a large market like New York City. Each participant is asked about demographics, media choices, purchase behavior, and attitudes and values during a 20-minute telephone interview.

The Stowell study of the New York City market identified nine different types of people. Group I consisted of affluent, well-educated professionals who were politically liberal and great patrons of the arts. They respond well to images of creative solutions, cultural events, classical music, and exotic vacation places. Some of the words they respond to are "innovative," "elegant," and "uncompromising." Contrast them with Group IV, a younger, less well educated, and lower income group. They are content in their jobs and optimistic about their chances for advancement. Since most of them are unattached, they like nothing better than to socialize with friends either at home or out on the town. They respond to images of young people partying, fast pace, and excitement. Some of the words that work with them are "fun," "outrageous," "maximum," and "power."

On the other hand, Stowell's study of the Fort Wayne, Indiana, market, found only four psychographic types. The Stowell reports also contain clues as to the most effective creative approaches for advertising directed at each group:

Group I is young, well educated, and affluent, and makes up 23 percent of the Fort Wayne population. They like going out for entertainment, they work long hours, are ambitious in their careers, and are politically liberal. In products they are innovative and look for style and quality.

Attractive images	Commitment to excellence, creative solutions.
Alienating images	Simplistic explanations, very traditional people.
Key words	Responsive, speed, excitement, science, precise.

Group II are affluent, older, conservative people who comprise 22 percent of the population. They spend free time at home with their families or in family-oriented social activities, they are content with their position, and more politically active than other groups. They have strong feelings of patriotism and are conservative in both their political and personal values. As consumers, they want high-quality merchandise that is sophisticated and practical.

Attractive images	Economic growth, images of strength and power
Alienating images	Liberals, nontraditional lifestyles, avant-garde fashions
Key words	Productivity, experienced, control, comfort, elegant, luxurious

Group III makes up 28 percent of the population. They have average incomes, are not too ambitious, and their values are traditional and family oriented. They clip coupons and hold conservative views toward social welfare programs.

Attractive images	Traditional family scenes in contemporary setting, women nurturing husbands and children.
Alienating images	People who show disregard for family values, avant-garde lifestyles.
Key words	Family, home, trusted, popular, affordable, best value, homemade.

Group IV makes up 27 percent of the population. This group is older, either retired or employed in dead-end jobs. They hold little hope that their lives will improve and are cynical about public officials. For recreation they either watch TV or play cards, and they are highly religious.

Attractive images	Safety, security, nostalgic scenes from country's past.
Alienating images	Men and women in nontraditional roles, images of speed, fast pace, high technology.
Key words	Guarantee, no-risk, old-fashioned, reliable, standard, experienced.

With the above information, the creative department has the beginnings of a successful ad campaign. Add data from the station's database, and the advertiser can find out what media each customer group is exposed to most and identify the optimal media mix.

It used to be that the completed ad or promotional campaign was the end of the story. Now, however, advertisers want to be assured their money has been well spent. More and more, they are asking for proof that advertisements and/or promotions had a positive effect on the bottom line. It's up to the researcher to determine:

What ads or promotions get results?

6. Track sales coming from targeted segments. Finding out how effective your communication efforts have been is a difficult task. Ideally, it requires a way to measure three things: 1) exposure to ads/promotions; 2) post-exposure sales; and 3) whether additional sales are from regular or new customers and where those customers are coming from.

The firms that maintain panels of American householders who record every commercial they watch and laser scan all subsequent purchases should be able to supply the above information. These single-source databases sold by scanner data firms were developed especially to solve the problem of determining ad/promotion effectiveness. But their data only cover certain products and certain advertisements or promotions in specific markets.

There is also the obstacle of cost. Household panel data, which are extremely useful for packaged goods giants such as Procter & Gamble, may not include the products of small or regional manufacturers and they may be unaffordable.

Many companies have to depend on their own resources to measure ad effectiveness. One way to do it internally is to more closely monitor sales after the ad and/or promotional campaign. Determining where your business is coming from is of primary importance. To do this, a researcher can segment sales by time period, geographic area of origin, and if possible, by source of information. For example:

• Companies that build proprietary customer databases can use the rate of return of customer questionnaires to accurately measure retail sales activity to a local level, and assess the performance of advertising and promotional efforts on a market-by-market basis.

• Segmenting sales by the **time period** immediately following the ad or promotion allows the researcher to identify sales occurring during the period of influence. To gather these data, a date and time must be attached to each transaction.

• Segmenting sales by **geographic origin** is especially useful in geography-based efforts. It allows the researcher to determine if the sales are coming from the target area. This requires either a customer address attached to the transaction or the general area of origin. For the purposes of some companies it may be enough to know that the sales came from a certain county or ZIP Code. These data are available through distribution points, outlets, or scanner-equipped stores if customer addresses are attached to sales receipts.

• Segmenting sales by the **information source** requires some type of two-way communication between the vendor and the customer. This communication could be in verbal form; *i.e.,* a clerk or an order taker asks the customer how she heard about the product, sale, or promotion. A company can also establish two-way communication with the customer by including a phone number, a coupon, or a mail-in form along with an ad or promotion that will make the customer eligible for a sweepstake or prize.

More companies are shifting money from advertising to promotions because of the measurement advantage of promotions. Promotions can be measured through coded coupons, numbers of mail-in rebates. There are a number of innovative ways companies use to measure promotion effectiveness that also work for some advertisers.

Coupons with codes on them will help identify not only the medium in which the ad appeared, but if they are direct mailed, they can identify the exact address of the customer. Companies specializing in customer couponing can design special offers to appeal to specific customers. These customized mailings identify the demographic segments who use the products. Mail the coupon directly to the areas targeted and then monitor the results of the campaign. Then when a customer comes into a store to redeem the coupon, the coupon identifies him as a new customer so clerks can give him the star treatment. A Personal Identification Number on the coupon also allows the company to measure response from each area targeted.

Now that AT&T, MCI, and US Sprint are offering caller identification services in many markets, 800 numbers not only produce inquiries, but they create an instant new prospect or customer database. The caller identification service traces incoming calls so quickly that the recipient of the call can tell the number the call originated from before even answering the phone. A company with a 800 number running in an ad or promotion can record the caller's number and ask for his general demographics to create a valuable database of new and prospective customers.

Case Study: Selling Gas Grills

Market Statistics, a New York-based demographic research firm, produces the Merchandise Line Report, based on census retail data, and two annual publications, *Survey of Buying Power* and *Data Service*. Its research specialists offered the following case study dealing with media planning.

The firm uses several specialized terms in its analyses:

• **Buying Power Index** (BPI) is a weighted average of a market's total population, total income, and total retail sales, all expressed as a share of the total U.S. population, income, and retail sales. It is a percentage, not an index number, which represents the share of the consumer's overall buying power in a specific market.

• **Performance Index** (PI) compares actual sales with expected sales. It's calculated by computing a Buying Power Index and then dividing sales by the BPI.

A major manufacturer of gas grills hired Market Statistics to determine whether the company should go ahead with its planned $2 million network television advertising campaign. There had been a general increase of business in the leisure category, which had translated into substantial gains in the company's sales. In the last season, they sold 500,000 units.

First, the researcher analyzed the company's past performance and found it inconsistent. Then past sales were measured by the Buying Power Index of the counties and the ADIs (Areas of Dominant Influence) where sales occurred. New York County, for example, was found to have a BPI of .8890, which meant that it should have accounted for that percentage (4,445) of the 500,000 units sold last season. But it didn't. It accounted for only 3,000 units. The researcher calculated that New York County had a Performance Index (actual sales against BPI) of 70, which was 30 percent below the expected level.

To determine the reason for the shortfall, New York County was compared with one of the company's high-performing counties—Orange County, California. Both counties had a similar number of households. Here's what they found:

County	Total Households (000)	BPI	Units	PI	Actual Units Sold
Orange	808.2	1.0361	5,180	110	5,698
New York	707.9	.8890	4,445	70	3,000

The next step was to take a closer look at each area's demographics to determine how they were different. The analyst needed to find out what factors influenced demand for the product and whether a more definitive customized BPI could be developed that would take these factors into consideration. That would help determine if television was the correct way to reach these markets.

First, the company analyzed its product registration card database created by National Demographics & Lifestyles to find out what other factors aside from number of households determined demand. One fact emerged: sales of gas grills were minimal among one-person households. Next, the company examined each county in light of this factor:

County	Total Households	1-Person Households	% 1-Person Households
New York	770,900	395,860	51.4%
Orange	695,800	175,238	24.5

One out of every two households in New York County is a one-person household, while that figure is only one out of five in Orange County. Obviously, this characteristic is a primary determinant of demand. Every other market was analyzed taking this into consideration. The results showed that consistently high-performing markets had low concentrations of one-person households. Other factors, such as having space to use a barbeque, also influenced demand. Sales were much higher in neighborhoods of houses than in areas with high concentrations of apartment dwellers.

The Solution: The researcher created a new BPI in which the absence of one-person households was appropriately weighted. The new county-ADI breakdown showed an interesting finding about the effectiveness of network TV. Under the old BPI breakdown, the top 50 ADIs would have represented a total potential of 68 percent of the company's U.S. sales. The new BPI showed total potential of 77 percent—an even greater concentration of sales in the top 50 ADIs. At that point, the advertising agency decided that network TV cast too wide a net, and they recommended instead a program using spot TV on a market-by-market basis.

This case study shows how demographic differences can affect the effectiveness of one medium or method of advertising over another. In this case, television was the medium of choice. But an extension of this analysis might have included a media preference analysis of current customers in the product registration card database. This analysis is most useful when it focuses on both media and favorite programs or subjects. If most of our existing customers, for example, read sports sections of newspapers or tune in to sports programs on local television and cable, using all three media would probably be the most effective way to reach potential customers.

Another way to proceed would be to use a geodemographic segmentation system. This identifies the high-use segments, their media preferences, and exposure times or sections read. Then the ability of media in the market to deliver target audiences would be analyzed, considering prices and penetration of key geodemographic segments. The following case study takes the cluster analysis approach.

Case Study: Selling a Packaged Good

Based in Stamford, Connecticut, Donnelley Marketing Information Services is a subsidiary of Dun & Bradstreet. Its connection to A. C. Nielsen, another D&B subsidiary, gives the marketing services firm direct access to Nielsen ratings data. The following case study uses data from NPD/Nielsen's SCANTRACK service and accesses the ratings data through Donnelley's TV Conquest product. Donnelley also produces ClusterPLUS, a cluster segmentation system that places all the neighborhoods in the country into one of 47 cluster segments.

Donnelley was hired by a major packaged-goods manufacturer (the client authorized release of this case only if the company and product specifics were omitted) to gather information about markets, marketing, and media for its planned line extension.

The product had traditionally shown mass appeal. Historically, the company's goal had been to gain 100 percent distribution at the retailer level and reach the consumer for the least cost. In hiring Donnelley, the company wanted to determine whether certain groups of customers were more inclined to buy the new product. Donnelley also wanted to find out whether these customers could be targeted more effectively with focused product placement and advertising.

The first step was to test market the product to identify exactly who the product appealed to most. Test marketing was conducted in three markets, and the results showed that the niche line extension appealed to a limited number of customers who were quite different from the customer profile of the overall brand. The problem was how to identify the consumers, where they lived, how they could be reached, and the markets and stores that had the most potential for success with the line extension.

Donnelley cluster-coded the test market results and determined that volume demand for the product would be concentrated in nine of their 47 cluster groups. These nine groups would account for 50 percent of the product's movement:

Cluster No.	Cluster Household	% of Households	% of Users	Index
1	Established Wealthy	1.30%	3.52%	278
3	Young Affluents with Children	2.08	5.50	264
19	Young Ex-Urban Families	1.96	4.88	254
37	Avg. Income Blue-Collar Families	1.59	3.78	238
36	Middle Income Hispanics	1.62	3.60	222
21	Rural Families with Children	3.76	7.55	201
12	Highly Mobile Working Couples	3.84	6.87	179
9	Non-Urban Working	3.99	5.98	175
6	Highly MobileYoung Couples	2.99	4.65	155

This identified the broad targets, but further analysis was needed to find reachable groups. Next Donnelley called up demographic information on the cluster groups including their likelihood to be professionals, Hispanics, married, parents, their median incomes, and length of residence. By doing so, the analysts were able to divide the nine segments into two target groups according to their demographic similarities:

Target 1 (clusters 1, 3, 6, 9, and 12) Affluent Mobiles "Designers"

Target 2 (clusters 19, 21, 36, 37) Dual Avg. Income Mobile Families & Hispanics

Next, Donnelley analysts wanted to find out which markets around the country contained the highest concentration of the targeted customer segments. The idea here was to reach the majority of the target market for the lowest possible cost. The analysts used data from SCANTRACK to identify the market that had the highest concentration of the clusters with the greatest propensity to buy the product. This identified the markets to be included in the initial roll-out of the product. Some of the most favorable markets were:

- Seattle
- Portland
- Sacramento
- Salt Lake City
- Dallas
- Houston

- Tucson
- San Diego
- Miami
- Minneapolis
- Detroit
- New York

Donnelley generated a map from the SCANTRACK data that rated every market in the country with an index that calculated the concentration of the cluster groups buying most of the product. Due to budget considerations, the company decided to roll into markets with indices above 110.

In Chicago, one of the original test markets, the sales effort was designed to gain more sales from a key food operator. Accounts and stores were compared to ZIP indices to determine which stores had the most potential. Every store in a chain could be analyzed and given an index showing its potential. This told the company which stores were situated in neighborhoods with high concentrations of the target customer clusters. Donnelley generated a map showing the entire Chicago market and indicated areas with high potential and locations of stores in those areas.

Next came the media segment of the analysis. Donnelley wanted to determine which media, programs, or subjects the targeted cluster groups were likely to use. To get a better idea about the target groups' likes and dislikes, the researcher looked at a combination of Mediamark and Simmons data indicating what other products they purchased. With this they found out that Target Group 1, the Affluent Mobiles, likes the following things:

Index	*Description*
199	Owns in-ground swimming pool.
185	Rented a car 3+ times in the last year.
175	Took a trip to Hawaii in last 3 years.
172	Stayed in a hotel/motel on domestic bus trip in last year.
158	Took 6 - 19 domestic plane trips in last year.
157	Belongs to a health club.
152	Sent flowers by wire in last year.
147	Went snow-skiing in last year.
146	Drinks imported white dinner/table wine.

This lifestyle information offers a "marketing snapshot" that the company can use to get a clearer picture of its target customer. These data could also help in the creative process of advertising message development.

Next, Donnelley researchers used Mediamark and Simmons data to find out what media the target groups preferred:

Index	Description
117	Magazines — Quintile 1
117	Newspapers — Quintile 2
114	Total TV — Quintile 4
113	Newspapers — Quintile 5
111	Outdoor — Quintile 1
109	Radio (Driving) — Quintile 2

The target groups are big readers of magazines and newspapers. They fall in the upper two quintiles of newspapers, making this medium an even stronger preference. Television usage is relatively low, but that wouldn't rule out targeted spot advertisements that played during programs on topics they enjoy.

Donnelley representatives said that they routinely use Mediamark or Simmons data as the first source because they provide a quick idea of the target groups' preferences. But in forming a media strategy, each high-use medium needs to be examined in more detail. For that, Donnelley goes to the best source available on each medium.

Because magazine usage was so high and Mediamark and Simmons are the best source for magazine information, Donnelley looked deeper into the Mediamark and Simmons data to find out which magazines the target clusters read most:

Index	Description
142	Business and finance magazines
142	*Smithsonian* magazine
137	Sports magazines
132	Epicurean magazines
131	*National Geographic* magazine
131	*U.S. News and World Report*
131	*Newsweek*

This report is telling in two respects. It reveals both the particular magazines the target group shows interest in and their favorite topics. This information could be applied to decisions about the newspaper sections and television programs or cable channels in which to place advertisements.

Like many packaged-goods manufacturers, this company had traditionally spent much of its advertising budget on television. Both the company and its agency were interested in using television, but they determined that spot TV rather than traditional network buys would be more efficient at reaching their target groups.

Using TV Conquest, Donnelley reviewed the Nielsen ratings data to determine which local television stations and which day parts reached the target groups most efficiently.

The researchers gathered the Nielsen Station Index (NSI) ratings for the Cincinnati market during February 1989 *(figure 11c.)*. The NSI report compares the total ratings for the station with the target group ratings, and indexes them to show the stations and day parts used most by the target groups. This report indicates that the company is going for frequency rather than reach because the data were generated for relatively inexpensive weekday time slots with lower ratings. Prime-time slots usually have higher double-digit ratings, and so come with higher prices.

To determine the best stations and time slots for ads, the company or the advertising agency would compare the last three columns of the NSI report. The index gives an immediate indication of which time slots have high viewership in the target clusters. Station WLWT's weekday 12:30 to 1 p.m. time slot shows the highest index of 231, indicating people in the target clusters are 131 percent more likely than average to watch that station at that time. This is useful for planning television buys, but the advertiser needs to further consider the target rating figure as compared with the DMA (Dominant Marketing Area, Nielsen's definition of a television market). The target rating shows the usage of the time period among the target clusters, while the DMA rating represents the Nielsen ratings that set the price for the time period. The advertisers look for the highest target rating with the lowest DMA rating to find the best television buy for the money.

Another big consideration, however, is the kind of program that runs in the time slot. Judging from the magazines preferred, the best programs would involve news, finance, sports, or even gourmet cooking. If the time period is occupied by a rerun of "Mister Ed," an ad run then will probably fail to reach the target cluster groups.

Donnelley researchers said this case study could have gone further into the media analysis had the client wished to pay for additional data on newspapers, outdoor advertising, or more television markets. But even as far as it goes, this case study illustrates the benefits of a media analysis for both the company and the advertising agency. A media analysis gives the company enough information to evaluate its present media mix, while a media analysis originated by an advertising agency allows the agency to justify its media decisions to the client.

Conclusion: As a result of Donnelley's analysis, the packaged-goods manufacturer was able to focus the product's rollout more precisely and

Figure 11c: NSI RATINGS FOR CINCINNATI

NICHE LINE EXTENSION
TARGET GROUP I AFFLUENT MOBILES
CINCINNATI
NSI RATINGS FEBRUARY 89

Sta	Day	Time	Title				Persons 25-54 TGT RTG	DMA RTG	Index
WCPO	MTWRF	9:00A - 9:30A	WCPO	/M-F	9:00A - 9:30A	2.2	1.2	182
	MTWRF	12:30P - 1:00P	WCPO	/M-F	12:30P - 1:00P	4.7	2.6	182
	MTWRF	9:30A - 10:00A	WCPO	/M-F	9:30A - 10:00A	2.2	1.3	167
	MTWRF	1:30P - 2:00P	WCPO	/M-F	1:30P - 2:00P	3.1	1.9	164
	MTWRF	1:00P - 1:30P	WCPO	/M-F	1:00P - 1:30P	3.7	2.4	156
WIII	MTWRF	12:00P - 12:30P	WIII	/M-F	12:00P - 12:30P	0.1	0.0	227
	MTWRF	4:00P - 4:30P	WIII	/M-F	4:00P - 4:30P	0.1	0.1	145
WKRC	MTWRF	7:30A - 8:00A	WKRC	/M-F	7:30A - 8:00A	3.8	3.1	124
WLWT	MTWRF	12:30P - 1:00P	WLWT	/M-F	12:30P - 1:00P	2.3	1.0	231
	MTWRF	2:00P - 2:30P	WLWT	/M-F	2:00P - 2:30P	3.7	1.8	202
	MTWRF	2:30P - 3:00P	WLWT	/M-F	2:30P - 3:00P	3.6	1.9	187
	MTWRF	3:00P - 3:30P	WLWT	/M-F	3:00P - 3:30P	4.4	2.5	174
	MTWRF	7:00A - 7:30A	WLWT	/M-F	7:00A - 7:30A	4.1	2.4	174
	MTWRF	12:00P - 12:30P	WLWT	/M-F	12:00P - 12:30P	4.0	2.4	166
	MTWRF	4:00P - 4:30P	WLWT	/M-F	4:00P - 4:30P	1.8	1.1	158
	MTWRF	3:30P - 4:00P	WLWT	/M-F	3:30P - 4:00P	4.1	2.6	158
	MTWRF	7:30A - 8:00A	WLWT	/M-F	7:30A - 8:00A	3.3	2.1	157
	MTWRF	11:00A - 11:30A	WLWT	/M-F	11:00A - 11:30A	2.6	1.8	145
	MTWRF	8:30A - 9:00A	WLWT	/M-F	8:30A - 9:00A	3.3	2.3	144
	MTWRF	8:00A - 8:30A	WLWT	/M-F	8:00A - 8:30A	3.1	2.2	142
	MTWRF	1:30P - 2:00P	WLWT	/M-F	1:30P - 2:00P	4.2	3.1	135
	MTWRF	1:00P -1:30P	WLWT	/M-F	1:00P - 1:30P	3.8	2.9	134
	MTWRF	11:30A - 12:00P	WLWT	/M-F	11:30A - 12:00P	2.0	1.6	129
	MTWRF	10:30A - 11:00A	WLWT	/M-F	10:30A - 11:00A	4.2	3.6	115
	MTWRF	9:00A - 9:30A	WLWT	/M-F	9:00A - 9:30A	5.3	4.8	111
WXIX	MTWRF	8:00A - 8:30A	WXIX	/M-F	8:00A - 8:30A	1.0	0.9	117

SOURCE: TV/CONQUEST®, Donnelley Marketing Information Services and Nielsen Media Research.

saved about $400,000 by better allocating merchandising resources. It cost the company less to introduce the product in only a third of the SCANTRACK markets rather than in the whole nation. And the company saved money by using spot TV rather than the costly national network television campaign it would have approved without the Donnelley target marketing information.

Whatever analysis method is used, the primary goal of advertising and promotion analysis is to gather the media preference data necessary to allow you to reach your target market cost-effectively. There are numerous ways to use the data—their power is limited only by the creativity and knowledge of the user.

CHAPTER TWELVE

Strategic Planning

STRATEGIC planning is as essential to business success as accurate bookkeeping or an effective management team. A good strategic plan gives business leaders the ability to see well into the future instead of just one month or two quarters ahead. Executives have the opportunity to comprehend the big picture and to weigh their business forecast in light of major legal, technological, or economic changes.

In today's highly competitive market, the concept of strategic planning must be expanded to include areas like human resources and customer satisfaction. Productive employees and satisfied customers may well provide the competitive advantage that makes the difference between breaking even and robust growth.

Strategic planning is greatly enhanced by consumer information. Analyzing demographic and consumption trends over time identifies changes occurring in a market and within key customer segments. Demographic projections and purchase behavior data give the business researcher a first-hand look at the future. Because of the accuracy of demographic projections, this look at the future is much more precise than any crystal ball could be.

Strategic planning consists of: 1) following market changes; 2) finding new market niches; 3) forecasting revenues; 4) strategic investments. It reveals:

- *How are my customers changing?*
- *How are all segments of the market changing?*
- *What are the fastest growing markets/customer groups?*
- *Are there products/services they will want that I can deliver?*
- *What sales growth can I expect from my existing markets?*
- *Judging from trends, in which departments or new lines of business should I increase my investment?*

Purpose: Make information-based business decisions now to maximize the company's long-term growth and future fiscal stability.

Tools: Demographic, purchase behavior data.

Formula: Forecasting revenue: % market share **x** size of market **x** revenue per unit = estimated revenue.

Concept: A long-term analysis of demographic changes and consumption trends along with market-specific information will give managers the basis for forming successful strategic plans.

Method: Identify major customer segments over time.

There are four broad goals involved in strategic planning: 1) following market changes; 2) finding new market niches; 3) forecasting revenues; and 4) identifying strategic investments.

Following Market Changes

The first step of strategic planning is to identify the effect of demographic and consumption changes on the present market. To identify market changes look at the consumption levels by demographic segment for a specific product or brand in light of broad demographic and consumption trends.

1. How are my customers changing? Information from a syndicated survey done by Mediamark or Simmons or in-house records will identify the heavy buyers of a product and whether or not that group has changed in the past few years. Reinforce these data with consumption figures from the Consumer Expenditure Survey to identify which groups purchased most of the product during the same period. This will tell you which groups are responsible for increases or decreases in sales

2. What is the impact of demographic or consumption trends? Once you have identified the current heavy, medium, and light buyers, review their demographics to predict how they will be affected by trends.

In some industries, such as the hard-liquor industry, consumption has declined nearly across the board. This has been due to changing tastes and growing sentiment against drug and alcohol abuse. The bed-linen industry is another example. People today buy sheets and pillowcases less often than they did a generation ago. Why? One of the side effects of today's busy lifestyles is that people change their bed linen less often today than housewives did 30 years ago, so less wear on the product means less need to replace it.

In other industries, revenues have increased, but the increase has been fueled primarily by the rising spending power of the baby boom or some other subgroup. The goal here is to identify the important segments of your market and to understand whether the changes in their buying habits reflect demographic or product usage trends.

Review the demographic trends discussed in chapter 2 and evaluate your industry in terms of the shifting age structure of the population and other broad demographic trends. This will identify places to concentrate on in your strategic planning.

Finding New Market Niches

If your present customers are not using your product like they used to, or their usage might decline as they age out of their present age group, it may be time to find another market.

Growth can be achieved even in a flat or slow-growing market by identifying and targeting the fastest growing population segments. The controversial move by R. J. Reynolds Tobacco Company to market Uptown, a new brand of cigarettes, exclusively targeted at black customers, was an example of a company going after a new market niche. The company's decision was based on the demographic facts—the higher growth projections of minority populations and higher overall smoking rates among blacks. The company was eventually forced to abandon the marketing campaign because of adverse publicity due to the negative aspects of the product. The Kool brand, however, has targeted ads specifically at blacks for years and sponsored jazz festivals featuring black artists. Reynolds was just taking niche marketing a step further.

Though the concept was sound from a marketing standpoint, Reynolds' experience underscores the difficulty involved in targeting product line extensions or new products exclusively at niche minority markets. The product has to be right. If the maker of nearly any other product with higher-than-average use among blacks had announced a national exclusive marketing campaign, the news probably would have been cheered as an example of the increasing purchasing clout of the black community. The message must also be right. McDonald's, Wisk detergent, Schlitz malt liquor, and many other companies have targeted successful advertising exclusively at black customers. The ads were careful not to reinforce ethnic or racial stereotypes.

Many of the most successful U.S. companies have grown and prospered by finding and successfully targeting emerging niche markets. In the 1970s, Pampers saw a need for a disposable diaper among busy new mothers, many of whom were working. This is the age in which entrepreneurs can get fat by helping customers get thin. Programs such as Weight Watchers, Nutri/System Inc., and Diet Center are doing well by providing ballooning baby boomers with weigh-ins, lectures, and special diet foods. So how does a researcher identify a potential niche market?

Method: Examine demographic trends to determine how market segments are changing. Use purchase data to determine changing consumption patterns. Evaluate product line to reposition an existing product or develop new products to match changes.

How are all segments of the market changing?

1. Identify fastest growing population segments within the market. Get a demographic trend report from a data vendor or consult the Census Bureau counts and projections. Examine the relative sizes of the market segments in question and look for significant growth or decline. Consider how these changes fit into broader trends such as the aging of the population and slower growth. Look at the demographic projections. Do these projections correspond with past growth trends? Which groups show continued growth five years from now? This will determine the high-growth groups that are worthwhile targets.

What are the fastest growing markets/customer groups?

2. Identify the groups whose consumption rates are growing. With Consumer Expenditure Survey figures over a five- or ten-year period, a researcher can chart consumption levels by product category and identify changes. Determine which groups show the most growth in their consumption of your product. Perhaps households headed by 35-to-44-year-olds have been spending $20 more a year on your product for the past two years than they did before. These data will reinforce your demographic research, which perhaps shows that the number of households in this age group is growing. This could be a niche market for you, but first you have to determine how well you already serve this market.

3. Are high-growth groups already served? Determining this requires a detailed customer profile, which includes heavy, medium, and light users of your product (see chapter 10). Compare your customer profile with the high-growth segments you have already identified. Is there significant growth among segments you don't serve? Is growth among your primary customer groups in a downspin compared with non-customer groups? If so, expect future trouble and look for high-growth groups with the most potential.

One way to do this is to rank each segment according to three variables: 1) their growth rate; 2) their consumption rates; and 3) how much of your product they buy now. Make three lists representing each variable. Let's suppose that the customer groups who top each list are different—Hispanics and one-person households are growing most in the market, but households headed by 35-to-44-year-olds have the fastest-growing consumption rates, and women between 18 and 24 currently make up most of your customers.

Once you have determined which segments have the highest potential, look at how well each top group does in the other categories. If the group is high in one category but low in another, they may not be a worthwhile target. For example, the fastest-growing group might have the lowest consumption rate in your product group. This would suggest there is low potential for your product with these customers unless you find a way to boost consumption. It may be better to concentrate on a group with high-to-medium rates in at least two categories.

The next task will be finding a way to increase consumption among the fastest growing groups while not alienating regular customers.

Are there products/services they will want that I can deliver?

4. How can I increase my coverage of the high-growth groups? Determining this requires a more extensive product or service analysis and primary research into what these potential customer groups want in a product and what it would take for them to buy your product in particular. This step cannot be done successfully without primary research in the form of surveys or focus groups to pinpoint exactly what these customers think. The results of this research and operational information about your business will determine whether you choose:

- To alter existing product to better meet the needs of the growing market.
- To reposition product either in terms of shelf arrangement, distribution, or image enhancement to appeal more to the target markets.
- Or to develop a new product to meet the needs of the emerging market.

Forecasting Revenues

The real test of a company's strategic planning is its ability to accurately forecast future revenues. Here again, demographics along with sales data provide essential clues. Demographic projections in combination with sales history and information about the size of the present market can be used successfully to forecast sales.

What sales growth can I expect from my existing markets?

Remember the market potential (territory) analysis at the end of chapter 9? This analysis is a valuable prerequisite to forecasting sales. In that analysis, we determined that out of five markets or territories, three were operating above potential and two were operating below potential. In market two we were selling 22 percent above potential. How much more can we expect to sell in the future? Can we reasonably expect another 10 percent sales increase next year? Probably not, but we can reasonably expect to increase sales in the two markets that are underperforming. We can allocate more of our advertising and promotional budget to those markets to try to bring them up to par. Our forecast will attempt to find the revenue increases we can expect if we bring all underperforming areas up to par.

To forecast revenue, we need to know our market share (share of total current market), the size of the market (number of customers in market), and the revenue per unit (average annual sales per customer). By manipulating these figures in the following way, a researcher can estimate revenues for the immediate future.

Formula: % market share **x** size of market **x** revenue per unit = estimated revenue.

When the size of the market is adjusted according to demographic projections and sales per customer are adjusted for inflation (and/or other anticipated changes), a researcher can reasonably forecast future revenues.

1. Determine your market share. Market share can be defined as the portion of total sales your sales represent in the market. For example, a regional furniture retailer with stores in a three-state area should not consider the national market as a benchmark in determining market share. Rather, the market should be defined as total furniture sold in the three-state area. A manufacturer that distributes nationally or regionally can forecast sales by nation or by each region served. Industry sales data are available from the state and federal governments, from sources inside specific industries, or from data vendors.

To calculate market share, divide your sales for the latest year by total market sales. If the total retail market for furniture in the three-state market is $1.5 billion and your total sales through stores and mail order are $300 million, you know that your market share is 20 percent.

2. Calculate the size of the market. Determine the demographic variables that affect demand for your product. In the case of our furniture store, we might define our market by the broadest demographics possible to include all future buyers. Perhaps we choose households headed by 25-to-64-year-olds that make more than $30,000 a year. By either hiring a data supplier or by doing our own research, we determine from census figures that 1.2 million households in the market will match our profile in the next year.

3. Determine the average value of each customer or transaction. Most businesses already have an idea of how much each customer is worth. This figure is a result of dividing the total sales for the latest year by the number of transactions for that year, or if possible, by the number of customers. Although using the number of customers is preferable, most businesses have no way of telling how many customers they have. The important goal here is to come to a reasonable estimate of what the average customer spends on your merchandise.

Our furniture business owner is lucky. He has sales records that include a date and the name and address of each customer. This allows the marketers to identify repeat purchases and to determine pretty accurately what the average customer spends in the stores. After a lengthy examination of the sales records, the researcher finds that the average customer spent $130 in our stores last year.

4. Calculate potential revenue: % market share **x** size of market **x** revenue per unit **=** estimated revenue. The equation would look like this:

$$0.20 \text{ x } 1.2 \text{ million x } \$130 = \$312 \text{ million}$$

By putting the formula to work, the furniture business finds that they can expect to make $312 million next year, barring any outside negative forces such as an economic downturn.

5. Forecast future revenues. Adjust either the market share or the size of the market to future projections and the formula can be used to forecast future revenues.

Market Share: Use the market potential analysis from chapter 9 to determine how well each market is performing. Our example showed that two areas were operating below potential. Suppose our market share is 20 percent. Next we have to consider how much it will increase if we brought the two underperforming areas up to potential. From examining the market potential matrix on page 122, we see that we need to see an 8.5 percent sales increase in the two areas to bring them up to potential. Suppose this increase would bring in $10 million in additional sales in the next year. After adding in the estimated increase, the new market share becomes 21 percent. Use the larger market share forecast to forecast future revenue.

Market share should also be adjusted if there are any changes in the company's operations or the competitive situation that might affect the bottom line. Suppose a competitor goes out of business, a new one opens up, or the company decides to ease credit terms. Researchers can estimate the possible effect these factors will have on the company's market share.

Market Size: By adjusting the size of the market according to demographic projections, an analyst can estimate the future size of the market and adjust the formula accordingly. For example, suppose after adjusting for the expected surge in households headed by 35-to-54-year-olds and the expected drop in 25-to-34-year-olds in the 1990s, the researcher determines that our market will include 1.5 million households by 2000. This figure can then be incorporated into the new equation to forecast revenues for 2000.

Strategic Investments

Which lines of business will offer the most growth potential and become the prime candidates for investment in the 1990s and beyond? That's a question with no sure and easy answer. Corporations pay trend watchers and marketing gurus handsome fees to offer bits of insight into the risky business of strategic investment.

However, there are important insights that can be gained from looking at the hard numbers. Demographic and consumption trends as revealed by census projections and the Consumer Expenditure Survey should be the foundation of any investment strategy. Understanding demographic changes can illuminate many of the consumption shifts that point to good investments.

Judging from trends, in which departments or new lines of business should I increase my investment?

1. Get to know the demographic trends. In some cases, a review of the population and income projections for the 1990s will be enough to spark ideas in innovative entrepreneurs. Shifting sizes of the age groups in the 1990s will produce dramatic change.

2. Identify broad consumption changes and their causes. Examine the Consumer Expenditure Survey to discover broad shifts in consumption. This method is admittedly time-consuming as consumption patterns emerge only after several years of figures are compared. The volume of data may be overwhelming, but there are answers to be found by crunching the numbers.

Look for broad shifts in behavior by examining consumption data from syndicated surveys or lifestyle research specialists such as Yankelovich Clancy Shulman.

Next determine whether the causes of the behavior shifts are related to demographics or lifestyles and attitudes. Understanding the cause of the change can help determine its longevity and whether it is a trend or merely a fad.

For example, some consumption changes are traceable to major demographic shifts. The failed revival of the miniskirt in 1987 was due largely to the rejection of the idea by aging baby-boom women. The same women who embraced the micro-mini when they were 22 decided no designer was going to induce them to look like fools when they were 42 and old enough to know better. Had the fashion mavens understood the demographics of their customers better, perhaps the failure could have been avoided.

H. J. Heinz's awareness of the demographic shifts gave it the foresight to purchase Weight Watchers in 1978, well before most of the rest of the food industry had recognized the true potential of the diet market. This foresight put Heinz at the forefront of a new market and positioned the packaged-food giant for a huge opportunity. As baby boomers' wallets expanded so did their waistlines, which meant growth in the diet frozen foods category. By 1988, Weight Watchers frozen-dinner entrees had knocked Stouffer's Lean Cuisine out of the top selling slot. The same year, Weight Watchers tipped the revenue scales at $1.3 billion, and its operating income of $100 million represented 14.5 percent of Heinz's operating income, according to *Fortune* magazine. For Heinz, it was the perfect investment to make at a time when Americans were showing growing concern about their expanding waistlines, high cholesterol levels, and limited time to cook.

Other consumption shifts are caused by softer changes in opinions and lifestyles. The consumption shift from brown to white liquor, the backlash against aerosols because of concern about the Earth's ozone layer, and the success of oat bran products are all examples of attitude or lifestyle-caused consumption shifts.

3. Examine your own business's capability to capitalize on the shift. This is easy to say, but much harder to do. This assessment requires cold objectivity, untainted by the desire to buy or the lure of profit potential. Entering a new market may transform the entire corporate culture and divert resources from areas essential for continued corporate health. It is essential that a new venture be evaluated against the strain it will put on the existing business.

But there is a flip side to this coin. Sometimes businesses that are perfectly positioned to jump on a new consumption trend miss the opportunity because they define their business expertise too narrowly.

4. Weigh demographic and consumption trends against the competitive environment. Once a potential new investment has been chosen, evaluate the demographic factors (whether the size of the market is growing or declining) against the consumption rate (whether people are buying more or less of the product or service) and view the results in terms of the competition. Is the field filled with competing companies, or are you considering an emerging business with few competitors?

One way to get an immediate graphic representation of this would be to draw a simple graph. Market growth is indicated from 0 to 100 percent growth up the left side, and consumption growth is indicated with a similar scale from low to high consumption across the bottom. Plot the potential investments on the graph according to how they fall on the growth and consumption scales. This is a quick and dirty way to rate the relative potential of various investments. Once the field has been screened and the top candidates identified, then rate each according to the competitive environment and the company's capacity to succeed in the new business. Obviously, the most positive investment would show a growing market, growing consumption, little competition, and compatibility with current interests. But good investments can be found even if all factors are not optimum now, as long as future growth looks promising.

Investment Intangibles

Some of the most important investments a business can make may never translate to the bottom line. But don't underestimate the need for company-wide commitment to customer service that nurtures employee excellence and good customer relations.

The satisfaction of employees and customers is so interrelated that it seems inconceivable that many firms still view them as separate problems—or fail to view them as problems at all. Every day many firms place their livelihood—the customers—in the hands of underpaid and often disgruntled front-line workers. The meeting may last only 15 seconds, but it may be the only chance the company gets to make a positive impression on the customer. Jan Carlzon, president of Scandinavian Airlines, says that moment of truth happens 50 million times a year for his company. For that 15-second interval, the front-line ticket seller *is* Scandinavian Airlines, the billing clerk *is* Macy's, and the order taker *is* the entire Burger King corporation in the mind of that customer. If the employee is rude, slow, or indifferent, the company just lost a customer to the competition.

That good impression in the customer's mind may be the most important asset any business can possess, yet it has no hard value. It can't be bought or sold, and it is tenuous and fragile. Once it is destroyed, it is often impossible to reestablish. It seems logical then that every company that deals with customers directly should initiate programs that help to ensure service quality.

This failure to recognize the importance of employee/customer relations could be the biggest strategic mistake of the decade for some firms. Consider the demographics involved. Households headed by 35-to-54-year-olds already control nearly half of all household income. Just imagine what will happen when the baby boom moves into that age group in the 1990s.

"They will demand good service and they will be able to pay for it," says Cheryl Russell, editor-in-chief of *American Demographics* magazine. "If they don't get it from your company, they'll get it from your competitor."

A study of the performance of 2,600 businesses over a 15-year period done by the Strategic Planning Institute of Cambridge, Massachusetts, illustrates the importance of customers' perceptions of quality to a business's financial performance. The businesses that were consistently high performers in several areas, including market share, asset turnover, and return on investment, were the ones that offered the highest quality. In addition, the study found that the quality of customer service was a primary determinant of how well customers rated the quality of the firm's goods and services.

How can a business move to safeguard its most important asset — the customer's goodwill? In their book, *Total Customer Service: The Ultimate Weapon* (Harper & Row, 1989), William H. Davidow and Bro Uttal offer a six-point plan for doing just that. Their suggestions:

1. Develop a strategy. Find out what customers expect. Segment customers by their service expectations to identify those needing high-touch and low-touch service. Set customer expectations by promising a little less than you can deliver.

2. Leadership commitment. No service strategy will work without leaders who drive it hard. Foster a service-oriented culture. Make customer service everybody's business. Declare war on bureaucracy.

3. Develop better people policies. Work ceaselessly to hire the right people. Train, train and, retrain. Motivate lavishly.

4. Make customer service a principle of design. Understand exactly how the core product or service can break down. Listen to what the service staff says about product or service problems. Share the work.

5. Backbone of service: infrastructure. Plan for the long haul. Match the infrastructure to the customer. Leapfrog the growth of sales and service to avoid lags between demand and ability to supply.

6. Measure the results. Let your customers say what counts. Design a system that balances process, product, and satisfaction measures. Make the measurement systems matter by tying them in to compensation, both psychic and monetary.

Investment in customer service is more important to strategic business planning now than at any other time in the history of American business. Several demographic and economic trends unique to this time period have converged to make this so:

- The baby boom is moving into its peak earning years and demands service.
- Seventy-five percent of the U.S. GNP now comes from the service sector.
- Domestic markets are growing more slowly than they have in the past.

- There are more competing products and companies in many fields, so consumers have more choices. If one fails to satisfy, they can easily try another.

- Customers perceive that service quality is falling, so companies that care about quality service can distinguish themselves in the customer's mind.

In analyzing the top service providers in *Fortune* magazine, Bro Uttal noted that the companies shared some key attributes. "They make outlandish efforts to hire only the right people, to train and motivate them, and to give them the authority necessary to serve customers well. They invest earlier and much more heavily than their competitors in technology to support customer service. They keep an especially sharp eye on the competition. And they constantly ask customers to rate the quality of service they have received."

Customers are demanding more quality and service, and the firms that can satisfy that demand are pulling away from their competitors. L. L. Bean will replace worn out bottoms of its Maine hunting shoes at cost for customers. American Express will buck bureaucratic hurdles to replace travelers checks lost in Cuba. Embassy Suites gives customers free breakfast and a daily cocktail hour and promotes employees who show a willingness to serve and embrace new responsibilities. Cadillac has engineers equipped with computerized drawings who walk its dealership mechanics through complicated repairs to assure that the repair gets done right the first time.

There is ample evidence that paying attention to quality and going that extra mile for the customers makes good business sense for the 1990s. Our plan for using customer information can become the basis of a workable customer service strategy. Before devising a strategy, a company has to find out what each of its customer segments demands in the way of service. Demographic and purchase behavior data will help segment customers, and psychographic research will identify their lifestyles and attitudes. Then it's up to the individual company to ask its customers directly through surveys what they think about the service and how they would like to see it improved. The top service-providing firms are the ones that ask and keep asking customers about service. The ones that emerge on the competitive edge in the 1990s will be the ones that truly value the customer.

Throughout this book we keep returning to one central issue: the customer is the most important ingredient for business success. The more you learn about your customers from your consumer information system, the better you can serve them. The better you continue to serve your customers, the better your chances are for long-term prosperity.

CHAPTER THIRTEEN

The Power of the Database

"Knowledge is power." —Francis Bacon, *Meditations Sacrae (1597)*

THERE IS NO turning back to the early days of the industrial economy, when the only customer information companies needed was a general idea of the location of population centers. An increasingly diverse population translates into increasing complexity at all levels of commercial enterprise. Changing attitudes and lifestyles require continuous monitoring. The important constant is that customers buy goods and services, and the more satisfied they are the more they keep buying. Being on the cutting edge of an industry today means knowing more about present and future customers than the competition does. Consumer information is the key to competitive intelligence.

Now that the spigot of consumer information is turned on full blast, the flow of consumer information will not diminish soon. Technological advances, greater competition in most markets, and a changing economy will spur demand for business information services. Veronis Suhler & Associates' Communications Industry Forecast 1989-1993 predicts that the business information segment of the communications industry will grow 10.5 percent a year during those four years. Consumer information in a sleeker form, tailored to customer specifics, undoubtedly will be the marketing tool of the 1990s.

Industry Consolidation

Growth of the information industry, increasing sophistication among data users, and technological advances mean more and better consumer information in the future. Data companies, like hardware stores, used to sell hammers and nails and leave it up to the client to build the house. That's not enough to stay competitive in today's data industry. The lower cost and increased accessibility of the raw 1990 census data require data firms to offer more than just numbers. They have to sell solutions to business problems.

The data industry is gearing up for the challenge. Three major forces are at work that bode well for the buyer: 1) the data are more accessible; 2) more companies are finding ways to link their databases and make compatible products; and 3) the industry is consolidating.

Mergers in the information industry have been sparked by intensifying competition. The best way to beat a persistent smaller competitor is to buy him out. But there is an up side to consolidation. By joining forces, providers of diverse databases increase the range of information they can provide to clients. The mergers have created giants and given some smaller research firms the ability to go after specific industries. Dun & Bradstreet, Equifax, and the Dutch company, VNU, are the revenue goliaths of the industry.

In 1989, VNU bought National Planning Data Corporation, a primary source of demographic data for many other firms, and Belden Associates of Dallas, a 50-year-old firm specializing in qualitative research for newspapers. VNU already owned Claritas, creator of one of the first geodemographic clustering systems, PRIZM. In addition, they purchased Birch/Scarborough, leader in radio and newspaper research; part of Market Metrics, maker of Supermarket Solutions targeted at the supermarket and packaged-goods industries; and Urban Decision Systems, another early demographic data company.

Equifax, of Atlanta, is one of the three leading U.S. credit bureaus, which together maintain records on 160 million Americans. Equifax reported revenues of $259 million in 1988. That same year, Equifax bought National Decision Systems (now Equifax Marketing Decision Systems), a full-service data firm that makes the VISION cluster system, the Infomark desktop system, reports, maps, and a wide range of other information products. Equifax integrated its credit data with previously existing NDS databases, thereby creating a whole new dimension of purchase data.

Information giant Dun & Bradstreet, with annual revenues of about $3 billion, provides over 3,000 business information products and services worldwide. D&B owns R. H. Donnelley, one of the largest direct-mail firms in the nation, as well as Donnelley Marketing Information Services, A. C. Nielsen, the largest U.S. research organization, and D&B Credit Services. These affiliations allow Donnelley to provide television viewing and purchase data through NPD/Nielsen's SCANTRACK services, and gives it access to D&B's reports on the financial condition of some 10 million companies. In addition, R. H. Donnelley maintains a list of names and addresses and data connected to 84 million U.S. households.

Some smaller firms are absorbing former competitors to better target a specific market. R. L. Polk & Company produces a nationwide consumer mailing list compiled from vehicle registrations, telephone lists, and other sources. Polk recently purchased National Demographics & Lifestyles, a firm with a 30-million name mailing list based on over a million monthly questionnaires. In addition, Polk owns part of Wiland Services, a direct-mail company, and Geographic Data Technology, a mapping company. Added capabilities from subsidiaries give Polk a better total product to offer its target customers—direct-mail firms and manufacturers of consumer durables.

Mergers give information providers additional talent and resources to target specific industries more effectively. The pooling of resources allows them to build and maintain larger consumer databases.

At the same time, data providers are more willing to integrate their products and services. This has been in response to complaints from companies that found themselves with lots of data but without solutions to their marketing problems. As corporate marketers embraced micro-marketing, simple demographics were not enough to successfully target smaller groups of customers. Now most data firms will link demographic databases with purchase behavior, media preference databases, and psychographic databases, and pull all the data together in integrated desktop systems. These systems use personal computers with mass storage capacity to give clients direct access to diverse databases right in the office. Equifax Marketing Decision Systems' Infomark, Donnelley's Conquest, Claritas's COMPASS, and National Demographics & Lifestyles' OASYS are examples of such systems.

The information industry's response to increasing competition has been to consolidate resources, integrate diverse databases, and act as marketing consultants—not just data vendors—for their clients. It seems to be the response of a maturing industry, led by companies that are learning to take their own advice: get to know the customers and cater to their needs.

The Dawn of the Database

The demand for customer information is still evolving. As marketing strategies focus on smaller and smaller segments of the population, companies demand more specific information on individual customers. One of the newest buzzwords among marketers is "database marketing," which is by definition a record of specific information on selected individuals.

There is not much difference between the database used in database marketing and the plain old customer or prospect list used by mail-order sellers of old. The difference is simply a matter of enhancement and use. Direct-mail lists were used by firms specializing in selling through the mails.

The customer or prospect database becomes more effective as it becomes more refined, that is, as more specific information about the customers is added to the database. For example, a list of the names and addresses of customers who have purchased products in the same category as yours is useful, but a list of customers who have purchased your product in the last six months is better. Finding out how much they bought, how often, and how much they spent is better still. And the database becomes even more useful if you can find out the customers' demographics, what other things they buy, their psychographic types, and what media they prefer. Not every database will require all this information. It depends on the product and the nature of the customers. Sometimes specific psychographic data, such as hobbies enjoyed, will be of more value than broad demographics.

This is really the essence of the consumer marketing model we have been describing in this book. A database is just a direct way to go about gathering and using the information. You start with the actual customers, rather than demographic and purchase behavior profiles of likely customers. If the information on actual customers is available, by all means use it.

As detailed in chapter 10, information on your customers comes from two-way communication with them. Some common methods companies use to compile lists are product registration cards, in-package rebates or coupons to be sent in or redeemed at a store, and inquiries through mail-in forms on ads, a number on a print or TV ad, or responses from a mass mailing. Even a billboard with a toll-free number can become a data-gathering tool in database marketing.

Direct Mail

The most obvious application of database marketing is still its original use. It makes it much easier to launch a successful direct-mail campaign. With such a database, big packaged-goods companies can target their coupons and promotions at the people who will buy the products. No more sending coupons for denture products to 25-year-olds or offers for second credit cards to single people.

Database marketing is being touted as a "revolution," the answer to marketers' dreams. It is an extremely powerful marketing tool, especially when used in conjunction with other media because it has the power to aim communication more precisely and reduce wasted ad dollars. But a database will not solve all marketing problems. It will fail to produce sales if it is not developed as part of an overall marketing plan or if its strengths and weaknesses are incompletely understood.

Philip Morris and its subsidiaries, Kraft Foods and Citibank, are a few of the corporations exploring database marketing. When marketing their Gold-card, Citibank used database marketing to identify prospects and target them for offers. The company found that "media synergy," or supporting direct mail with telemarketing, was crucial. And timing was everything. Positive responses were higher when the telephone call came after the direct-mail package arrived.

Philip Morris has been developing its 12 million-name database for a number of years. It started offering cigarettes by mail order in 1990 when it introduced its upscale brand, Cartier Vendome. A mail campaign targets smokers who are customers of upscale tobacco outlets. The offer gives credit-card holders the opportunity to order cigarettes and have them delivered through the mail. If the campaign achieves the success the company expects, direct marketers speculate that it will demonstrate the effectiveness of the technique and encourage other companies to try database marketing.

Telephones to the Rescue

Technology is rising to the challenge presented by escalating demand for more and better consumer information. More companies are successfully integrating 900 or 800 telephone numbers into their advertisements and using the responses as a means to get feedback on products and to compile data about prospects.

Americans' willingness to use the numbers is increasing too. AT&T reports that the number of 800 number calls soared to 7.03 billion in 1988, up from 1.9 billion in 1984. Calls to 800 numbers set up especially for customer service have also increased by 30 percent a year for the last three years, according to the Washington, D.C.-based research group, Technical Assistance Research Programs.

Even 900 numbers, which require the customer to pay for the call, are becoming widely used in promotions by top consumer companies. Revlon launched a $2 million beauty-care sweepstakes targeted at 52 million households in 1990. The sweepstakes included a one-day freestanding insert with a 900 number that ran in 220 general circulation newspapers. A 900-number hotline operated for three months, and callers recited the four-digit code on their insert to find out instantly if they won. Revlon created awareness, boosted brand loyalty among users, and got the names and addresses of hundreds of thousands of prospects—and the customers paid for the call.

Gannett Company's *USA Today* launched a 900-number weather hotline in 1989. The line offers tie-in benefits, according to Gannett officials. For example, a company sponsoring the hotline, such as a hotel chain, can record a message that gives the caller the option of being connected to the chain's reservation desk. Through the satellite messages offered by 48 Gannett newspapers, marketers can target their messages to specific geographic regions. A sun-care product company, for instance, could run a message where it's hot and sunny.

Gannett also pays its long-distance carrier for computerized phone listings of everyone calling the hotline. These data on computer tape can then be loaded into the company's computers and matched with other information in the database. So Gannett's weather report is much more than a service. It's an effective way of getting customers' phone numbers—and the customers themselves are paying for it.

The major communications companies are making it easier to get phone numbers. Thanks to the caller identification services now offered by the major telephone companies in many areas, 800 and 900 numbers can build an instant database. Caller identification is an instant call trace; the number of the caller is flashed on a display while the phone is ringing. Companies can use these new data to identify the caller's location. Catalog or mail-order firms can use the information to call up the customer's account and serve the customer more efficiently.

The power of the telephone goes far beyond electronic publishing or the ability of 800 and 900 numbers to inform, entertain, advertise, and gather information. Telephone's ability to deliver one-to-one information is now in its infancy, but consider the possibilities:

- Through fax, it can deliver mail;
- Through interactive computer technology and on-line information services, it can provide a household with library and information services;
- Through fiber optic technology, it can deliver video images;
- And, of course, it can transmit the sound of a voice.

All this points to the probability that telephone numbers will become an even more important tool for advertisers who want to know and communicate with customers, not merely with telemarketing, but with customized messages for people who subscribe to specific information services.

When this medium is up and running in all its futuristic glory, it may not look anything like the telephone of today. But the telephone number will be the password necessary to send customized messages to people you want to reach. Growing interest in databases and the potential power of the telephone can only mean one thing: companies that lead in developing computerized customer information databases will be the marketing communications leaders in the next century.

Managing Data in the 1990s

This is the age of one-to-one marketing, and that's not going to change. One-to-one marketing requires more and better use of data and sophisticated ways of recording, filing, integrating, and applying them. This will require corporations to make significant investments in modernizing and streamlining their data processing and marketing information departments.

New uses for computer technology, such as home shopping, will complicate the task of integrating diverse corporate databases. In 1989, 50,000 households signed up for a new IBM/Sears service called Prodigy. It allows customers to bank, shop, and get information through their home computers. IBM and Sears hope the service will gain better mass appeal than such consumer-oriented videotex systems as CompuServe or The Source. Prodigy is reportedly cheaper and easier to use than its precursors. It costs $150 for the software kit to use with a modem, plus a $10 monthly fee. The service is expected to reach more than 50 cities by mid-1990.

A service like Prodigy presents the retailer with an opportunity to get more information about customers. When they shop by computer, they provide purchase information; when they access information, they reveal something about their likes and dislikes; and when they bank, they show something about their finances. The companies have no plans to use this information, but because it's all on computer record, the possibility exists.

Evolving technologies mean it's important for companies developing databases to view their systems as open-ended, so they can expand and take on new information and functions as the company's needs evolve. They must also keep three basic rules in mind: 1) there must be an overall plan and commitment by the management; 2) the system has to have the right capabilities for the jobs required of it; and 3) employees require training and support once the system has been introduced.

We spoke in earlier chapters about the need to devise a corporate marketing strategy and to build a consumer information system to fit into that overall strategy. This requires the company to hire the right people and facilitate communications between them. There should be an overall database manager who is part marketer or at least able to understand the needs of the user departments. Most importantly, marketing and other departments that will use the system must have continual input as the corporate database system is developed, software is created, and revisions are planned.

The computer system should be easy to use and learn. Its incorporation into daily operations should be done in phases, so new users can get comfortable with the system. Users should be supported with advanced training on the word processing, mapping, and spreadsheet software. The ultimate goal is for the database system to become the marketer's most valuable tool, something used daily to help generate ideas and facilitate decision making.

Building, updating, and using the computer system is only one hurdle along the route to better use of consumer information. A key hurdle, that this book can help you surmount, is the misunderstanding and misuse of consumer information itself. Both research specialists and novices will benefit from a thorough understanding of what consumer information is, where it comes from, and how it can be used.

Marketers and planners of the future will have to take the lead in using consumer information. They'll have to be masters of consumer information because they'll need to know what market segments to target, what data they need to do it, and exactly where to go to get that information.

The 1990 census will add billions of new numbers to the already substantial output from scanner cash registers, people meters, panel diaries, syndicated studies, and market research reports. The marketer of the 1990s will have to be extraordinarily skilled at processing vast amounts of data and making sense out of them, because out of that ocean of numbers must come not only a better understanding of consumer markets, but precise measurements of marketing efficiency. Marketers who are able to present consumer information that produces results—higher sales, increasing market share, and effective communication—will be the ones who become indispensable to their companies even while marketing departments suffer cutbacks.

Slower population and market growth, product proliferation, and the increasing demand for quality and service make the competitive environment tougher in the 1990s. The only response is intelligent use of consumer information. Growth can be found in slow-growing markets by understanding the demographic trends. Customer groups can be targeted precisely if you have information about their purchase and media behavior. Messages aimed at target groups can be designed to hit their mark like well-crafted arrows through psychographic research.

As knowledge about the uses of consumer information grows, consumer information is going to work its way into nearly every aspect of business decision-making. In the age of one-to-one marketing, the only defense against encroaching competitors is the old business axiom, "know thy customer." The deeper that knowledge, the better prepared the business is for any shift in the market. With enough information on the customers, businesses can step forward confidently in this period of fragmentation and embrace the changes.

Information Providers

Here is a partial list of the many firms that can help you analyze your current and potential customers.

Multi-Service Demographic Firms

CACI
9302 Lee Highway, #310
Fairfax, VA 22031
(703)218-4400, (800)292-CACI

Claritas
201 North Union Street
Alexandria ,VA 22314
(703)683-8300

Donnelley Marketing Information Services
70 Seaview Avenue
Stamford, CT 06902
(800)527-DMIS, (203)353-7000

Equifax Marketing Decision Systems
539 Encinitas Boulevard
Encinitas, CA 92024
(800)877-5560; (619)942-7000

Market Statistics
633 Third Avenue
New York, NY 10017
(212)986-4800

National Demographics & Lifestyles
1621 Eighteenth Street
Denver, CO 80202
(800)525-3533; (303)292-5000

National Planning Data Corporation
P.O. Box 610
Ithaca, NY 14851
(607)273-8208

Urban Decision Systems
P.O. Box 25953
Los Angeles, CA 90025
(800)633-9568; (213)820-8931

Lifestyle Research

Langer Associates, Inc.
19 West 44th Street
New York, NY 10036
(212)391-0350

Yankelovich Clancy Shulman
8 Wright Street
Westport, CT 06880
(203)227-2700 or (212)752-7500

Values and Lifestyles (VALS) Program
SRI International
333 Ravenswood Avenue
Menlo Park, CA 94025
(415)859-4324

Media Specialists

The Arbitron Company
142 West 57th Street
New York, NY 10019
(212)887-1300

Birch/Scarborough Research
12350 N.W. 39th Street
Coral Springs, FL 33065
(305)753-6043

Information Resources, Inc.
150 North Clinton Street
Chicago, IL 60606
(312)726-1221

Mediamark Research, Inc.
708 Third Avenue
New York, NY 10017
(212)599-0444

Mendelsohn Media Research, Inc.
352 Park Avenue South
New York, NY 10010
(212)684-6350

The NPD Group, Inc.
900 West Shore Road
Port Washington, NY 11050
(516)625-2302

Nielsen Media Research
Nielsen Plaza
Northbrook, IL 60062
(708)498-6300

Simmons Market Research Bureau
380 Madison Avenue
New York, NY 10017
(212)916-8900

Demographically Enhanced Lists

Metrodirect
901 West Bond Street
Lincoln, NE 68521
(800)228-4571

National Demographics &
Lifestyles
1621 Eighteenth Street
Denver, CO 80202
(800)525-3533; (303)292-5000

R.L. Polk & Company
6400 Monroe Boulevard
Taylor, MI 48180
(313)292-3200

SmartNames, Inc.
176 Second Avenue
Waltham, MA 02154
(800)424-4636; (617)890-8900

Federal Agencies

Bureau of Economic Analysis
U.S. Department of Commerce
1401 K Street, N.W.
Washington, DC 20230
(202)523-0777

Bureau of Labor Statistics
441 G Street, N.W.
Washington, DC 20212
(202)523-1221

National Center for Health
Statistics
3700 East-West Highway, Rm. 157
Hyattsville, MD 20782
(301)436-8500

U.S. Bureau of the Census
Data User Services Division
Washington, DC 20233
(301)763-4100

Market Research & Tools for Analysis

Impact Resources
125 Dillmont Drive
Columbus, OH 43235
(614)888-5900

Leigh Stowell & Company, Inc.
Market Place Tower
2025 First Avenue, #310
Seattle, WA 98121
(206)726-5550

Market Facts
676 North St. Clair Street
Chicago, IL 60611
(312)280-9100

Maritz Marketing Research
1395 North Highway Drive
Fenton, MO 63026
(314)827-2325

Market Metrics
18517 William Penn Way
Lancaster, PA 17601
(717)397-1500

Market Opinion Research
243 West Congress
Detroit, MI 48826
(313)963-2414

**Marshall Marketing &
Communications, Inc.**
1699 Washington Road, #500
Pittsburgh, PA 15228
(412)854-4500

National Analysts
400 Market Street
Philadelphia, PA 19106
(215)627-8110

NFO Research, Inc.
2700 Oregon Road, Box 315
Toledo, OH 43691
(419)666-88000

Spectra Marketing Systems Inc.
120 S. Riverside Plaza, #1760
Chicago, IL 60606
(312)715-0606

Survey Sampling
One Post Road
Fairfield, CT 06430
(203)255-4200

Opinion Polling Firms

The Gallup Organization
100 Palmer Square, #200
Princeton, NJ 08542
(609)924-9600

Louis Harris & Associates
630 Fifth Avenue
New York, NY 1011
(212)698—9600

The Roper Organization
205 East 42nd Street
New York, NY 10017
(212)599-0700

INDEX